D0309080

R

bT                2.95

150 RECIPES FROM THE TEAHOUSE

茶館菜譜一百五十例

# 150 Recipes from the Teahouse

## Vivienne and Jenny Lo

*faber and faber*

LONDON · BOSTON

First published in 1997
by Faber and Faber Limited
3 Queen Square London WC1N 3AU

Photoset by Parker Typesetting Service, Leicester
and Mitaka Ltd, Leamington Spa
Printed in England by Clays Ltd, St Ives plc

All rights reserved

© Vivienne and Jenny Lo, 1997
Photographs © Graham Kirk, 1997
Drawings © Hilary Re'em, 1997

Vivienne and Jenny Lo are hereby identified as author of this work in accordance
with Section 77 of the Copyright, Designs and Patents Act 1988

A CIP record for this book is available from the British Library
ISBN 0-571-17797-2

10 9 8 7 6 5 4 3 2 1

To father and mother
(cold tea and savoury noodles)

Thanks are due to Alan Yau and wagamama for showing us how to realize our dream; to our chefs Tim Diep, Kenneth Kam and Victor Huang; to Friederike, Xun, Lili, Guang, Youlan and their mothers; to Kim for good sense and outrage; and to Robert for all the free vegetables.

# Contents

# Illustrations

The dishes shown in this book were prepared and photographed in Jenny Lo's Teahouse. The bowls and plates are hand-thrown by Hilary Re'em especially for use in Jenny Lo's Teahouse. The drawings are by Hilary Re'em.

*Kenneth Lo*

# Foreword

For a year now my two daughters, Jennifer and Vivienne, have been asking me about my grandmother's teashop on the bustling South Street of our ancestral hometown, Fuzhou. It is all so long ago now, seventy years or more since my last visit, that the images have become a little hazy. Of course, Fuzhou was still medieval at the beginning of the century. From the leafy, hilltop suburb where we lived amidst lavish colonial splendour it was a half-hour journey by rickshaw or sedan chair to the teashop, and the milling crowds in the heart of the city. The journey took us across the glistening, yellow-brown Min River, over the countless ancient stone arches of what always seemed to me to be the longest bridge in the world.

As for my grandmother herself, she was our oldest ancestor, and not really a grandmother at all, but the second wife of my paternal grandfather. (My natural grandmother had died while my grandfather was stationed in London.) She suffered with rheumatic pains and spent her days reclining on a couch. Her two personal maids, one still a child, were clad in blue batik jackets and loose trousers and fussed around, massaging her aching limbs or pounding her with a soft pummel. She was a skinny little thing and seemed very old. In the summer, she would sit out on the veranda where I, her favourite grandchild, would cool her with the swing fan. The swing fan had a six-foot wooden frame upholstered with thick beige woven cotton and was hung from the ceiling. Whenever I tugged on the the rope pulley the fan sent gentle gusts of wind back and forth along the veranda.

The afternoon was the best time to visit her apartment as she would have her supper early, and being quite old her appetite had decreased, so that she never quite managed to finish her meal, leaving plenty for us to scavenge. Being a practising Buddhist she was mainly a vegetarian, although she did eat seafood. No doubt she felt that if she did not harm living things, her chances of entering one of the better Buddhist heavens would be improved when the time came. Her maid prepared fabulous vegetarian soups from turnips and mushrooms. One of her favourite dishes for 'high tea' was a hotpot of leeks, French beans, oysters and noodles, cooked over charcoal at the table.

Despite her age and frailty grandmother still had a very astute mind and was at the helm, managing what was left of the family fortune. Twice weekly the bookkeeper would report to her about her two businesses, the pawnshop and the teashop. She would issue instructions and discuss stratagems with him. Occasionally, we would accompany her on her visits to town by sedan to oversee the shops. The varnished wooden facade of the teashop, intricately carved, opened out on to the street, the shop being bounded by a high counter where one could sit and watch the world go by. From there we could silently look down on the customers buying tea. Behind the counter were a few shop assistants who, naturally indulgent of the boss's children, addressed us as 'the little masters'. They wore a uniform of black embossed satin jackets and skullcaps, some with the old imperial plait still hanging down behind. Twenty different kinds of tea were kept in wooden drawers at the back of the shop and the customers could sample their choice in earthenware teapots that were kept brimming with fresh tea. The teashop was steeped in a strong aroma of jasmine flowers, tea and varnished wood.

My most vivid memories of the teashop centre around the many festivals that exploded on to the streets of the city. Whether it was the New Year Festival, the Spring Festival, the Dragon Boat or the Harvest Moon Lantern Festival, we would use the shop-front as our private gallery, a vantage point from which we could enjoy safely the ghoulish processions, the clashing of cymbals and the report of firecrackers. In the background there was always a phalanx of relatives who would never fail to congregate for any celebration. Everyone came in their best costumes. The gentlemen wore black satin gowns and skullcaps with coloured topknots that denoted their official rank. The ladies were clad in more colourful robes with rectangular embroidered panels gathering their skirts. Over the top they would wear short jackets, delicately finished with trim and piping.

A few years later, after starting at the Anglican missionary school on Nantai island, I became acquainted with a larger range of teahouses. Eking out the reward money for my fine brushwork and calligraphy, or for a perfect recitation of one of the *Four Books*, the Confucian classics, I would often drop in to a riverside teahouse to have a bite before returning home, much in the same spirit that English children visit the sweetshop. I had an immense appetite, and was always ready for a small bowl of chicken noodle soup or tossed aromatic noodles in sesame paste, lightly sprinkled with fresh chopped chives or spring onions and washed down with a cup of Wulong, the speciality tea of Fuzhou. All the dishes were moreish, like eating peanuts. It was poor man's food, but we still considered it an indulgence. After all, it was tasty and wholesome, and every bowl was spiced with the joy of being of independent means.

Living so close to the river, many of those teahouses were riverside bars. When the fishing boats came home, you could buy a basket of fresh crab claws for a few pennies – the crabs conveniently discarded their claws when caught. The claws were boiled and cracked open and, with the tender pinkish white flesh dipped in a marinade of vinegar or soy sauce with chopped ginger or garlic, made for an orgy of gastronomic delight. Sitting at the tables we would while away the time watching the ebb of the river reflecting patterns that moved lazily across the walls of the shop. In the background the continuous ticking sound of the proprietor's fingers flicking the beads of the abacus back and forth lengthened each moment, while on the sampan parked nearby, his wife was busy preparing the family's meals, or sorting the endless array of goods and chattels that were kept on board.

Mencius, Confucius's disciple, was able to state that 'the gentleman distances himself from the kitchen' which, of course, does not mean that he is aloof from his chefs, but simply that he was not to go near the abattoir or the messy business around the wok! I heartily approve. Although I have been known to venture into the kitchen, I am much happier behind the typewriter and have always enjoyed a good relationship with my chefs. From Qingqing, our head chef at Lo Lodge in Fuzhou whose animated tales of the exploits of the Monkey King first drew me into the kitchen, to the various generations of chefs at Memories of China – Kam Po But, Tim Tang and latterly Mr Lam – creative conversations with the professionals have always been the secret of turning out Chinese haute cuisine. My own extensive experience of eating well, and an understanding of western ways, has enabled me to shape their skill into an accessible art by choreographing and finishing the dishes on the one hand and by translating and interpreting recipes on the other.

My children are quite another kettle of fish. They have their mother's barbarian blood, and are therefore much more inclined to get their hands dirty. Although I have never seen them slaughtering their food, I shouldn't wonder if they have. Anne, being a farmer's daughter and a Protestant, is a workaholic and has little respect for the typewriter. When we were building Memories of China she would quite often work all night, and was equally happy clearing the drains in the kitchen as she was chairing the board meetings. I could only sit at home and type her notes of encouragement.

All my children have an extraordinary capacity for hard work. Since the opening of the Teahouse, both girls have learnt how to be fire chefs, something I never dreamed of doing and, traditionally, not women's work. Hard work has given them a love of the most basic and nourishing of food. This we can all share. Years ago, before we opened Memories of China, Vivienne and I would often talk of opening a soup kitchen under the arches at Waterloo station. Good, basic Chinese food was intended to feed the black-haired masses and can easily be adapted for fast food. Unfortunately, in England Chinese fast food too often results in bland and over-cooked slop. The Teahouse sets out to remedy this.

Vivienne is a health professional, originally an acupuncturist and now completing her PhD in the history of Chinese medicine at London University. She has gone into the theory of eating for health in some depth. Jenny, on the other hand, has all the know-how and experience gained from fifteen years of running the family business – both the restaurants and my cookery school. Together, they have the perfect qualities to translate the best of Chinese food for the next generation. People have no time or money for banquets, but still demand quality. Their food is cheap, healthy, fast and elegant.

Over the last few months I have been working with them to perfect the quintessential Chinese dishes. We are convinced that the ultimate menu will offer no more than five or six dishes; so far we have narrowed the menu down to about ten, and experience and feedback from the Teahouse will help us towards our goal. Some of the dishes are already quite magnificent. Just lately, on several of these hot nights, I have awakened from visions of eating a large plate of their black bean seafood with fresh, hand-drawn, egg noodles tossed with crispy mangetout and red and green peppers. Simply heavenly!

Kenneth Lo (July 1995)

# Introduction by Vivienne Lo

## Tea

Nobody really knows when tea-drinking was first invented in China. Tradition attributes the discovery of the tea plant to Shen Nong, the Divine Farmer, who taught people how to cultivate the land rather than to hunt and gather. He is said to have tasted every plant, and so identified all the herbs and grains that were fit to eat. One day while boiling his drinking water, a custom he also sought to establish, a sprig of the wild tea plant accidentally fell into his pot, and so it was that tea-drinking first began.

Through a selfless process of trial and error Shen Nong discovered that tea leaves were an antidote to the toxic effects of seventy-two herbs. The tea plant, which originated as an evergreen shrub in the mountains of South China, became part of the therapeutic cuisine. A handful of young tea leaves would simply be added to a cauldron of rice broth or soup together with vegetables, ginger and onion. They were thought to 'gladden the heart', reduce the need for sleep and alleviate bladder ailments.

Extensive cultivation of the tea plant by the third and fourth centuries brought tea to a larger proportion of the population, and by the fifth century the Emperor Wu sanctioned its ritual usage in official worship. Fine teas, often gathered from the single buds of wild tea plants, were reserved for the imperial court as part of the provincial tribute. Good tea became so prized that by the eighth century a group of tea merchants commissioned the writer Lu Yu, an orphan brought up in a Chan Buddhist temple, to compile the *Chajing Tea Classic* in which every detail of proper tea-drinking was exhaustively set out. More important to the ritual development of tea was its usage in Chan Buddhism, the origin of Japanese Zen, where it was served next to meditation halls in order to heighten mental acuity.

Traditions of tea production and tea-making were to change radically over the centuries. In the T'ang dynasty tea was ground with a pestle, while in the Song dynasty tea was made by grinding the leaves to a powder and pouring on boiling water. The tea was then whisked to a white froth with a special tea whisk. During the Yuan dynasty (1279–1368) the Mongols brought their barbaric practice of drinking tea with cream and spices – a habit that was not to outlast their rule – but they also introduced the practice of steaming and hand-rolling the leaves, which preserved the green colour and enhanced the flavour. It was not until the Ming dynasty (1368–1644) that the leaves began to be steeped in small teapots as they are today.

Tales of tea-drinking began to reach Europe during the sixteenth century and the first consignment arrived in Holland in 1610, where it was hailed for its laxative qualities. It was not until forty years later that Thomas Garaway, a coffee-house proprietor, began to offer it in London, extolling its healing virtues: 'being drunk with milk it strengtheneth the inward parts'. From the very start tea with milk was established as the British norm. By the end of the seventeenth century tea was a popular beverage drunk at all levels of European society, although fine teas were still expensive and very highly prized.

To begin with, tea was taken after dinner as a digestive. Four o'clock tea-time with sandwiches and cakes became a tradition in the mid-nineteenth century drawing-rooms, where elaborate rituals mirrored the desire for style and elegance in society. Chinese porcelain had caused a sensation when it first arrived with the tea consignments from China, and showing off the family teaware was an essential part of the British tea ceremony.

In time, tea became the single most important export from China, shifting the balance of payments strongly in favour of the Chinese. The West seemed to have little to offer the proud Middle Kingdom, and even if it did China was not going to open her doors to unrestricted foreign trade. She preferred to remain in the position she had adopted for so long and in which she was so comfortable. China did not trade, the Emperor merely gracefully received the tribute from outlying barbarian nations. This time China had underestimated the barbarians. The situation was not allowed to remain so for long. After centuries of trade the English finally came up with Indian opium, a product that could be smuggled by stealth through the coastal regions and that the Chinese could be persuaded to desire in bulk.

The shameful trading practices of the British spawned a new kind of nationalism among Chinese youth. Commissioner Lin Zexu was one of their great heroes. He ensured everlasting fame for his patriotism when he ritually mixed 20,000 cases of British opium into salt-water ponds filled with lime. His outrage is clear in his letter to the 'Barbarian Queen' (Victoria) complaining about

those who smuggle opium and seduce the people of China to smoke it
. . . In your honourable country people are forbidden to smoke the drug;
it is clearly from knowing the harmful effect . . . Is there a single thing
from China that has harmed a foreign country? Now tea and rhubarb, for
example; foreign countries cannot get by without them . . .

It was a well-known fact in China that the English could not
survive without the laxative effects of tea and rhubarb! Commissioner Lin's remonstrations were ultimately in vain and the
Opium Wars (1839–42) soon ensued. China suffered a crushing
defeat and was forced to sign the Treaty of Nanjing, which opened
up five ports to foreign trade: Fuzhou, Ningbo, Shanghai, Amoy
and Canton.

## Journeys to the West

If it had not been for tea perhaps our family would never have
ended up in London. Fuzhou, our ancestral home, had always
been a bustling harbour which was one of the gateways to the
South China Sea, but it was the tea trade that transformed it into
an international port, able to service large sea-going vessels like
the tea clippers that raced between Pagoda Anchorage on the Min
River and Greenwich on the Thames. Between the 1860s and
1920s three generations of our family sailed this route, establish-
ing London and Fuzhou as the foci of nineteenth and early
twentieth-century family enterprise.

Tea had been planted for eleven centuries in the hills around
Fuzhou, and gained official recognition when the rare rock teas
from the Wuyi mountain range were honoured in the provincial
tribute list. There were many varieties and qualities available. To
begin with, most tea was green tea. Green tea is so called because
it is only dried in a wok and rolled along its length, a process that
leaves it thin and papery. Different techniques give the tea
varying degrees of twist. Some are tightly curled and others
almost flat. Steeped in boiled water, the leaves swell and uncurl.

The best green tea comes from the neighbouring province,
Zhejiang, and in particular from the hills around Hangzhou. The
straw-coloured liquid with its thirst-quenching properties is ideal
for a hot day, and with the lowest caffeine content of all teas it is
good after an evening meal and will never keep you awake.
Jasmine, nowadays the most famous tea from Fuzhou, is a
fragrant, light green tea flavoured with the freshly picked jasmine
flowers that the mountain women of Fujian wear in their hair in
the spring. It is most frequently served weak, without milk or

3

lemon, as a digestive after a large meal, and being low in caffeine is also suitable as an evening drink.

The partly fermented Wulong Black Dragon teas from the Wuyi mountain range were the result of a process developed in the early Qing dynasty. Wulong was subjected to a new and prolonged fermentation which, rather than involving alcohol, simply meant that the leaves were put through a special rolling which battered and crushed the leaves before they were spread out cold to oxidize in the air. Finally the tea was tossed and dried in several stages in a hot wok. Subtle changes in the colour and a new strength of flavour inspired a new tea practice of brewing the tea in the tiniest of teapots and savouring it in minute teacups. The Iron Goddess of Mercy, the cream of the Wulong teas, is a delicate, light tea served hot and black. It is lower in caffeine than full black teas, with a flavour that has been likened to peaches. It is at its best served on warm afternoons or after an evening meal.

With the opening of the treaty ports the western merchants and tea planters began to build European-style homes around the old city of Fuzhou. To escape the city heat they chose an area on the top of the highest slopes on Nantai island, across one stream of the golden brown Min River and beneath the shade of the pine trees. They brought with them all the comfort and luxury of their life in Europe. They also brought religion and Christian missionary schools. But trends in the West were soon to have a radical effect on trade in Fuzhou. Although many westerners enjoyed the semi-fermented teas, the fully-fermented teas were better suited to the combinations of milk and sugar that inevitably found their way into the European brew. By 1860 the focus of the trade had shifted to India and Ceylon, where the fully-fermented black teas were stronger in flavour and more under the control of the westerners. Fuzhou and South-east China could not adapt with the speed necessary to sustain the market.

With the decline of the tea trade in the last quarter of the nineteenth century, many of the British migrated to Ceylon and Assam, leaving their European villas for those Chinese who aspired to western ways. As the Commissioner of Foreigner Affairs, grandfather was left with little to do, and spent his life in the greenhouse growing orchids and rambling in the hills. On Sundays there was always roast for lunch and every day at 4.30 p.m., without fail, tea was served on the veranda. He had a silver teapot from which he poured a smoky flavoured tea, probably

Lapsang Suchong, a specially guarded tea from the foothills of the Wuyi mountain range – a brand that they could get from step-great-grandmother's teashop on South Street in the city of Fuzhou.

## Growing up with Tea and Noodles

As well as being steeped in classical Chinese education father was also suckled on the cold leftover breakfast tea with milk left outside his parents' room in the morning. After his first long trip to England in 1919 at six years' old, he never managed to feel completely Chinese again. After a life of international travel his return to Fuzhou at nine left him sharply aware that his hometown was still a medieval backwater, and that his time there was merely a stepping-stone to better things. He remembered his hometown most fondly through the dishes and delicacies available: the sounds, sights and smells of the snacks by the sports ground, or the small cafés and restaurants down by the river where he could buy a delicious stir-fry of sesame paste, spring onions and noodles.

In voluntary exile during the 1930s, like all emigré Chinese father would always gravitate towards Chinese restaurants as if they were an umbilical cord through which spiritual sustenance could be derived. Tea and noodles not only served to assuage the immediate hunger, but also to fill the loneliness. For a short spell as consul during the war he worked as mediator between seamen and shipping agencies. Ironically, it was this period that helped to establish him in his later profession. The seamen organized themselves into informal unions based around their native districts, languages and regional food. Each union had its own clubroom that would also double as a restaurant and take pride in serving authentic food to remind its members of home. When father was eventually denied the chance to continue his position in the Civil Service, he began to fulfil his destiny as ambassador for Chinese culture in the only and most obvious way left to him. As purveyor of knowledge about Chinese food he would become a Chinese cultural ambassador, and influence the West in as great a way as the ancestors that he so esteemed. He embarked on a life of eating his way home.

As Chinese food inspector for the Egon Ronay restaurant guide, he could formalize his passion for the comfort and familiarity of restaurants and even be paid for the pleasure. In his middle years he travelled the length and breadth of the country sampling all the Chinese food available. Consequently as children we spent long hours crawling around under the tables of good-quality Chinese restaurants, listening to endless anecdotes about food and banquets he had eaten.

As adults there is nothing Jenny and I find so boring as sitting in fancy restaurants for long periods of time talking about food. We have both developed a passion for plain, good, no-fuss, home cooking, whether it is Sunday roast, spaghetti bolognaise or long-braised skirt of beef and noodles. For Jenny it was tea that was always her comfort food. Tea was always served at home as a response to any event of emotional magnitude – births, deaths, pregnancies, marriages and divorces all came with a cup of tea and a pat on the shoulder. In fact, Jenny is said to have been weaned on tea and boiled eggs. She took her tea with milk and sugar and her eggs plain – if father could be prevented from creeping up behind and dowsing them with soy sauce, a habit he could never be persuaded out of.

I never did like tea as a child and so it was a consolation that I was denied. There was something cloying about it that was bitter, rancid and insipid all in one. Of course that was tea with milk, the way it was served at home after the tradition that grandfather had established in Fuzhou. It was the milk bit that I was unconsciously objecting to – the memory of that free half-pint of poison that was administered at school every morning at 11 a.m. still torments me.

For me, there was nothing so reassuring as the sight of father at the kitchen door with a bowl of noodles dripping with long-cooked pork or skirt of beef. Through all the pain and trauma of growing up in Surrey with no contact with Chinese culture, no Chinese language, friends or family, it filled my heart with joy and calmed my spirit. In time I also came to appreciate the fine teas of Fuzhou served hot and plain. And since tasting the light liquor of the Goddess of Mercy I am a complete convert to the semi-fermented brews of the Wuyi mountain range.

## Teahouses

Even though we were bored by endless Chinese banquets, grow-ing up in restaurants left us with quite a refined palate. In a sense we were spoilt, so much so that we never considered going near the local takeaway. Both the local Cantonese families and the food that they served to English customers were strangers to us. Even the fish and chip shop was more familiar. Takeaway food was always covered in shiny brown sludge, slimy concentrations of soy and cornflour that oozed out between the cardboard and aluminium of the packaging. What was missing was the middle range of food – food still appropriate to an everyday diet yet not produced to the scale or cost of a banquet. It is to this kind of food that this book is dedicated.

In China, there are many kinds of establishment that have been known as *chadian* (teashops) or *chaguan* (teahouses). Some are described in the chapters that follow and these are generally characterized by the cheapness and quality of the food rather than the size and splendour of the menu. Very often a teahouse will only serve one dish in which it specializes, or serve a style of lunch-time snack, like Cantonese dimsum, the steamed and deep-fried wrapped dumplings. At its most simple a teahouse will be a place where people congregate to sip different qualities of tea and pick at dried snacks such as nuts, dried fruits and bean curd.

Historically speaking, the term *chaguan* teahouse often refers to a brothel. Zhou Mi (1232–1308) writing in *Old Affairs of Hangzhou* describes three classes of prostitution. The third and best brothels were referred to as teahouses, and were the best places to find educated female company to entertain a party or participate in a special occasion or ceremony. Many of the courtesans resident in the teahouses were skilled in poetry, dancing and singing, and so the teahouses were frequented by high officials, wealthy merchants, and writers and artists who were rich or had rich patrons. As soon as a guest had come in and drunk his first cup of tea, he had to pay several strings of cash for the pleasure of the fine company.

A similar sort of society was to be found in the famous flower boats of the Ming dynasty, where guests could feast with female companions, enjoy fine singing and dancing and spend the night on the water. The boat itself was a magnificent structure with a great hall where the orchestra played surrounded by red-lacquered carvings, gilded wooden pillars and silken drapes. One could expect a lavish feast and flowing wine.

Even in nineteenth-century Beijing the teahouse known as the Jiangnan (South of the Yangzi) teahouse, doubled up as a brothel as well as being a patisserie. But there were as many kinds of teahouse in those days as there are now. Most districts had a large one that could guarantee savoury dishes, some light entertainment and good conversation. A cheap menu with simple bowls of noodles and minced pork would be on offer, cooked on a fire behind the counter. The customer could sit inside at traditional teahouse benches and stools or in the inner courtyard where there were hooks for hanging birdcages and showing off your favourite pet.

Our own concept of the teahouse is defined loosely as a place to rest and eat which serves homely food and lots of different teas. In Jenny Lo's Teahouse there is no Peking duck in pancakes, or steamed sea bass. We don't stand on ceremony. On the other hand we are not interested in the chop suey connection – the mishmash compromise between Chinese chefs and the undiscerning western public. In choosing recipes for the Teahouse our aim was to make the finest tastes of the East accessible, attractive and commonplace to the ordinary British palate.

Like the teahouses of pre-revolutionary Beijing, where people from all professions and persuasions could afford to eat, Jenny Lo's Teahouse is a place where customers can easily chat to each other, but can equally well eat alone and keep themselves to themselves. While providing a friendly and interesting atmosphere we also hope to inspire some of the more spiritual and ceremonial qualities of the Japanese teahouse, as we have described in Chapter 5. This is principally conveyed through design. Bold graphics and motifs, modern applications of traditional Chinese themes, are set against a blank background emphasizing the empty space, the Zen principle. Careful attention is also paid to the choice of utensils and teaware, to respect the themes of the tea ceremony. By combining the themes of meditation, congregation, teahouse and temple we hope to provide a sanctuary from the stress and demands of modern life, a place of nourishment for body and spirit.

The success of Jenny Lo's Teahouse is testimony to our idea. Customers come in lunch parties, but there are many who choose to eat alone, especially women who find that the environment allows them the freedom to be independent. Our food has a reputation for being comfort food, not in the sense that it encourages stuffing to fill some gaping emotional emptiness, but more as a food that is comfortable to the digestion and healthy enough to leave you full of life and energy.

## Recipes

Jenny has selected, written and tested the recipes in this book. Many of them have come directly from the mothers and cooks of our friends who still live in China. As with all orally transmitted recipes they are prone to leave out critical stages which the original chef believes to be part of the natural repertoire of every cook. Jenny has been well-placed to identify the pitfalls and simplify the recipes. She began her working life in 1980 running the administration for the cookery school, Ken Lo's Kitchen, and for our parents' first restaurant, Memories of China, in Ebury Street. During a period of over ten years she worked closely with such well-known chefs as Mrs Fei, Terry Tan, Sri Owen, Lesley Downer, Deh-ta Hsiung, the Memories' chef But and of course our father, for whom she was editorial assistant. In the run-up to opening the Teahouse Jenny and chef Tim Diep were responsible for all the creative work behind the dishes that finally make up the menu.

My own interest in food began at an early age and has since never abated, but until recently I studiously remained outside the family business. As an acupuncturist I have regular conversations with my patients about the relationship between diet and health and this is my special area of interest. The recipes here are chosen for many criteria, but not the least of these is that many are both good to eat and good for you. Our choices will reveal a concern for less red meat and more fresh vegetables served in delicious, clear, home-made stock. There is an emphasis on steaming, grilling and wok cooking. Some raw salad is served. While we have a chapter exclusively devoted to oriental dietary therapy, western dietary principles also influence our choices: over-salting, additives and MSG are avoided, along with deep-frying for long periods or adding too much oil.

Most of our recipes show concern for authenticity. We will use black beans where it might be easier to use black bean sauce, or fresh stock where you can use bouillon powder, agar agar when gelatine is easier to use. We are not advocating being slaves to any ideal or even to our own recipes. Many authentic Chinese dishes taste revolting. While most of our recipes came directly from friends or friends' mothers and represent their home-cooking, we have tampered with them where we feel that they will not suit the western taste, or where unnecessary quantities of MSG, oil or salt are used. Short-cuts usually go unnoticed by all except the expert, although it is well to know how the original tastes before trying to make the short-cut. Hence this book. We have tested and re-tested the recipes and they do taste pretty authentic and are cooked in more or less the original way. If you are a novice to Chinese cooking try them out and learn how the food should taste before going off to the supermarket to make the short-cuts.

All the recipes in the book have servings indicated. Except for the recipes designated as one-pot dishes, they are all designed to be eaten in conjunction with a selection of other dishes.

## The Essential Chinese Kitchen

When I look at demonstration cooking on the television and the immaculate designer kitchens I cannot help wondering whether anyone ever really eats in them. Everything gleams, as if you could eat your dinner off the floor without fear of contamination. I do envy the large stainless steel industrial gas hobs that are fashionable these days, but other luxuries we can do without. For most of our dishes all you need is a wok, a tureen or large casserole and a ladle. That's the beauty of it.

A steamer can also come in handy, especially if you like fish, and you can buy bamboo basket steamers of various sizes. I use a large one which fits in my wok, but there is no reason why any other kind of steamer should not be used. A fish kettle is fine for fish steaming, and one of those stainless steel steamers that opens like petals and adapts to different sizes of saucepan will do fine for vegetables.

## Ingredients

Tasty Chinese foods can be turned out with very few ingredients. For me, the essentials are ginger, soy sauce, rice vinegar, sesame oil and some kinds of stock. Lately I am also inclined to keep a jar of hot bean sauce by the cooker. All the other ingredients necessary can be found or improvised from the larder. At the back of the book under 'The Essential Larder' (see page 260) you will find many substitutes for common ingredients where they are not available.

Major supermarkets have begun to stock acceptable proprietary versions of black bean sauce, yellow bean sauce, teriyaki, hoisin and barbecue sauces. Provided that basic techniques are mastered, there is no reason (apart from additives) why these substitutes cannot be used in day-to-day cooking. To progress to the stage where a simple stir-fry is a dish of excellence, with fresh crunchy vegetables in a savoury coating rather than soggy bean sprouts and brown sludge, it is good to spend a period of time aiming at authenticity.

Any attempt at authentic Chinese cooking will require at least one visit to an oriental supermarket (see the list on page 272). To be really authentic you will have to include a visit to a restaurant in Chinatown with the family. Make a day trip of it: it is not feasible to rush in armed with a list and expect to be out in ten minutes. Have a good dimsum lunch first, before visiting the supermarket, and take your time to savour the experience – it is an Aladdin's cave of colours and smells.

You will also need to have some idea of what you are looking for, as the English name printed on the packaging, if any, may not be consistent. Study the list at the back of the book. I always have to stand and stare at the shelves for a while before my eye alights on the thing I want. If you cannot find something, don't be afraid to ask, and don't be put off when the shop assistant looks at you blankly. That is the standard response. It can seem that there is a strange conspiracy not to sell you anything. Persevere. You have to believe that the ingredient is there underneath your nose, and if it is on this list it almost certainly is. Repeat the name of the ingredient in as many different ways as possible, and show them the Chinese characters at the back of this book. Failing that there will certainly be someone there who speaks good English and they can be sought out. At least they won't expect you to speak Cantonese. Jenny, who is often mistaken for being full Chinese, but only speaks a little Mandarin or modern standard Chinese with a heavy South London accent, is always barked at in Cantonese at the till. Probably she is being asked 'Cash or cheque?' When she doesn't respond appropriately the assistant is apt to mutter 'Can't speak, can't speak!' and give her the look saved for the much pitied and the disinherited.

The following is a list of all the ingredients that you will need to become a consummate Chinese chef, arranged in the groupings that you will find them. For more information on particular ingredients see The Essential Larder (page 260).

BOTTLES AND JARS
Soy sauce (light and dark)
Oyster sauce
Sesame oil
Chilli oil
Rice vinegar
Shaoxing wine
Hot bean sauce

TINS
Yellow bean
Hoisin sauce

Bamboo shoots (sliced)
Water chestnuts (sliced)
Lychees
Sweet red bean paste
Ginko nuts

### DRIED SPICES AND SEEDS
Five-spice powder
Whole five-spice
Sichuan peppercorns
Star anise
Sesame seeds

### DRIED FOODS
Wood ears (black and white fungus)
Dried prawns
Hair vegetable (facai)
Chinese mushrooms
Black beans
Dried rice stick noodles
Dried river noodles (hofun)
Fen si noodles
Bean curd skins and sticks

### VEGETABLES
White Chinese radish (daikon or mooli)
Bak choy
Chinese leaves
Ginger
Garlic

### IN THE REFRIGERATOR
Fresh river noodles (hofun)
Fresh oil noodles
Fresh wun tun noodles/skins
Bean curd (silken and plain)

With these ingredients in your larder you will be able to prepare most of the dishes in this book. If you can do them well we will offer you a job in the Teahouse! Naturally, fresh food has to be bought on the day that you want it. Bean curd and fresh noodles such as river noodles (hofun) and fresh egg noodles (oil noodles) cannot be kept for more than a couple of days. Vegetables and roots such as Chinese white radish and ginger will last a little longer.

## Buying Noodles

There is a wide selection of dried noodles available in Chinatown, as well as an increasing variety on the shelves of major super-markets. Egg noodles are easy to find in all shapes and sizes. The finest dried egg noodles can be boiled then shallow-fried to make a crispy nest on which all manner of delicacies can be stacked. This is the classic Cantonese noodle sold in most Chinese restaurants in Britain.

The ubiquitous Singapore noodle is probably single-handedly responsible for popularizing dried rice noodles. This rice stick noodle only needs to be soaked for a short while before being stir-fried. It is quite different to the thicker, softer river noodle (hofun), which is one of our favourites.

Most difficult to fathom are the fresh noodles. Dried noodles simply cannot compare with them. The fresh Japanese egg noodle or ramen that we use in our soup noodle dishes is not available retail, though a vacuum-packed version can be bought in good specialist Japanese supermarkets. Alternatively, fresh spaghettini will do, but remember not to fully cook them because they continue to cook in the soup broth. In general Italian pasta should be more al dente than its Chinese counterparts.

River noodles (hofun), the flat, soft rice noodles, are commonly available in Chinese supermarkets. Sometimes you can find river noodles with specks of prawn and sausage which add flavour and interest. In general, the supermarket river noodle is not so good as the version that comes directly in plastic bags from the factory somewhere in the back streets behind Soho's Gerrard Street. If you can find the unmarked back door it is a sight to see the great stainless steel machine being fed at one end with raw rice and water, and producing great skeins of soggy white noodles at the other. If you cannot find river noodles, wide flat tagliatelle, par-boiled, are the preferred substitute.

Finally, yellow egg oil noodles and white noodles are easily found in the refrigerators of Chinese supermarkets. Again, the quality is not so good as that supplied directly to the trade, but it is infinitely superior to dried egg noodles. A version of this noodle is now sold in leading supermarkets, together with an instant sauce. Due to its oily nature the oil noodle can be added directly to a stir-fry without pre-cooking, and without much sauce or oil to toss it in. The white noodle is also important to Beijing and Sichuan cooking. Unlike the oil noodle it must be blanched before serving.

## Basic Cooking Techniques

There are many cooking techniques to learn in the broader field of Chinese cookery, but most are already familiar to the European cook. Deep-frying in batter, shallow-frying, roasting, braising, stewing, boiling, marinating, barbecuing and steaming need no introduction. The only difference is the combination of ingredients. Red-cooking, for example, is simply stewing with soy sauce for varying periods over a low heat. Deep-fried battered foods might then be braised in a small amount of stock and other flavourings. Marinated foods may be roasted, deep-fried or shallow-fried. Often pre-cooked foods are assembled at the last minute, sometimes brought together in a savoury unifying sauce. There is no mystery or magic to the methods. Only stir-frying is different. As most of the dishes in this book contain an element of stir-fry, it is as well to begin to learn.

### A GUIDE TO STIR-FRYING

*The Wok*  In stir-frying it is traditional to use a tempered iron wok, the word that is the romanization of the Cantonese pronunciation for pot. You can use a large, thin-bottomed frying pan instead, but the essence of the technique is that the food is cooked quickly, over very high heat, in very little oil. Woks come in various sizes. The largest are used for preparing food in restaurants and are not necessary for domestic cooking. For a family, a wok of about 35cm (14 inch) in diameter is sufficient for stir-frying, deep-frying, simmering and steaming. It is best to purchase the round steel stand that goes with it, to prevent the wok rolling around on the stove. A traditional wok must be seasoned by brushing it with a thin coat of oil and heating it over a low heat, turning to make sure that the oil heats all over. Wipe it clean with kitchen paper and repeat the process. Finally rinse it and dry over direct heat. To clean a wok it is best simply to use running water and a fine bristle brush. You can buy various bristle and bamboo implements for cleaning the wok in a Chinese supermarket, but an ordinary bristle brush for cleaning vegetables is sufficient. Brush away anything that is sticking to the wok and rinse under running water. Then dry over direct heat. Regular use will prevent it rusting, but otherwise be sure to keep it oiled.

Because of the need to change the degree of heat suddenly it is not easy to stir-fry over an electric stove. The distance created by the stand removes the wok from the source of heat. A compromise is to keep two hobs at different temperatures and to move the wok from one to another, but without a stand this may be dangerous at home. Electric woks are an acceptable substitute.

A long-handled ladle is usually used along with the wok as an extension to your hand. It helps to turn and flip the food. A perforated spoon or flat metal sieve with a handle is also useful to strain oil, which is often used over and over again.

*Oil*   The quality of the oil is critical to the success of stir-frying, and by this we do not mean using the finest virgin olive oil. Olive oil, butter and sesame oil burn at quite low temperatures and are useless for stir-frying. Sesame oil can be used to flavour, but the thick concentrated Chinese version overpowers the flavour of the food. It is better to use a bland oil that can also withstand high temperatures, such as soy, sunflower, vegetable or groundnut oils. Lard is traditional and imparts a rich flavour and a glossy sheen, but is generally considered to be unacceptable these days.

To begin, the wok must first be heated before adding the oil so that it moves freely. Cold oil clings to a cold wok and makes the food stick. The oil must be swirled around to coat as much of the surface as possible. When the oil is on the point of smoking it is ready.

Oil is generally flavoured by being used and re-used (although it must be acknowledged that recent medical research blames the re-using of oil as the cause of several diseases). In stir-frying, ingredients are often deep-fried for a few seconds before pouring off the oil. The best way to manage this is to have an oil bowl covered with a strainer next to the cooker. When the food has been adequately deep-fried the contents of the wok can be poured through the strainer and left to drain thoroughly while you go on to the next stage. To re-claim the oil strain it thoroughly into a wok. Heat it together with some fresh ginger and a sliced spring onion. Let the onion and ginger brown before discarding. Cool the oil and store it in a sealed container.

*Preparation*   It is true what they say about Chinese food taking forever to prepare and no time to cook. The cutting is arduous, but does not require any particular skill. To cook through quickly, lean meats must be cubed, minced or sliced thinly and uniformly, against the grain, to break up the fibres. Vegetables must be cut with a sensitivity to how long they take to cook; Chinese leaves cook quickly, so need not be cut too finely; carrots are harder and need to be cut into julienne strips.

Once cut, the meat is often marinated in soy sauce, rice wine, sugar, salt or cornflour. Marinating helps it to absorb flavoured liquids, and prevents it from shrivelling and drying when it is coated with searing hot oil. Chicken, prawns and fish are sometimes marinated in egg-white, cornflour and oil or just cornflour and oil for 30 minutes. They are then deep-fried in hot oil for a few seconds before being drained and added to the stir-fry at the appropriate moment. These marinades help to tenderize the meat or fish and give them a smoother texture.

Stir-frying is the perfect way to bring out the best in vegetables. It is possible to cook them to perfection without losing any of their fresh crunchiness and taste. Some slightly harder vegetables may need to be blanched and drained before stir-frying. In general, you should always wash and dry vegetables before cutting. Throwing wet vegetables into hot oil will certainly get you into trouble.

Since the final stir-fry happens at great speed, the ingredients should be prepared first if you are a novice so as not to distract your attention when it actually comes to cooking. Sometimes all the wet ingredients and flavouring agents will be mixed in advance. Most Chinese chefs will have their bottles of sauce and flavouring ingredients lined up within arm's reach of the hob.

*Tossing the Wok*   Stir-frying can be divided into several stages, depending on the ingredients and the particular process chosen. Father and chefs of his generation always talked about flavouring the oil, which involves heating a little oil in the wok and adding flavouring agents such as garlic or ginger. We find that garlic added directly to hot oil burns easily, and this then ruins the whole dish. It is better to add the flavouring agents at a later stage with the vegetables,when they still have a chance to flavour the oil. If a recipe does suggest adding ginger to the oil first, fry it on its own for just a few seconds before adding other ingredients.

More commonly we find that chefs will add a quantity of oil to the wok in order to deep-fry the meat, poultry, fish or seafood for a few seconds before draining and setting aside. The vegetables are then scattered into the wok so as not to reduce the heat of the oil. This is the start of the stir-fry. By tipping the wok and drawing it towards the body and then thrusting it forward again, all the contents of the wok spin into the air and fold over on themselves. A heavy iron spoon completes the action by flipping the food over. Clearly, it takes a little time to master the wrist action, and it is more difficult on a domestic cooker, but it is fun to try. The crucial idea is that the ingredients are tossed, turned and flipped in generous sweeping motions – anything to make them move around the wok without sticking and burning. They must end up cooked evenly and coated on all sides with oil and sauce.

The seasonings, and any stock, soy and other liquids are all added during the middle stage of the stir-fry. When the contents of the wok are brought back to the boil the heat is turned down to a strong simmer and sometimes the wok is covered. The contents are now left to steam vigorously. Timing depends on the particular ingredients, but this middle stage should not exceed a few minutes. As we always try to avoid adding too much cornflour to our sauces, the dishes can be reduced by simmering at this stage. When crackling sounds can be heard this is the moment when the liquids are about to dry up.

Finally, garnishes that do not need cooking, such as julienned cucumber, coriander and finely sliced spring onion, are added to the wok with sesame oil to flavour and finish the dish. This is also the point at which cornflour solution is added, if it is used at all, to thicken and glaze any remaining sauce.

Stir-fried food must always be served immediately. It cannot be left to sit. This is one of the reasons why it is difficult to produce at a sit-down dinner if you are making a number of dishes and expect to sit down too. I find that at meals with Chinese families the women are constantly in the kitchen, and only sit down at the end of the meal when the stir-fried dishes are definitely looking weary! At home, it is best to stir-fry for a family meal where one or two dishes will do for everyone.

## Simple Stock-making

One of the most frustrating conundrums of this book is that many of our dishes specify freshly-made stock. In the kitchens of a good restaurant or in traditional family homes a stockpot is always kept just below a simmer, but what do you do in modern households where life is not regular and everyone is out all day?

There is no doubt that if you are making a clear soup there is nothing comparable to the broths described below, but if you are simply adding a tablespoon or two to stir-fry or stew you can be forgiven for using ready-prepared stock powder or even water, depending on the strength of the other ingredients. Most restaurants simply use the ready-prepared stock bases provided by oriental suppliers. The problem is the ingredients. Most powders and bases still use MSG and other undesirable flavourings, although there are some which are more aware of customers' demands for additive-free products. Vegetarian bouillon powders now available in health-food shops are light years ahead of the yeast pastes that father had to put up with during his early years of writing cookery books, but the dominating flavour is still salt. If you like a seafood flavour the Japanese bonito flakes may be to your taste. Or if you live near a good supermarket, a better solution are the freshly-made beef and chicken stocks sold in cartons and stored in the refrigerator section.

### BASIC CHICKEN STOCK

If you have the time, then there is nothing like a home-made chicken broth. Use a whole chicken, then remove the best pieces after 30 minutes for use in one of the recipes that requires pre-cooked chicken. If you use a free-range chicken the stock will taste infinitely better and definitely will not require much seasoning. The markets serving Afro-Caribbean and Jewish communities are the best bet for well-flavoured chickens. Pork bones are a necessary evil and make a big difference to the flavour. If you object you will probably have to beef up the stock with some proprietary bouillon.

1 large free-range chicken
500 g (1 lb) pork bones
3 cm (1¼ inch) piece of root ginger, sliced
1 spring onion, trimmed
1 teaspoon white peppercorns
4 litres (7 pints) water
dash of oyster sauce (optional)
salt and sugar to taste

Remove the fat from the cavity and cut off the parson's nose. Rinse the chicken in cold water, cleaning all blood from the cavity to prevent the broth becoming cloudy. Joint the chicken and cut the wings, legs and back into 2.5cm (1 inch) pieces.

Place the pork bones and all the chicken except the breast in a large heavy pan. Cover it with cold water and bring to a brisk boil. Turn off the heat immediately and strain, pouring the water away. Return the pork bones and chicken to the pan with the vegetables, peppercorns and oyster sauce. Pour on the water and bring to a brisk boil. Add the chicken breast. Turn the heat to low and skim off all impurities from the surface. When the stock is clear turn up the heat and bring back to the boil. Adjust to a gentle simmer, preventing the stock from returning to a full boil. After 30 minutes remove the breast and take the meat off the bones. Return the bones to the pan. Simmer for a further 3 hours, stirring occasionally. Skim the surface from time to time to keep the broth clear.

Let the broth cool, then strain through a fine or muslin-lined sieve. Discard the meat and bones and strain again. Skim the oil from the stock if it is to be used straight away. Season lightly to taste with salt and sugar, remembering that there will be further seasoning when the final soup is prepared. The stock will keep for 4–5 days in the refrigerator and for about 3 months in the freezer. Leave the fat on the top to seal, removing it before you use the stock.

VEGETARIAN STOCK

Jenny Lo's Teahouse must be one of a handful of establishments that prepares a clear vegetarian stock every day for its customers. There are any number of variations, including turnip, cabbage, leeks, onions, courgettes and garlic, but be careful not to use ingredients such as celery which give the stock a turbid colour. One interesting addition is a little deep-fried Sichuan pickle, which will give the stock a hot, spicy flavour.

1 large Chinese white radish, chopped
4 large carrots, chopped
handful of coriander and parsley stalks
3 cm (1 ¼ inch) piece of root ginger
2 bay leaves
3 litres (5 pints) water
bouillon powder, to taste (optional)
salt and sugar to taste

Place all the ingredients except the salt and sugar in a large pan. Bring the water to a rolling boil then turn the heat down, skimming any impurities from the surface. Simmer for 3 hours, then strain through a fine or muslin-lined sieve. Season lightly to taste with salt and sugar, remembering that there will be further seasoning when the final soup is prepared. If you eat fish then a dash of fish sauce is a good, delicate addition to the broth.

*Uncle Walter*

# 1 Recipes from the Northern Teahouse

I love Beijing. In Beijing human lives are painted vividly in grey, against an urban background that is as wide and deep as the sky itself. From the market-lined boulevards where you have to dodge bicycles and grey trucks to the tiny grey hutongs with their huddled dwellings, its scale never ceases to impress me. Temples and city gates frowning on the horizon serve as an eternal reminder that in the face of might and history, each individual is of very little consequence. The relics of antiquity seem to say that imperial grandeur may not be long gone. Perhaps it never even went. But despite the towering edifices designed to intimidate, the surety of political corruption and the scale of human tragedies, ordinary life in Beijing is filled with the colour and diversity of all four seasons.

For me, Uncle Walter is Beijing. To look at he is the image of my father, although much more unkempt. Their lives, however, could scarcely have been more different. Father and Uncle Charles escaped the Japanese war and fled Yanjing and Qinghua universities to attend Cambridge and Harvard respectively. From there, regardless of the inevitable struggle of the disinherited, they continued to enjoy a lifetime of daily tennis, educated company and international travel. And they were always to be found where the best food was being served. Father, in particular, was accomplished at living well on a shoe-string. Life was not to be so glamorous for Uncle Walter. Being the third brother, the least academic and the last to graduate to the capital from Fuzhou, he was always left out, and consequently was just a little too late to escape the looming invasion. Since the late 1930s he has lived on his own, eking out a living either by sponging off relatives or teaching a little English, which he speaks perfectly in 'Voice of America' style.

For thirty years Uncle Walter has lived in a shabby ground-floor room off Changanjie (Boulevard of Eternal Peace) in the heart of the city. In the next room along the passageway live a tailor and his family of six, who share the gas ring and sink. In the last ten years, since he has accumulated a little money from relatives overseas, Uncle Walter has acquired a bed and a lightshade. Lipton tea and disposable razors are scattered across his calico tablecloth along with the other luxuries of life. Maps paper the bare, peeling walls. Every morning he takes his daily constitutional along the route also taken by the tanks in June 1989 when they rolled into Tiananmen to crush the student demonstration. It is about a three mile round trip. Since he was knocked down in a cycling accident he has walked with slow deliberation, leaning heavily on a walking stick.

Despite the frailty of age and illness, Walter launches himself across Changanjie without looking to left or right, sending bicycles scattering in all directions. Having crossed the cycling lanes he will rest a moment to catch his breath before making a beeline across the wide central avenue where trucks thunder past without slowing down to acknowledge old-age pensioners. He never wavers or hesitates, never stops to look at what has just missed ending his life. In winter, he proudly sports the old Barbour that I sent him one Christmas. (He is even prouder now that he knows that the more worn and stained it looks, the more he resembles the Queen of England.)

The main purpose of his daily expedition is to bump into a group of British or American tourists and have a chance to practise his English or pontificate on the state of the Chinese economy. Changanjie is also where the Friendship Store and most of the expensive hotels are located, so his chances of such entertainment are quite high. I believe he would move away from the centre of town if it was not for these chance meetings, or if he was not waiting for a relative from overseas to drop by and take him out to dinner. Every few years or so one of us does.

From a western, or even a traditional Chinese, point of view, Walter's life is a shambles. He has had very little money, no wife, children or close family nearby to care for him, and the barest of physical comforts. But being gentle, naturally frugal and, most important, insignificant have stood him in good stead. When the Red Guards came knocking in 1966 Walter invited them in and gave them a cup of tea and a warm bowl of water to wash their feet. After all they were only children, and being revolutionaries was exhausting work. All along he was polite and courteous. As a teacher, he could not completely avoid 'correction' during the Cultural Revolution. At the kangeroo court the children in charge were particularly interested in why he had been given a foreign imperialist, capitalist name. When he answered that he was given the name Walter in 1919 by an English doctor who couldn't spell Xiaoyue on the medicine bottle, the whole court collapsed in a fit of giggles. Anybody called 'Wotou' – Chinese for turnip head – could not be taken seriously. Walter was let off with writing a voluminous confession of guilt.

But despite the poverty of his existence Walter never seems depressed. Years of hardship have taught him to derive great satisfaction from the simplest of pleasures. And, being a Lo, the greatest of these is eating. He is a connoisseur of the teahouses and cafés of Beijing. As evening draws on in the red brick compound where he lives, the row of hard metal stands which hawk meat, fruit, vegetables and clothing shut up shop and a number of small cafés open their doors to the locals. Out in the compound dusty faces brush past in the half-light and the smell of supper wafts through the cooling air. There is a timeless tranquillity in the certainty with which daily life repeats itself. The sonorous din of daytime buying, bargaining and vending has calmed to a murmur. At 6 o'clock the small cafés offer the cheapest, and some of the best, basic fare to be had in Beijing. Some are more decorous than others. Most still have simple benches beside the rough, rusty formica-topped tables and bare concrete floors where cigarettes are stubbed out in great quantity. There is very little light to read the menu. With a group of friends, the effect is to make the gathering even more intimate. The waitress, amused at the presence of foreigners, waits impatiently for the order and manages to be friendly without being either deferential or rude. Walter presides over the table.

I always suggest braised aubergine and stir-fried greens. He chooses mandarin fish and mushu rou and together we decide upon the long-cooked belly of pork. He, indulgently, worries about cholesterol and tells me about an article he has read about the beneficial effect of eating broccoli and drinking green tea. Perhaps if we order everything, the green things will cancel out the saturated fat. Here in the sanctuary of the compound we sink into the comfort that comes of being family, without expectation of grand conversation, etiquette or the burden of having to decide who does the washing-up. Bones pile up on the table.

For the same price as our five-course meal we can buy chocolate cake and percolated coffee on the other side of Changanjie. Flanking the glass doorway, the waitresses, wearing long brocade split-leg dresses, are also on patrol. They don't like the look of Walter. The dandruff and food stains on his worn lapels mark him out as a local. Nevertheless they smile graciously. The high bridge of my nose and indeterminate looks are sufficient to suggest that I might harbour credit cards about my person. Walter is in seventh heaven.

Once the eating has concluded the party is naturally over and we slowly walk Walter home to his compound. By this time there is little left to say. For now, the business of eating and the pursuit of the next meal is suspended and replaced by a feeling of well-being, with the prospect of a good sleep before the merry-go-round begins again.

Almost all Chinese, whatever their social status, live by and for their bellies. I have not yet met a Chinese anorexic. It must be a legacy of the fear of going hungry, engendered by being one of so many million in an uncertain environment. As anyone who works with Chinese people knows, eating comes before every-thing else. When the clock strikes 12 noon or 6 o'clock nothing will keep self-respecting Chinese at their desks. And in Beijing you can rely on there being good food to satisfy hunger and assuage anxiety.

A good friend will always agree to eat with you, just as you can always expect to be well fed by them on another occasion. Eating cannot be a solitary affair, but must be shared with the people you love or are doing business with; it increases the pleasure. Talking about food is also an integral part of the ritual. Even the familiar greeting is not the equivalent of the formal 'How are you?' that students of Chinese always learn first and use inappropriately, but 'Have you eaten yet?'

Now that Beijing is surrounded by greenhouses and market gardens, food in the little cafés is no longer quite so determined by the vegetables seasonally available in the adjacent street market. In the old days it would be brought into town on sturdy legs, by peasants swinging heavily laden baskets on either end of a long pole. Nowadays I suppose it thunders down Changanjie in those grey trucks. But quantity and price still vary according to the season. All the seasons in Beijing are reliably distinct.

After a long, frozen winter, spring comes slowly to the North China plain. A bitterly cold wind gradually dries out the ground. Nothing has yet begun to grow and food becomes expensive. Only a few decades ago the quality of life would depend upon how well the winter stores were laid in the cold holes. After the top layers were peeled off, life became a constant round of carrots, cabbage, turnips and potatoes. Cheap food remains the same. Dust, blown from the loose silt of the Yellow River plain, blocks the nose and irritates the eyes. The rasping guttural sound of people retching on the streets gains new heights. But soon the light rains arrive and the insects awaken – butterflies, green cicadas, beetles and locusts busy themselves in the courtyards. Lamb replaces mutton.

Beijing has many good lamb dishes. One of the most refreshing snacks in the dusty northern spring are the pancakes rolled with steaming 'jiu cai', a cross between chives and bean sprouts, fried with tender lamb and savoury piquant sauces. Of course Mongolian hotpot is the essence of northern family celebration. Its secret is that everyone does the cooking themselves. Wafer-thin slices of lamb are plunged into a hotpot full of broth brought to a rolling boil at the table. Each diner mixes three or four savoury dips, some chilli hot, some spicy with ginger and garlic, and others with the nutty taste of sesame. Once the meat is finished, bowls full of noodles and sliced cabbage are emptied into the broth and the pot is covered and allowed to simmer for five minutes.

Then there is the barbecue of lamb that my father was so fond of. For him, the gloom of a cold night in Beijing was dispelled by sitting around a blazing charcoal burner in the company of four or more good friends. It evoked the campfires and camaraderie of nomadic life. For centuries East Market had been the place for the most fun and entertainment. You could buy antiques, paintings and scrolls, eat snacks and sweetmeats while watching open-air theatre, dance, or listen to Beijing Opera. This is how he described the barbecues at East Market in his autobiography:

The most enticing delicacy was Mongolian Barbecue of Lamb. Slices of lamb were dipped in egg before being grilled over a blazing fire and eaten with a spicy sauce. It was a feast fit for any Mongolian prince!

In the second phase of spring a warmer wind blows and new plans and projects, harboured throughout hibernation, begin to take shape. Fresh hope seems to break through the ground with the new seedlings. Despite, or perhaps because of, the suppression of 'superstition' during the decades of continuing revolution, a lot of activity can still be seen in the graveyards around the time of the Qingming festival. It is time to sweep the graves and courtyards and appease the ancestors with suitable offerings of food and a family picnic.

Around the Forbidden City there are still beautiful family houses with rooms that open out on to a central courtyard filled with winter jasmine and the whites and pale pinks of flowering peach, pear and plum blossoms. Fine latticework of the imperial age can still be found there, but it is often in a sad state of disrepair, and now that the compounds house several families, rather than perhaps a famous courtesan or wealthy bureaucrat, cabbages and maize are planted alongside the sunflowers.

As spring turns to summer, the grain begins to ripen and activity on the plains around Beijing increases. Apples, tomatoes, spinach, cucumbers and water melons pour into town. Life and the living-room move out on to the street, ahead of the dog-days of midsummer when no one can withstand the tyranny of the sun. It is then that everything stops. Chilled green or jasmine tea quenches the thirst. Even better is the sour prune soup (cold boiled prune juice), icy and tart, that used to be wheeled round the streets late in the tranquil nights of summer, and can be bought in bottles straight from the refrigerator at the corner shop.

In old Beijing there were three kinds of teahouse. First, there was the teahouse from Jiangnan (south of the Yangzi River), probably a euphemism for a brothel. The other special pleasure of the Jiangnan teahouse was that it served cakes. Another kind served savoury dishes: both teahouse and restaurant rolled into one. Finally there was the literary teahouse, where tea-drinking was accompanied by traditional story-telling and Shandong fast tales. Lao She (1899–1966), the famous playwright, described one such teahouse in the introduction to his famous play *Teahouse* (1957; translation by John Howard Gibbon):

Large teahouses are no longer to be seen in the capital, but a few decades ago every district in Beijing had at least one, where in addition to tea, simple snacks and meals were served. Every day bird fanciers, after strolling about with their caged orioles and thrushes, would come in to rest awhile, enjoy a pot of tea, and compare the singing abilities of their birds. Go-betweens and those who had deals to discuss also frequented such teahouses. In those days there would often be quarrels between gangs, but there were always friends about to calm things down. The two sides would crowd around these mediators who would reason first with one side then the other; then they would all drink tea and down bowls of noodles with minced pork (a speciality of the large teahouses – cheap and quickly prepared), hostility transformed to hospitality. In sum, the teahouse was an important institution of those times, a place where people came to transact business, or simply to while away the time.

In the teahouses one could hear the most absurd stories, such as how in a certain place a huge spider had turned into a demon and was then struck by lightning. One could also come in contact with the strangest views; for example, that foreign troops could be prevented from landing by building a Great Wall along the sea coast. Here one might also hear about the latest tune composed by some Beijing Opera star, or the best way to prepare opium. In the teahouses one might also see rare art objects newly acquired by some patron – a jade fan pendant, recently unearthed, or a three-colour glazed snuff bottle. Yes, the teahouse was indeed an important place; it could even be reckoned a kind of cultural centre . . .

Just inside the main entrance is the counter and a cookstove. The room should be large and high-ceilinged with both oblong tables and square ones, and traditional teahouse benches and stools. Through the window an inner courtyard can be seen with more benches and stools under a high awning. In the teahouse and under the awning there are hooks for hanging bird-cages. Pasted everywhere are notices: 'Don't discuss state affairs'.

For me the teahouses of Beijing are those around Uncle Walter's compound. But street food is also a great entertainment. The best is to be found at breakfast-time in the steaming roadside cafés where you can take a place at any time of the year. You can find hot sweet potatoes, tea eggs, warm soya milk with oil sticks (the Beijing equivalent of the Spanish churros) or almond tea. There are also many hot griddle cakes stuffed with sweet red bean paste or nuts and covered with sesame seeds.

Lao She compared loving Beijing to loving your mother: words can't really express the feeling. When you think of something charming, like the fine food she produces, it brings a faint and private smile to your face, but if you think of her frailty and deteriorating health it can bring you to tears. For me loving Beijing holds something of that quality. Perhaps it is Uncle Walter. Perhaps it is inheriting my father's memories of the early 1930s, undoubtedly the happiest years of his life. Whatever the reason Beijing, solemn, dusty but vivid, has a way of getting under your skin.

# Breakfast in Beijing

杏
仁
茶

**Almond Tea**

Almond tea used to be peddled on the streets of Beijing at
daybreak. It is not really a tea, more a sweet, light soup that
gently awakens the digestion. It might be likened to having
warm milk for breakfast, without being so heavy or rich. Add or
subtract water, so that you can drink the final product from a
bowl. It should not be as thick as porridge. The same recipe can
be made with walnuts: when drunk daily, it is thought to
rejuvenate the skin.

200 g (7 oz) ground almonds
20 g (¾ oz) glutinous rice powder or plain ground rice
1 litre (1¾ pints) water
sugar, to taste

Put the almonds and rice powder in a blender or food processor.
With the motor running, slowly add the water to make a liquid.
Pour into a pan and add sugar to taste. Place over a medium
heat, stirring continuously. When the liquid boils turn down the
heat and simmer for 10 minutes, stirring to prevent it sticking.
Add more water if the mixture thickens too much. Serve in
small bowls for breakfast with a griddle cake or doughnut. It can
also be served as a dessert, or a filling drink.

豆
腐
漿
和
油
條

## Soya Milk and Oil Sticks

Vivienne cannot decide whether soya milk and oil sticks or hot chocolate and churros are her favourite breakfast. It depends whether she is waking up in Spain or in the dusty streets of Beijing. The soya milk can be drunk plain, as it is naturally sweet, or it can be sweetened to taste. It should be warmed, but not boiled, and seems to taste better from a bowl rather than a cup. Oil sticks are essentially the same as the Spanish churros, or doughnuts, but without the sugar. As we cannot find a recipe for them, and the only one we've heard of contains unacceptable ingredients, try the griddle cakes on the following page instead.

一品燒餅

## Beijing No 1 Griddle Cakes
MAKES 20

From starting with the simplest recipe we now go on to one of
the most difficult in the book! Beijing has many kinds of griddle
cakes that are sold in cafés or at the roadside. As there is no
concept of a four o'clock tea-time, they are eaten at breakfast-
time, or any other time between meals. The cake they most
closely resemble is the English Eccles cake. Griddle cakes come
with assorted fillings and are particularly abundant around the
New Year. The filling we have used needs a tart-flavoured jam.
In Beijing it would be haw jam, but blackcurrant jam or
cranberry sauce would be an acceptable alternative.

500g (1 lb) self-raising flour
8 tablespoons cold water
4 tablespoons vegetable oil, plus extra for frying
sesame seeds to coat the cakes

STUFFING
50 g (2 oz) walnuts, roughly chopped
150 g (5 oz) sugar
1 teaspoon lemon juice
pinch of salt
4 teaspoons blackcurrant jam or cranberry sauce
2 tablespoons sesame oil or tahini

Sieve 320 g (10 oz) of the flour into a bowl and slowly mix in the
water until you have a sticky dough. Cover and set aside for 30
minutes.

Meanwhile, sieve 160 g (5½ oz) of the flour into a mixing bowl
and make a well in the centre. Gently heat the 4 tablespoons of
oil in a pan. When the oil is hot, pour it slowly into the well and
work it into the flour, pushing and squeezing with the fingertips.

To make the stuffing, toss the walnuts with the remaining
flour in a bowl, then mix thoroughly with the rest of the stuffing
ingredients.

Turn out the reserved dough on to a floured work-surface and shape into 2 sausages. Cut each one into 10 pieces. Press each piece flat, then roll out into 10 cm (4 inch) rounds with a rolling pin. The round should be thinner at the edges, so roll around the edges again. Shape the oiled flour into another sausage and divide into 20 pieces. Place each piece at the centre of a round of dough and press down with the fingers, flattening it so that it makes a smaller yellow round on top of the original round.

Place a teaspoonful of the stuffing at the centre of each round. Draw the sides up and gather together as if making tiny pleats. When you have what looks like a tiny drawstring purse press the opening together. Then turn the bun in the palm of one hand alternately nipping in and pressing down on the opening until it can no longer be seen. Press the cake as flat as possible without making the bottom layer of dough so thin that you can see through it. Sprinkle the sesame seeds on a plate and press the bottom of the cake on to the sesame seeds.

Brush a heavy frying pan or griddle with oil and fry the cakes in batches over the lowest heat possible. Cook for about 5 minutes on one side until the cake browns underneath, pressing down with a spatula, then turn and cook on the other side. If the heat is too high the outside will burn while the inside will not be cooked. The sesame seeds may drop in the pan and burn, so scoop them out when they do. Brush the pan with more oil from time to time. If the seeds burn badly then the pan may have to be washed once or twice before all the cakes are cooked.

## 蔥油餅 Spring Onion Cakes

MAKES 20

Friends from Beijing will make onion cakes to go with any family meal. They are a perfect accompaniment to clear soups and vegetable dishes and are always a favourite with children. In the elegant tree-lined streets of north Shanghai street vendors ringing handbells still hawk a deep-fried version for breakfast. If 20 is too many for one sitting the dough can be kept wrapped in the refrigerator for up to 48 hours. Rolling the pancakes thinly makes them crisp, and avoids the centre being stodgy.

400 g (13 oz) plain flour
125 g (4 oz) self-raising flour
400 ml (14 fl oz) boiling water
10 tablespoons finely chopped spring onions, green part only
2½ teaspoons salt
150 ml (¼ pint) vegetable oil

Sieve the flours together into a bowl. Pour the boiling water into the flour in a thin stream, stirring and mixing thoroughly. Leave to stand for a few minutes, then add enough cold water to mix into a pliable dough. Knead for a few minutes, then cover with clingfilm and leave for 30 minutes.

Divide the dough into 5 pieces and roll each piece into a 30 cm (12 inch) pancake. Sprinkle each pancake with an even layer of chopped spring onion and half a teaspoon of salt. Drizzle 1 tablespoon of oil evenly over the top, then roll the pancake into a long sausage. Divide the sausage into 4 equal segments and pat each segment into a round. Flatten the rounds with the palm of the hand, then roll them out into 10 cm (4 inch) pancakes. Try not to let the spring onions poke through the dough.

Heat some oil in a heavy frying pan, varying the amount according to taste. Less oil will make the pancake like a chapati, while more is often to the taste of the children.

Shallow-fry each pancake until brown underneath, pressing down with a fish slice, then turn and brown on the other side. The cooking should take about 5 minutes.

# Vegetable and Vegetarian Dishes

紅燒茄子 **Red-braised Aubergine**

SERVES 4

This is one of the dishes that we always order when we eat with Uncle Walter. It is best eaten with plain boiled rice and one or two other dishes such as one of the egg dishes, the greens and the onion cakes.

8 tablespoons vegetable oil, plus extra if needed
3 cloves garlic, crushed
2 small aubergines, halved and sliced diagonally in 2.5 cm (1 inch) pieces
½ red pepper, cored, seeded and cut into thin strips (optional)
2 tablespoons light soy sauce
1 tablespoon sugar
½ tablespoon rice vinegar
chopped coriander, to garnish

Heat the oil in a wok over a high heat. When it begins to smoke slightly add half the garlic and then the aubergine. Stir-fry for 30 seconds then turn the heat down and continue stirring, adding a little more oil if necessary.

When the aubergine is cooked through and quite soft, add the red pepper and stir for a further minute. Add the soy sauce, sugar, vinegar and the remaining garlic and stir for another minute. Turn into a serving dish and sprinkle with chopped coriander.

涼
拌
粉
絲

## Spicy Silk Noodle Salad

SERVES 4

This is a very popular family dish which makes a deliciously pungent starter, or an accompaniment to more bland dishes. Being cold and quick to prepare it is especially good in the summer. The main work is in assembling the ingredients. Fen si noodles are made from a green bean and taste quite unlike any other. They most closely resemble rice noodles, although they are more translucent. Take care when buying them: they are often known as green bean silk noodles.

half a packet, about 125 g (4 oz), fen si noodles
1 carrot, cut into matchstick-sized slivers
1 spring onion, finely sliced
2 cloves garlic, crushed and finely chopped
1 tablespoon tahini
2 tablespoons water
pinch of salt
2 tablespoons dark soy sauce
1 tablespoon rice vinegar
1 tablespoon sesame oil
¼ hot chilli, finely chopped
small bunch of coriander, roughly chopped
coriander sprigs, to garnish

Place the noodles in a bowl and pour on enough boiling water to cover. Leave to soak for a few minutes until just soft but still al dente, then drain, rinse under cold water, then drain well. Divide the noodles between 4 bowls. Mix together the remaining ingredients and pour over the noodles. Garnish with coriander sprigs.

鍋塌豆腐

## Battered Bean Curd

SERVES 4

Being a vegetarian, our friend Joanna was very apprehensive about going to Beijing. She was well prepared for her hair to fall out from eating nothing but plain boiled rice for three months. The first month studying Ming dynasty case histories at the Beijing medical college did nothing to dispel her anxiety – no food, no friends and nowhere to go – just the greyness of the dormitories and only Uncle Walter to keep her amused. Then she found the café behind the campus where the proprietor and his wife served up every dish on the menu with bean curd instead of meat. From then on everything took a turn for the better. Although, in her words, most of the dishes seemed to be drowned in 'brown sludge', each one tasted good and distinctly different. Now that she is back in London she can't wait to go back for more!

500 g (1 lb) or one cake bean curd, cut into 2.5 cm (1 inch) cubes
1 teaspoon salt
5 egg yolks, beaten
1 teaspoon sesame oil
pinch of black pepper
1 tablespoon cornflour
2 tablespoons vegetable oil
1 small Spanish onion
3 cloves garlic, finely chopped
1 stick celery, finely chopped
25 g (1 oz) Sichuan pickle, finely chopped
20 g (¾ oz) sesame seeds, lightly toasted
handful of fresh coriander leaves, chopped
1 spring onion, chopped

Sprinkle the bean curd with half the salt and leave for 30 minutes. Season the egg yolks with the remaining salt, sesame oil and black pepper. Dust the bean curd with the cornflour and dip each piece into the egg batter.

Heat the oil in a wok, add the onion and stir-fry for 1 minute.

Add the garlic and arrange the bean curd pieces around the base of the wok. Turn the heat to medium and brown the bean curd on each side, moving the pieces carefully to prevent them sticking. Mix the celery, pickle, and sesame seeds into the batter. Pour the mixture into the wok, sprinkle with the coriander and spring onion and leave until the egg is set and slightly brown. Remove with a spatula and serve immediately.

爆
炒
醋
辣
白
菜

## Hot and Sour Cabbage

SERVES 4 AS A SIDE DISH

This recipe livens up a familiar vegetable and is not at all difficult to make. Putting the salt in first helps seal the water into the cabbage and keeps it crisp.

1½ tablespoons vegetable oil
12 Sichuan peppercorns
3 dried red chillies, thinly sliced into rounds
½ teaspoon salt
1 small white cabbage, cut into 3cm (1½ inch) squares
1 tablespoon rice vinegar
½ teaspoon sugar
drop of sesame oil
coriander leaves, chopped, to garnish

Heat the oil in a pan until it just begins to smoke. Drop in the peppercorns and when their aroma escapes add the chillies, stirring for a few seconds. Add the salt, followed by the cabbage. Stir-fry over a high heat for 30 seconds, then add the vinegar, sugar and sesame oil. Turn for 2 minutes then serve immediately, sprinkled with fresh coriander.

小
白
菜

## Stir-fried Bak Choy

SERVES 2

The simplest way to cook bak choy, mustard greens, Chinese
leaves or spinach is simply to blanch them for about a minute in
boiling water, then turn in hot oil with some oyster sauce and
garlic for 30 seconds. This is how it is churned out in most fast
food establishments. Sometimes the second stage is omitted and
the oyster sauce poured cold over the blanched greens. Simply
tailor the cooking time to how tough the vegetables are, but be
careful not to overcook. The taste can be improved by stir-frying
from the beginning, as below. Green cabbage can also be used,
but increase the cooking time a little. The red bean curd cheese
can be omitted, but it would be advisable to replace it with a
tablespoon of dark soy sauce. Children who find boiled greens
inedible are often converted by the addition of garlic, a little soy
sauce and oil.

3 tablespoons vegetable oil
2 cloves garlic, crushed
1 teaspoon red bean curd cheese
250 g (8 oz) bak choy, leaves and white stems cut into short
strips 4 cm (1½ in) wide or 400 g (13 oz) spinach, hard stalks
removed
1 tablespoon good stock
pinch of salt
½ teaspoon sugar

Heat the oil in the wok, swirling it around until it starts to
smoke. Add the garlic and red bean cheese and crush together.
Then add the white part of the bak choy or all the other greens.
Stir-fry for 30 seconds, then turn down the heat. Add the
remaining green part of the bak choy with the stock, salt and
sugar and turn up the heat as high as possible, turning together
for another minute. Serve as a side dish with rice, or add oil
noodles at the last stage and garnish with coriander leaves for a
good lunch.

涼
拌
蕃
茄
黃
瓜

## Cold-tossed Tomato and Cucumber Salad

SERVES 4

Although this is a summer salad it can be served with any
selection of dishes, or even as an appetizer. It is attractive and
colourful and looks very effective served in a dark bowl.

1 medium cucumber, halved lengthways and cut into 5 mm (¼
inch) slices
1 tsp salt
200 g (7 oz) cherry tomatoes, halved
1 tablespoon sugar
2 tablespoons rice vinegar
1 tablespoon sunflower oil
1½ tablespoons sesame oil
Thai mint or coriander leaves, to garnish (optional)

Place the cucumber slices on a plate and sprinkle evenly with
the salt. Leave for 30 minutes, then pour away the excess juices.
Mix the tomatoes with the cucumber in a salad bowl. Combine
the sugar, vinegar and oils and mix thoroughly. Pour over the
salad and toss until well coated. Garnish with mint or coriander
leaves, if using.

# Egg Dishes

## 雞蛋西紅柿 Egg & Tomato Splash

SERVES 4

Vivienne's son Aaron, who is sometimes a vegetarian, demands this dish whenever Lily comes to dinner. Lily comes from Beijing and, being a Buddhist, is a more consistent vegetarian. She invariably ends up cooking for him. Of course, this dish could just be scrambled eggs with tomato, or it could be tomato omelette, but in fact it is neither. There is something very attractive about the vibrant yellow and red garnished with green. A variation of this dish is to replace the tomatoes with spinach: stir-fry 500 g (1 lb) of young spinach with a little salt and garlic until it is soft before returning the egg to the wok. Serve with rice (or toast!).

2 large spring onions, white part only, finely sliced
½ tsp salt
4 free-range eggs, beaten
3 tablespoons vegetable oil
5 tomatoes, quartered and seeded
1 teaspoon sugar
2 tablespoons water

Mix the spring onions and salt with the egg. Heat 2 tablespoons of the oil in a wok over a high heat. When it is just beginning to smoke pour in the egg mixture. As it swells stir quickly to prevent it burning. As soon as the egg turns a golden colour scoop it out of the pan with a slotted spoon and set aside. Turn the heat down. Heat the remaining oil in the wok. Add the tomatoes, sugar and water and simmer until the tomatoes are soft. Return the eggs to the wok, breaking them up with a fork, and mix with the tomato. Serve immediately.

賽
螃
蟹

## Competing with Crab

SERVES 3

Beijing is quite far from the sea, so it has few fish and seafood specialities, apart from the river crab that are hard to get hold of these days. No wonder they come up with concoctions like this! You have never tasted scrambled eggs quite so good, and the colour of the radishes even brings a hint of crab to the appearance of the dish. If you want to impress your guests, cook the yolks as below and steam the whites separately until they are solid. Then cut up the whites and add to the dish at the end. The white looks like crab meat whilst the yolk resembles the shell. Serve with a selection of other dishes and rice.

4 eggs
½ teaspoon salt
1 teaspoon sugar
5 tablespoons vegetable oil
1 tablespoon white wine vinegar
1 teaspoon oyster sauce
1 teaspoon Shaoxing wine
2.5 cm (1 inch) piece of root ginger, finely chopped
thinly sliced radishes, to garnish

Beat the eggs with the salt and sugar. Heat the oil in a pan and when it just begins to smoke pour in the egg. As the egg swells stir it quickly to prevent burning. When it is just beginning to turn firm add the vinegar, oyster sauce, Shaoxing wine and ginger. Turn again in the wok for a few seconds and serve, garnished with slices of radish.

# Meat dishes

爆
炒
羊
肉
片

## Flame-fried Lamb & Spring Onions

SERVES 2

This has always been a favourite in Beijing cafés. Most chefs add a teaspoon of cornflour blended with a little stock at the final stage, but we prefer to reduce the liquid. You will find it easier to slice the meat very thinly if it is slightly frozen first.

225 g (8 oz) lean lamb, sliced wafer-thin
4 tablespoons vegetable oil
1 teaspoon dark soy sauce
½ tablespoon light soy sauce
1 teaspoon yellow bean sauce
½ teaspoon chilli sauce
pinch of salt
½ tablespoon vinegar
2 teaspoons sugar
pinch of freshly ground pepper
1 tablespoon finely chopped root ginger
3 cloves garlic, crushed and finely chopped
6 large spring onions, green part only, sliced lengthways then chopped into 2.5 cm (1 inch) sections
½ carrot, thinly sliced on the diagonal
25 g (1 oz) mangetout (optional)
1 teaspoon sesame oil
½ tablespoon stock
½ tablespoon Shaoxing wine

Place the sliced lamb in a shallow dish, add 1 tablespoon oil and turn to coat. Leave to marinate for 30 minutes. Mix together the soy, yellow bean and chilli sauces, salt, vinegar, sugar and pepper.

Heat the remaining oil in a wok until it starts to smoke. Add the lamb, ginger and garlic. Stir-fry for 10 seconds, then turn down the heat and stir-fry until the meat changes colour. Immediately pour off as much of the oil as possible. Add the vegetables and sauce mixture. Turn up the heat to high and mix together for 20 seconds. Add the sesame oil, stock and wine and stir for another 10 seconds. Serve immediately on a bed of rice.

宮
爆
雞
丁

## Gongbao's Chicken Chunks

SERVES 3–4

This dish is fairly universal and very versatile. It is widely available in the back-street cafés of Beijing and is the tastiest of the ubiquitous 'brown sludge' dishes that our friend Joanna described. Pork or prawns may be substituted for chicken, and the nuts could be peanuts, almonds or walnuts. The chilli can also be varied or omitted altogether. Ding Gongbao was posted as an officer of the imperial court to Sichuan. For his leaving party he instructed his chef to entertain his friends with a new dish, the first in a great lineage of Gongbao dishes. Serve with rice and a vegetable dish.

350 g (12 oz) chicken breast, skinned, boned and cut into 2.5 cm (1 inch) cubes
2 tablespoons dark soy sauce
1 teaspoon cornflour
1 tablespoon Shaoxing wine
2 teaspoons sugar
pinch of salt
3 tablespoons vegetable oil
75 ml (3 fl oz) hot chicken stock (see page 18)
4 dried chillies (optional)
1 tablespoon finely chopped root ginger
1 small green pepper, cored, seeded and cut into 2.5 cm (1 inch) cubes
2 teaspoons red wine vinegar
50 g (2 oz) cashew nuts or pine nuts, toasted
1 teaspoon sesame oil

Place the chicken in a shallow dish, add 1 tablespoon of soy sauce and turn to coat well. Leave to marinate for 30 minutes. Blend the cornflour with the wine, remaining soy sauce, sugar and salt.

Heat 2 tablespoons of the oil in a wok until it just begins to smoke. Add the chicken and stir-fry until it changes colour. Add the stock and stir-fry for 1 minute, then pour the chicken and stock into a bowl and set aside. Wipe the wok clean with kitchen paper.

Add the remaining oil to the wok over a high heat and swirl it around till it begins to smoke. Add the chillies, stirring and pressing them into the oil until they darken. Add the ginger and green pepper to the wok and turn together. Return the chicken mixture to the wok and stir-fry together for 1 minute. Stir the vinegar into the cornflour mixture and pour over the chicken and peppers. Scatter in the toasted cashew nuts and stir until well coated with the sauce. Sprinkle with sesame oil and serve immediately.

北
京
炸
醬
麵

## Beijing Zhajiang Noodles

SERVES 3–4

This dish is quick to prepare and makes a good family meal. Everybody will love it. It was probably the main dish sold at the beginning of this century in the Beijing Teahouse. White noodles (see page 266) are easy to find in the refrigerators of Chinese supermarkets. They are naturally greasy, so it is important not to add too much extra fat. Otherwise, the dish is very flexible – you can use any kind of lean meat and add vegetables according to taste. Harder vegetables such as carrots should be sliced very finely and added at an earlier stage in the cooking.

500 g (1 lb) fresh white noodles or wun tun noodles
2 tablespoons vegetable oil
1 onion, finely chopped
2 slices root ginger, finely chopped
300 g (10 oz) minced pork
2 cloves garlic, crushed
1 tablespoon yellow bean paste
1 tablespoon soy sauce
4 tablespoons stock (see page 18)
10 cm (4 inch) piece of cucumber, cut into long strips
4 spring onions, chopped into 6 cm (2½ inch) sections and sliced lengthways
½ teaspoon sesame oil
½ tablespoon Shaoxing wine

Blanch the noodles briefly, rinse and drain them. If using wun tun noodles, boil for 2 minutes, then drain. If using dried egg noodles, cook according to packet instructions, but remove from the heat just before they are ready – they should be al dente. Keep warm.

Heat the vegetable oil in a wok until it starts to smoke. Add the onion and ginger and stir-fry for 1 minute, then add the pork and garlic. Stir-fry together for 3 minutes then turn down the heat. Add the yellow bean paste and soy sauce. Stir-fry on a high heat for another 3 minutes, stirring constantly to avoid sticking.

Then add the stock and cook for a further 3 minutes. Finally, add the cucumber and spring onions with the sesame oil, wine and noodles. Toss well together for another 10 seconds, then serve immediately.

木
樨
肉

## Mushu Rou Yellow Cassia Roll

SERVES 2

As we deliberately avoided giving a recipe for Peking duck we
felt we should still acknowledge the northern habit of wrapping
food in little pancakes at the table. We believe our father enjoyed
this dish more than he enjoyed Peking duck. The yellow cassia
blossoms are represented by the scrambled egg, which produces
a tapestry effect when contrasted with the black wood ears and
mushrooms. The pancakes can easily be bought and steamed for
a few minutes to reheat while you are preparing this wonderful
dish.

125 g (4 oz) lean pork, cut into matchstick-sized shreds
$1\frac{1}{2}$ tablespoons light soy sauce
4 dried Chinese mushrooms, soaked in hot water for 30 minutes
1 small handful wood ears, soaked in hot water for 30 minutes
12 stalks golden needles (tiger lily buds), soaked in hot water for
30 minutes
4 tablespoons vegetable oil
1 spring onion, sliced into 3 cm ($1\frac{1}{2}$ inch) sections
$2\frac{1}{2}$ tablespoons stock (see page 18)
3 eggs, beaten lightly
$\frac{1}{2}$ teaspoon sugar
1 tablespoon Shaoxing wine
1 teaspoon sesame oil
bought pancakes, to serve
plum sauce

Place the shredded pork in a shallow dish, sprinkle with the soy
sauce and turn to coat well. Leave to marinate for 20 minutes.
Meanwhile, drain the dried mushrooms, wood ears and golden
needles. Discard the tough stalks, then cut the mushroom caps
and wood ears into shreds the same size as the pork. Cut the
golden needles into 3 cm ($2\frac{1}{2}$ inch) sections.

Heat 2 tablespoons of oil in a wok, swirling it around until it
smokes. Add the mushrooms and pork and stir-fry for $1\frac{1}{2}$
minutes. Add the wood ears, spring onions, golden needles and

stock. Toss together for another minute and then remove from the heat.

Heat the remaining vegetable oil in a small pan and pour in the beaten eggs. Cook over a steady heat until they begin to rise, then break up the egg into little pieces with a fork and transfer to the wok. Add the sugar, wine and sesame oil and turn together briefly. Pile the mixture on to a warmed serving dish. Serve with warmed pancakes and plum sauce. Each guest spreads a pancake with a little plum sauce, spoons on some of the mixture and rolls up the pancake. The dish is equally good served with rice.

## Lamb and Leek Manchurian Pot-cooked Noodles

京
蔥
羊
肉
麵

SERVES 4–5

This is a substantial dish which was a favourite with our father.
The savoury meat makes a magnificent addition to the noodles,
which are turned together at the end of the process.

650 g (1¼ lb) boned leg of lamb, cut into bite-sized pieces
1½ teaspoons salt
pepper, to taste
1 tablespoon cornflour
4 tablespoons vegetable oil
3 slices root ginger, finely shredded
3 cloves garlic, crushed and finely chopped
900 ml (1½ pints) stock (see page 18)
400 g (13 oz) young leeks, cut into 3 cm (1¼ inch) sections
300 g (10 oz) oil noodles
3 tablespoons light soy sauce
4 tablespoons Shaoxing wine
few drops of sesame oil

Rub the lamb pieces with salt and pepper and toss in the
cornflour until evenly coated. Heat the oil in a casserole and add
the ginger and lamb. Stir-fry for 5 minutes, then add the garlic
and stir together. Add the stock and bring to the boil, then turn
down the heat and simmer for 1 hour.

Add the leeks to the casserole, then bring back to the boil.
Simmer for 5 minutes. Add the noodles and sprinkle with the
soy sauce and wine. Simmer for another 2 minutes until heated
through. To serve, sprinkle with pepper and sesame oil to taste.

*Red Braised Aubergine* (p. 33)

陳
皮
燒
牛
肉

## Tangerine Beef and Mushroom Stew

SERVES 4

This tangy stew is cooked so slowly and gently that the meat should melt in your mouth. Serve with rice and a vegetable.

5 large dried Chinese mushrooms, soaked in hot water for 30 minutes
½ tablespoon dried tangerine peel, soaked in hot water for 30 minutes
3 tablespoons vegetable oil
500g (1 lb) stewing beef, cut into 2.5 cm (1 inch) squares
200 ml (7 fl oz) hot stock (see page 18)
½ tablespoon rock sugar
1½ tablespoons dark soy sauce
1½ tablespoons Shaoxing wine
4 cm (2½ inch) length root ginger
1 small Spanish onion, finely sliced
600 ml (1 pint) water
6 pieces deep-fried dried bean curd

Preheat the oven to 200°C, 400°F, Gas 6. Drain the mushrooms and tangerine peel. Discard the tough stalks and slice the mushrooms.

Heat the oil in a wok over a high heat until it is smoking. Add the beef and turn till it is browned on all sides. Pour off the oil. Add enough of the hot stock to cover the meat and simmer for 2 minutes. Transfer the beef and stock to a casserole. Add the sugar, soy sauce, wine, ginger, onion, tangerine peel, mushrooms and water. Bring to the boil, then cover and place in the preheated oven for 30 minutes. Reduce the heat to 150°C, 300°F, Gas 2 and cook for another 2–2½ hours.

Strain the cooking liquid from the casserole into another pan. Remove the tangerine peel and ginger and discard. Return the casserole to the oven to keep warm. Add the bean curd to the cooking liquid and bring to the boil. Simmer to reduce until the liquid thickens, then pour over the meat and mix together. Serve hot.

陳
皮
燒
鴨

## Tangerine Duck

SERVES 4–6

This is a warming, homely stew to keep out the Beijing winter freeze. The tangerine peel gives a slightly bitter flavour which counteracts the richness of the duck.

1 duck (2 kg/4 lb)
3 tablespoons soy sauce
1½ tablespoons vegetable oil
2 Spanish onions, sliced
4 large pieces dried tangerine peel, soaked in hot water
for 30 minutes
1 litre (1¾ pints) water
juice of 2 oranges
4 cm (1½ inches) piece root ginger
lettuce leaves, to serve
1 teaspoon salt
2 teaspoons sugar
1½ tablespoons oyster sauce
1 tablespoon cornflour blended with a little water

Preheat the oven to 200°C, 400°F, Gas 6. Dry the duck inside and out with kitchen paper, then rub with some of the soy sauce and all of the oil. Place the sliced onions in the cavity of the duck.

Place the duck on a rack over a roasting tin and cook in the preheated oven for 30 minutes, turning once.

Drain the tangerine peel. Bring the water and orange juice to the boil in a large casserole and add the duck, tangerine peel and ginger. Bring back to the boil, then simmer for 1½ hours, turning the duck from time to time.

Remove the duck from the casserole and drain. Joint the duck, then cut into small, bite-sized pieces. Arrange the duck pieces on a bed of lettuce leaves. Remove and discard the tangerine peel and ginger. Reduce the liquid in the casserole by boiling vigorously. Add the salt, sugar, remaining soy sauce, oyster sauce and cornflour. Simmer until the sauce has thickened, then pour over the duck. Serve with rice.

# Bread and Dumplings

包
子
## Steamed Savoury Dumplings

MAKES ABOUT 20

As an alternative filling for these delicious dumplings try a piece of Honey Roast Pork (see page 251). They can also be made with a sweet filling, using red bean paste.

15 g (½ oz) dried yeast
250 ml (8 fl oz) warm water
1 teaspoon sugar
400 g (13 oz) self-raising flour

SAVOURY FILLING
6 dried Chinese mushrooms, soaked in hot water for 30 minutes
500 g (1 lb) minced pork
2 tablespoons light soy sauce
1 teaspoon salt
1 teaspoon sugar
½ teaspoon pepper
2 tablespoons water
½ small Chinese cabbage, blanched, drained and chopped
2 teaspoons sesame oil

Mix the yeast in a small bowl with 4 tablespoons of the warm water and the sugar and leave to stand until it froths. Sift the flour into a bowl and make a well in the centre. Pour in the yeast mixture with the remaining warm water and mix to form a dough. Turn out on to a floured board and knead well. Return to the bowl, cover and leave in a warm place until the dough doubles in size.

Meanwhile, make the savoury filling. Drain the mushrooms, discard the tough stalks and chop the caps into small pieces. Put the minced pork in a large bowl. Add the soy sauce, half the salt, the sugar, pepper and water and mix well. Mix the mushrooms and cabbage with the remaining salt and the sesame oil, then mix into the minced pork.

Knock down the dough and knead well, then leave to rise in a warm place until about half the size again. Divide the dough into about 20 balls, then roll out each ball into a 6 cm (2½ inch) flat round. Place about 1 tablespoon of the savoury filling on each round. Gather up the edges and pinch to close over the filling. Alternatively, for a sweet filling, form the dough into a shell shape, fill with 2 teaspoons of sweet red bean paste and pinch the edges to close.

Cut greaseproof paper into rounds the size of the dumplings and press one on to the base of each dumpling. Place the dumplings in a steamer, keeping them well apart, and steam for 12 minutes.

鍋
貼
## Guo Tie

SERVES 8–10

When you are invited to a guo tie party don't be surprised if you get roped into making them yourself! These dumplings have been popularized in Japanese noodle bars, but they are very much part of any gathering of northern family and friends. Students from Beijing are particularly fond of them, while in Xian they can be found cooked in dustbins.

Though we have attended many guo tie parties, we have never seen anyone making the skins so, even though cookery books usually provide a recipe, we think it unrealistic to ask Europeans to go to all that trouble! It is easy to buy the skins in Chinatown, although our chefs prefer the thinner Japanese variety. The rest is fun.

1 packet of guo tie skins, defrosted
4 tablespoons vegetable oil
200 ml (7 fl oz) hot water

MEAT STUFFING
150 g (5 oz) shelled prawns (optional)
225 g (8 oz) finely minced lean pork
2 slices root ginger, finely chopped
2 spring onions, finely chopped
1 tablespoon light soy sauce
1 teaspoon sugar
1 teaspoon salt
pinch of pepper
2 tablespoons vegetable oil
⅔ bunch of watercress, finely chopped

ALTERNATIVE VEGETABLE STUFFING
25 g (1 oz) dried wood ears, soaked in hot water for 30 minutes
25 g (1 oz) dried Chinese mushrooms, soaked in hot water for 30 minutes
50 g (2 oz) fen si noodles
150 g (5 oz) bean curd, chopped
2 spring onions or a handful of Chinese chives, finely chopped

25 g (1 oz) coriander leaves, finely chopped
2 tablespoons vegetarian oyster sauce
3 tablespoons vegetable oil
1 teaspoon sesame oil

DIPS
2 tablespoons shredded root ginger
5 tablespoons vinegar
2 tablespoons soy sauce (optional)
chilli oil (optional)

To make the meat stuffing, mix the prawns, if using, into the minced pork. Add the ginger, spring onions, soy sauce, sugar, salt and pepper, oil and enough water to make the mixture cohere. Add the watercress and mix together thoroughly.

To make the vegetable stuffing, drain the wood ears and mushrooms and discard the tough stalks. Finely chop the caps and wood ears and place in a bowl. Soak the fen si noodles in boiling water for a few minutes until soft, but still al dente, then drain. Chop the noodles finely and add to the bowl together with the remaining stuffing ingredients. Mix well.

Peel apart the guo tie skins and place a teaspoon of the meat or vegetable stuffing in the middle of each one. Fold into a half circle and seal the edges. Repeat until all the stuffing has been used up. Mix the dip ingredients together and leave to marinate.

Heat 3 tablespoons of oil in a wok over a high heat. Swill the oil all around the pan. Arrange the dumplings evenly over the surface and turn down the heat to medium. Cook for $2\frac{1}{2}$ minutes, until the bottom of the dumplings are browned. Pour the hot water down the side of the wok. Cover and steam over a high heat until almost all the water has evaporated. Heat the remaining tablespoon of vegetable oil and gently trickle down the side of the wok. Lower the heat and continue to cook, covered, until all the water has evaporated. Remove from the heat. Use a fish slice to gently loosen the dumplings from the bottom of the pan. Arrange the dumplings on a dish browned side upwards. Serve with the dip.

饅
頭

## Mantou

MAKES 12

Mantou are fluffy white buns that, along with rice and noodles, form part of the staple diet in northern China. They are best eaten alongside a dish with plenty of gravy to soak up.

15 g (½ oz) dried yeast
275 ml (9 fl oz) warm water
450 g (15 oz) plain flour
pinch of salt
1 tablespoon sugar
1 tablespoon vegetable oil
1 teaspoon baking powder

Mix the yeast in 2 tablespoons of the warm water and leave in a warm place for about 15 minutes until frothy. Sift the flour into a large bowl and mix in the salt and sugar. Make a well in the centre and pour in the yeast and the remaining warm water. Stir until the dough comes away from the sides. Turn out on to a floured surface and knead for 5 minutes, dusting with more flour if necessary. Work in the oil. The dough should be soft and springy. Return the dough to the bowl, cover and leave in a warm place for about 2 hours until it has doubled in size. Turn the dough out on to a floured surface and shape into a rectangle. Sprinkle evenly with the baking powder, then fold in half and knead again for 5 minutes, dusting with flour whenever necessary.

Divide the dough into 2 pieces, then roll each piece into a 18 cm (7 inch) long sausage. Cut each sausage into 6 pieces and place on a baking sheet spaced well apart. Cover and leave again in a warm place for about 20 minutes, or until they double in size. Place the buns on a damp cloth over a heatproof dish in a steamer and steam over fast boiling water for 15 minutes. Turn the heat off and leave to cool before removing from the steamer. Repeat until all the buns are cooked.

# Desserts

## 三 不 沾 Three Don't Stick

SERVES 6

This doesn't stick to the pan, the chopsticks or the teeth, but the recipe should carry a public health warning. Give it a miss if you are diet-conscious or squeamish. Our official food taster told us it was an absolute abomination, but the children demolished it in seconds. This is a rare indulgence which people from Beijing eat with their meal. We recommend picking at it after a meal instead of chocolate mints, but don't eat too much. An authentic speciality of the famous Tong He Ju restaurant in Beijing.

30 g (1¼ oz) cornflour
5 egg yolks
40 g (1½ oz) sugar
75 g (3 oz) lard or butter

Blend the cornflour to a smooth paste with a little water, then mix in the egg yolks. Blend in the sugar. Heat 50 g (2 oz) of the lard or butter in a pan over a medium heat. Add the egg mixture, stirring continuously. Divide the remaining lard or butter into 4 pieces. Add the pieces slowly, mixing in each one until very thick. Stir until the mixture comes away from the sides of the pan. Remove and eat while still hot.

杏
仁
豆
腐

## Almond Junket

SERVES 4

Our father used to make this by adding gelatine to almond tea (see page 28) and replacing the water with evaporated milk. That made a heavier junket than the one we have included here. This light junket is a perfect summer dessert, and is especially good with fresh fruit salad.

800 ml (1¼ pints) water
200 g (7 oz) ground almonds
15 g (½ oz) agar agar
25 g (1 oz) gelatine
3 tablespoons sugar
1 teaspoon almond extract
100 ml (3½ fl oz) evaporated milk

Gradually add the water to the ground almonds in a pan, mixing slowly. Bring to the boil, then simmer for 5 minutes. Add the agar agar and simmer for 2 minutes. Stir in the gelatine and sugar and continue to simmer until dissolved. Strain through a sieve into a bowl and add the almond extract and evaporated milk.

Pour into a shallow dish and refrigerate for about 4 hours. It should keep for about 4 days. The jelly can be cut into diamonds or squares and should be served with a mixed fruit salad – perhaps kiwis, strawberries or melon with a few tinned lychees or loquat.

糖
葫
蘆

## Apple and Walnut Treat

SERVES 4

This is a treat that used to be available on the streets of Beijing. These days you can still find caramelized crab apples and haw apples, but we have only ever read about them being sold interspersed with walnuts. This is our re-creation of the traditional snack. Crab apples are ideal, as their tart flavour contrasts sharply with the toffee, but unless you have a crab-apple tree, we suggest using cooking apples instead.

125 g (4 oz) plain flour
120 ml (4 fl oz) cold water
1 egg, beaten
4 medium-sized cooking apples, peeled, cored and quartered, or
500 g (1 lb) crab apples, left whole
2 tablespoons sesame seeds
vegetable oil, for deep-frying
200 g (7 oz) shelled walnuts, blanched

CARAMEL
2 tablespoons vegetable oil
225 g (8 oz) sugar

To make the caramel, heat a pan over a high heat, then add the oil. Swirl it around the pan then turn the heat down. Pour in the sugar and stir with the back of a spoon until it melts and foams. The mixture will turn golden brown. Be careful not to let the sugar burn. Keep hot.

Mix the flour with the water and beaten egg and beat to a smooth batter. Halve each apple quarter, dip the pieces in the batter, then sprinkle with sesame seeds. Heat the oil in a wok to 180°C, 350°F or until a cube of bread browns in 30 seconds. Deep-fry the apple pieces in batches for 2½ minutes. Remove with a slotted spoon and drain on kitchen paper.

When all the apple pieces have been fried and drained dip the apples and walnuts one at a time into the caramel coating, using a fork. Coat thoroughly, then pull them out and dip quickly into a bowl of iced water. Serve immediately.

# Family Celebration

火
鍋

## Mongolian Hot-Pot

SERVES 6–8

For us, this is the family dish of Beijing. On Vivienne's first trip with daughter Pearl, Auntie Meng-qi arranged this as a farewell treat. We say 'arranged' because she had to bribe a chef in one of the famous Beijing restaurants to buy the lamb. It cost her a good week's wages, but it was worth it. We ate like the royal family. Walter was simply glowing. The beauty of the Hot-Pot is that the food tastes so fresh, for it is cooked at the table, and you can flavour it with many different dips. The same principle applies in the Mongolian barbecues that have become popular recently, but has the advantage that you drink the hot broth afterwards, settling the digestion.

As this dish is cooked at the table it can only be properly cooked in a conventional Chinese charcoal hot-pot which can be bought at major supermarkets. An electric wok will do instead.

225 g (8 oz) squid, cleaned
400 g (14 oz) fen si noodles
1 medium Chinese cabbage, cut into 4 cm (1¾ inch) wide strips
2 kg (4 lb) leg of lamb, frozen, then cut into 6 x 2.5 cm (2½ x 1 inch) paper-thin slices
225 g (8 oz) raw tiger prawns, peeled and deveined
6 eggs, beaten
2.5 litres (4 pints) stock, plus extra if needed (see page 18)
2 slices root ginger
3 spring onions, cut into 3 cm (1½ inch) lengths
4 dried Chinese mushrooms, soaked in hot water for 30 minutes
1 tablespoon dried shrimps

Cut open the squid and score it diagonally, making a wide diamond pattern, then cut it into 4cm (1¾ inch) squares. Pour hot water over the noodles to cover and leave to soak for 5 minutes, until soft but still al dente, then drain and place in 2 bowls. Arrange the cabbage in 2–3 large bowls. Spread the lamb in a single layer over 7–8 medium-sized dishes. Arrange the prawns, squid and beaten egg in individual dishes. Each person should have a bowl, a side plate for a soup spoon and a pair of wooden or bamboo chopsticks.

Bring the stock to the boil at the table with the ginger, a handful of spring onions, the mushrooms, dried shrimps and some of the cabbage. When it is nearly boiling add one dish of sliced lamb. While the broth comes to a rolling boil each guest makes up a dip from the sauces on the table (see page 62). After boiling for less than a minute, turn the heat down to a simmer. Each guest should then retrieve what food they can find in the pot, dip it into their dip and eat it at once. The lamb may be dipped in beaten egg before being dunked in the dip.

From this point on each person makes their own selection of raw food and adds it to the pot. Replenish the stock when it runs low. As the cooking progresses the stock becomes richer and richer. When everyone has had their fill, add the noodles and the remainder of the vegetables to the hot-pot. Simmer together for a few minutes and then ladle into everyone's bowl.

## Uncle Walter's and Auntie Meng-qi's Dip

1 tablespoon dark soy sauce
1 tablespoon light soy sauce
3 tablespoons tahini
sugar, to taste
2 tablespoons Shaoxing wine
½ tablespoon of the juice from a jar of red fermented bean curd
½ tablespoon shrimp or fish sauce
2 cloves garlic, crushed and finely chopped
1 tablespoon chilli sauce
1 tablespoon hoisin sauce
1 tablespoon finely chopped Chinese chives, coriander and
spring onions

Mix all the ingredients thoroughly except for the chives,
coriander and spring onions, and leave to stand for a while,
blending with a little water into a smooth paste. Adjust to taste,
adding more water if too salty. Just before serving, add the fresh
herbs and spring onion.

# 2 Recipes from the Sichuan Teahouse

## The Perils of the Road to Shu*

Ah, alas, what terrors, how dangerous how sheer!

There are more perils on the road to Shu than on an ascent into the
blue skies.

When Can Cong and Yu Fu opened up a kingdom how boundless it
was!

Forty-eight thousand years ago, there was not one homestead as far as
the frontier of Qin.

To the West facing Mount Taibai a bird-way cuts through the E Mei
ranges.

When in landslides and avalanche sturdy soldiers perished, they set
sky-ladders and linked hanging ways in the rock.

Above, the lofty heights where six dragons repelled the sun; below,
the crashing waves and swirling currents.

The yellow crane cannot complete its flight and the monkeys lament
as they struggle to clamber through.

How Green Mud Pass weaves and turns, with nine bends every
hundred steps, it twists by crag and chasm.

Reaching for Orion, passing the Well Star, I look up and gasp for
breath,

Then holding my breast, I sit and heave a long sigh . . .

Sir, roaming westward when will you return? I fear the way and rocks
cannot be scaled!

You can only see sad birds that call on ancient trees, male chasing
female, round and round the woods

And hear no sound but the cuckoo calling at the moon, mourning the
empty mountain.

There are more perils on the road to Shu than on an ascent into the
blue skies! Just to hear of it will drain the blood from your cheeks.

Not a foot separates mountain peak and sky where withered pines
pounce over rearing cliffs;

The clamour of flying rapids vie with rushing torrents smashing on
cliffs and circling rocks, like thunder in ten thousand valleys.

How awesome is this place! Oh no! Traveller from afar, what brings
you here? Sword Ledge is a lofty rugged spot: should one man block
the Pass, ten thousand could not break through.

Even the guardians are strangers to you – they could transform
themselves into jackal and wolf.

Li Bai (AD701–762 )

* Shu is an ancient name for the region that now approximates to modern Sichuan.

All my images of Sichuan are hazy, just as the province itself is cloaked in rainless skies of clouds and mist. It is said that 'dogs bark at the sun' because, like the rainfall, the sun is a stranger when it finally arrives for the sixty-five blistering days of midsummer heat. Sichuan is often likened to the Kingdom of Heaven, a mountain stronghold in the sky where red pandas still roam the hilltop bamboo groves and a Buddha over 200 feet high has been hand-carved into the rock face. But the way to heaven has always been hard, hampered by rapids and perilous gorges, gorges which are themselves nearing extinction, soon to be blocked forever by the Gezhou Ba dam.

Geographically speaking the central basin of Sichuan, which nestles in a bend of the Yangzi, is the largest, most fertile and most densely populated of China's provinces. To the west the land rises into hills which form the eastern gateway to Tibet. Mount E Mei stands sentinel, towering 6,500 feet above the plain. Along the pathway to its summit, seventy temples serve plain Buddhist vegetarian food, but in the foothills of the Tibetan plateau there is little agriculture, little to eat but barley, wheat and wild medicinal herbs. To the north and north-east of the central basin the Yangzi flows through 120 miles of limestone gorges on the three-day journey to Wuhan in the east. At the beginning of the summer rainfall sudden, huge rises in the water level hasten the current and make the rapids and gorges perilous to navigate.

In contrast, on the central alluvial plain which is irrigated by canals and the upper reaches of the Min River, the mild winter climate and hot summers create conditions that have made Sichuan the most fertile granary of China. Scattered throughout the plain are sandstone hills, neatly layered with terraced fields full of rice, wheat, barley, sweet potatoes, broad beans, ground-nuts, cotton, grapes and apples. Everything is grown intensively and consequently there are plentiful pigs and poultry, and no room to graze sheep and lamb. There are oxen, originally bred for haulage in the Zigong rock salt mines to the south but also used for beef. Although the plain is completely landlocked there is an abundance of fresh-water fish and fowl in the rivers, ponds and tributaries.

With such a rich larder it is no surprise that many popular tastes originated in Sichuan. The 'one hundred dishes and one hundred flavours' of the various culinary traditions of Sichuan are quite familiar to the metropolitan westerner, particularly in the

USA where Sichuan cuisine is well-known as a distinct genre of restaurants. It is more difficult to find specialist restaurants in England, although many Sichuan dishes are incorporated into the standard Chinese menu. The most characteristic flavour comes from the ruddy Sichuan peppercorn which, like the Sichuan summer sun, is in no hurry to reveal itself. At first it is deceptively mild and tasty and then, when you are least expecting it, its heat suddenly explodes, clearing the sinuses and numbing the brain.

Sichuan peppercorn is universally used, but it has engendered three particular styles of cooking which can be identified by the terms Ma La, Cuan La and Jiao Ma. The Ma of Ma La can mean 'numb' and may refer to the numbness following the explosion of the peppercorn. The La of Ma La simply means chilli hot. The heat of the combined peppercorn and chilli are the predominant feature of this stir-fried dish, although the taste is filled out with soy sauce and ginger. Cuan La simply means 'sour and hot', a tangy effect achieved with the addition of plenty of vinegar. A third type of heat is not from the Sichuan peppercorn, but from ginger juice.

Jiao Ma pepper and sesame is a cold dressing assembled with Sichuan peppercorns and sesame oil or paste and used to throw over pre-cooked food. Nuts – peanuts, sesame, cashew, walnut and pine – are commonly used in Sichuan cooking. 'Weird flavour' hot and nutty sesame sauce is used to dress poultry.

Another style of local cooking is suspiciously described as 'fishy'. As this does not make for comfortable translation, it is usually left as Yuxiang. Ironically, there is no fish at all in the sauce. It is a term used for dishes that are spiced with the deep red-brown hot bean sauce and combined with a touch of sweet and sour. Dry stir-fry is a distinctive process which can be combined with various flavours, but first produces a chewy texture in the meat or vegetables. The main ingredient may be tossed over a high heat in spicy flavoured oil, and without a wet sauce, until it is quite dry and crusty.

Sweet and sour is also a common combination in local cuisine, along with several other types of cooking that are shared with the rest of China. Because it is over one thousand miles from the sea and the Yangzi was until recently the only means of contact with the outside world, the more rugged elements of northern nomadic fare cannot be detected in Sichuan. Dishes such as barbecued lamb are not as popular as in Beijing. But Beijing and

Sichuan do share similar dishes as a result of the movement of officials and magistrates between the cities. One representative example is the style of cuisine that scatters toasted nuts over slivers of meat cooked in a tart, savoury sauce, as developed in the kitchens of the imperial official Ding Gongbao, and known as Gongbao's this or that dish.

With the humid climate it is difficult to keep food fresh, so it is little wonder that innovative ways for preserving food originate in Sichuan. Food is commonly salted, dried, spiced, pickled or smoked. Rock salt from the local salt mines and chilli are used to preserve mustard greens and roots which have become an essential feature of flavouring in all regional Chinese cooking. The knobbly stems of the mustard greens or cabbage are dark and crisp and combine a hot and salty flavour which is an excellent addition to soups, noodles or salad. The root is pickled in brine and needs to be shredded or diced before use. Tea smoking is also native to Sichuan.

To the west of the plain Chengdu, the capital of Sichuan, is the main cultural centre of Sichuan. It is a square city that used to be bounded by city walls and four gates, but now has only the River Jin flanking two of its sides. It is said that Chengdu used to be one of the most beautiful cities of China, that it has the majesty of Beijing but is gentler and greener. In the older parts of the city wooden porches still line the wide avenues and the second floor still overhangs pavements which throng with life and commerce. For ten years Chengdu, at the vanguard of China's commercial reforms, has been alive with basket-weaving, cobblers, artisans and all kinds of entrepreneurs plying their trade.

Modernization and industry have sadly changed the old charm of the city, but its colour is still provided by the many peoples on the streets. Ethnically, most are related to the Han peoples who arrived in successive waves as displaced populations or forcible resettlements orchestrated by different rulers keen to break down regional resistance. Many are descendants of immigrant families from Hubei and Guangdong who were relocated at the end of the Ming dynasty in a vain attempt to retain control. Amongst the minority races there is a large community of Tibetans and the handsome Yi, a race of mountain farmers with their pointed caps and capes. Many other groups including Muslim, Sufa and Mossa congregate in Sichuan, but it is only the Muslims that appear to have had a lasting influence over the cuisine. Sesame and sweet desserts are said to have been brought from the Middle East and there is still a delicacy that is known as Persian candy. Sichuan beef dishes also originated in the Moslem communities.

It may be that the Sichuan peppercorn is responsible for forming the local personality. If my girl-friends from Sichuan are anything to go by, the Sichuanese appear small and delicate in build with mild manners. They also have a warm and generous nature. A common saying suggests that the Sichuan 'mountains are beautiful, rivers are beautiful and girls are beautiful'. That may be, but my experience of the women is that as well as all these attributes they, like the peppercorn, do not reveal themselves immediately, preferring to wait to let you feel the full force of their determination and single-mindedness. Another common, self-declared, image is that Sichuan people are 'rat-like', by which they mean resourceful, difficult to pin down and a little peppery with their tongues!

In Chengdu more than anywhere in China street life and street food is still a living tradition. Before 1949, like the teahouses everywhere in China, Chengdu chadian were the stage for political debate and all kinds of social intercourse. With the special status of Sichuan as the outlying region most prone to uprising and last to toe the party line, many teahouses were shut down during the Cultural Revolution. There are four main types of teahouse. The most attractive of those that remain are to be found in the parks where people drink tea and eat nuts and dried snacks in the open, sheltered by tall bamboo groves. From time to time hawkers appear, selling flowery bean curd from pitchers swinging at the end of a long pole slung over the shoulders. Only jasmine tea is available, in three grades determined by the quality of the flowers that are mixed in with the fragrant green leaves.

In the mornings old men can still be seen out with their bird-cages, and on holidays families congregate to while away the time with their children, playing cards and gossiping. After the shift is over the factory workers can also be found reclining on the long bamboo couches. Travelling entertainers and fortune-tellers seem to appear spontaneously in the open-air teahouses. The local opera house has a teahouse of its own, but scaled-down operas with two to three performers have replaced the traditional operas on the street. Story-tellers, who used to spout revolutionary tales, have returned to the folk-tales. Equally often the more traditional forms of entertainment are replaced with karaoke.

A second type of teahouse lurks in the back streets of old

Chengdu and is mainly a drinking club exclusively for men. Smoking and drinking is still considered undignified for women although time is transforming gender roles. The drinking clubs are now surrounded by a multitude of hairdressers, where women can perm, crimp or colour their hair to look like westerners. Expensive Maotai rice wine is on sale, but there are also many types of cheap wine to oil the gates to oblivion – Five Grain Liquor, Lu Zhou Old Wine and Wenjun Wine, named after a legendary Song poet famed for romantic poems. With no liquor laws alcoholism is commonplace amongst men. Inside the wineshops the atmosphere is thick and the decor shabby and dark, with low wooden beams, benches and tables. Dishes such as 'Husband and Wife Offal Pieces', a mixture of lungs, tripe and intestines in a spicy sauce, and boiled beef are the kind of macho fare available, designed to boost the head for alcohol.

A third type of teahouse serves a Sichuan version of the famous Mongolian hotpot or fire pot, claimed to be the ancestor of them all. It is known as the Yin and Yang fire pot on account of the two pots of stock bubbling away in holes carved into each table. Below the pots a gas or charcoal fire keeps the stock just simmering. One of the stocks is coated with a layer of chilli oil, and is the pot where more bland food, raw seafood and bean curd are cooked, while the other is for dipping every kind of meat, offal, eels and quail's eggs. The hot 'Yang' fire pot is really hot and few can eat much of it. The Yin and Yang fire pot serves as the centre of after-work social life and relaxation, where friendly groups can rest and chat.

The last type of teahouse is really the restaurants at the bottom end of the scale that also serve their food at wooden tables and benches. They can be divided into the rice restaurants and the noodle restaurants and all tend to serve a limited menu. Of these some, like the Dan Dan Noodle Shop and the Zhong family Shuijiao (steamed dumplings) are famous for serving just one dish. The Chen family Mapo Doufu and the Lai family Tang Yuan have become world-famous. Old Pockmarked Mrs Chen used to serve her hot bean curd and minced meat outside the old south gate to people coming and going from work in the town. The family continued the tradition. In the last decade the shop has had a facelift and, with the prosperity from gourmet pilgrimages, has begun to serve almost everything including twenty different types of bean curd. The Lai Tang Yuan has also expanded its menu, and serves a set menu of delicious small dishes including dan dan noodles, white fungus soup, dumplings and pastries, but still only serves the delicious sticky rice balls in sweet soup as a takeaway. Each rice ball is stuffed with a different sweet filling, from the most delectable black sesame seeds through red bean paste, rose-flavoured and marmalade to peanut butter and the very dubious sweet dried shrimp. These days the bewildering choice on offer at the Lai family's Soup Ball restaurant has to compete with a simpler solution on offer upstairs: Colonel Saunders has just opened another Kentucky Fried Chicken.

If the Kingdom of Heaven itself is under threat from American culinary imperialism, the extinction of the panda and the blocking of the gorges, elsewhere its fiery spirit lives on as the flavours of the Sichuan teahouse steadily invade the West. The recipes in this chapter are drawn from all four styles of teahouse tradition and have mostly been provided by Mrs Zhou, the kind and talented mother of a dear friend Xun. Many of them are standard recipes that you will know from the classic Chinese menu, but there are also many exquisite street delicacies that you are not likely to have encountered before.

# Vegetable and Vegetarian Dishes

魚
香
茄
子

## Fragrant Yuxiang Aubergine

SERVES 4

Aubergine is absolutely delicious served with the Yuxiang 'fish fragrance' method of cooking. The garlic is meant to be especially strong in this dish. Serve with rice or tossed with noodles.

3 tablespoons vegetable oil
2 pickled red chillies, finely chopped, or 1 teaspoon hot bean paste
2.5 cm (1 inch) piece of root ginger
4 cloves garlic, finely chopped
1 large aubergine, cut into small cubes
1½ tablespoons light soy sauce
3 tablespoons water
1 spring onion, finely chopped
1 tablespoon sugar
2 tablespoons vinegar

Heat the oil in a wok until it begins to smoke. Add the chilli, ginger and garlic and stir-fry. Add the aubergine and fry for 2 minutes. Add the soy sauce and water and cover, simmering for a further 2 minutes. Add the spring onion, sugar and vinegar and continue to mix together until the liquid has reduced.

## Sweet Potato Crisps

香
酥
茗
片

SERVES 4

This is a snack for the children which can be served with nuts, candied fruit and sunflower seeds. Alternatively, you can serve it with drinks or even as a pre-starter. The original recipe had ten times as much sugar, but the sweet potatoes themselves seem sweet enough. We have left a couple of teaspoons to be authentic!

1 tablespoon peanuts
1 tablespoon walnut halves
1 tablespoon sesame seeds
2 teaspoons white sugar
vegetable oil, for deep-frying
500g (1lb) sweet potato, thinly sliced into rounds
2 teaspoons brown sugar

Dry-fry the nuts and seeds in a wok until golden brown, starting with the peanuts. Roll the back of a large spoon over the peanuts while they are in the wok to loosen the skin. The skins can then easily be removed although it is not absolutely necessary. Finely chop or grind the nuts and seeds and mix with the white sugar.

Heat the oil in a wok. When it begins to smoke add a handful of the sweet potato and deep-fry for just over a minute until the water has evaporated and the potato begins to brown. Remove with a slotted spoon and drain on kitchen paper. Repeat until all the sweet potato has been fried. Return all the potato slices to the wok and deep-fry again until the chips are golden. Add the brown sugar to the oil and continue to fry for a few seconds. Remove again with a slotted spoon and drain on kitchen paper. To serve, sprinkle the nut mixture over the chips.

甜
酸
黃
瓜

## Crunchy Sichuan Pickle

2 medium cucumbers, finely sliced
200 g (7 oz) Chinese leaves, finely sliced
1 large carrot, thinly sliced
200 g (7 oz) white Chinese radish, thinly sliced
2 cloves garlic, crushed and finely chopped
4 teaspoons salt
4 dried chillies, seeded and cut into shreds
6 tablespoons gin
300 ml (½ pint) rice vinegar
200 ml (7 fl oz) water
50 g (2 oz) sugar
1 tablespoon crushed Sichuan peppercorns

Sprinkle the vegetables with the garlic, salt, chillies and gin and leave to season for 2 hours. Mix together the vinegar, water, sugar and peppercorns.

Place the vegetables in a jar and pour on the vinegar mixture. Cover and let it stand for 2 days, turning the vegetables once a day.

醋
溜
黃
瓜

## Hot & Sour Sesame Courgette

SERVES 2–3

As Huang gua, which can be compared to a tough cucumber, is not available in the West, this dish is improvized by using courgette, the closest vegetable commonly available.

225 g (8 oz) courgettes, thinly sliced
1 teaspoon salt
3 tablespoons sesame oil
1 teaspoon Sichuan peppercorns
2 dried red chillies, seeded and sliced
1 cm (½ inch) piece of root ginger, finely chopped
1 clove garlic, crushed and finely chopped
1 tablespoon rice vinegar
1 teaspoon soy sauce
2 teaspoons sugar
1 spring onion, finely chopped

Place the courgette slices in a shallow dish, sprinkle with the salt and leave for 15 minutes. Rinse and pat dry on kitchen paper.

Gently heat the sesame oil in a wok. When it is hot add the peppercorns and chillies and stir till they brown. Scoop out with a slotted spoon and discard. Add the ginger and garlic and stir for 1 minute. Add the courgettes and stir again for another minute. Add the vinegar, soy sauce and sugar and toss together until the courgettes become soft. Finally sprinkle in the spring onion and stir and toss together. Serve immediately.

辣
椒
炒
扁
豆

## Chilli French Beans

SERVES 4

225 g (8 oz) French beans, halved
1 tablespoon vegetable oil
1 green or red chilli, seeded and finely sliced
2 cloves garlic, crushed and finely chopped
1 tablespoon light soy sauce
½ teaspoon sugar
½ teaspoon sesame oil

Blanch the beans for 30 seconds, drain and then refresh under cold water and drain again. Heat the vegetable oil in a wok over a high heat and add the chillies to flavour the oil for 30 seconds. Then add the garlic. Turn in the oil and immediately add the French beans. Add the soy sauce and sugar and stir-fry for 3 minutes until well seasoned. Sprinkle with sesame oil and serve.

干
炒
豆
腐

## Dry-tossed Bean Curd

SERVES 2

This simple dish must be the most basic of the bean curd dishes. The amount of salt is characteristic of Sichuan and can be reduced to taste or where salt is contra-indicated in a diet. The dish can be served as a snack, or as one of 23 dishes served with rice.

4 tablespoons vegetable oil
350 g (12 oz) bean curd, cut into 3 cm (1½ inch) squares
1 teaspoon ground sea salt
1 spring onion, finely chopped

Heat the oil in a wok until it begins to smoke. Gently place the bean curd in the wok. Brown the pieces on each side for 5 minutes over a high heat, being careful not to break up the bean curd too much. Add the salt and turn until the pieces are golden brown. Add the spring onion and stir once again. Strain off the oil and turn out on to a warm dish.

麻
辣
豆
腐

## Pepper and Chilli Mala Bean Curd

SERVES 2

The silken bean curd is softer and more delicate than the standard variety available in Chinatown. It is easily available in good health food shops and is often described as Japanese bean curd, the softer texture being more popular in Japan. In China, soft quality bean curd is made with peanuts as well as soy beans. The chilli in this dish should be varied to taste. Serve with rice, or for a lunch-time snack try it with a slice of brown bread.

1 tablespoon vegetable oil
1 teaspoon hot bean paste
225 g (8 oz) silken bean curd
2 large spring onions, cut into 5 mm (¼ inch) pieces
2 tablespoons dark soy sauce
1 tablespoons light soy sauce
pinch of ground Sichuan pepper

Heat the oil in a wok with the hot bean paste. When it begins to smoke, add the bean curd. Gently break up the curd into large chunks and turn for a minute over a high heat. Turn down the heat, add the spring onions and soy sauces and simmer for 5 minutes. Turn out on to a serving dish and sprinkle on the Sichuan pepper. Stir before serving.

羅
江
豆
雞

## Luojiang Spiced Bean Curd

SERVES 2–3

This delicious savoury snack comes from a Buddhist temple in
Luojiang, a small town outside Chengdu. In the 1920s it won a
prize for the local region.

1 tablespoon vegetable oil
2 slices root ginger, finely chopped
5 g (¼ oz) sesame seeds, toasted
2 tablespoons soy sauce
125 g (4 oz) dried bean curd skins or sticks (see page 261), soaked
overnight

Heat the oil in a wok until it begins to smoke, add the ginger
and stir-fry for 30 seconds. Add the sesame seeds and soy sauce
and stir to mix thoroughly. Drain the bean curd skins and cut
into 12 cm (5 inch) squares. Place a tablespoon of the sesame
seed mixture along one edge of each square. Fold over the ends
and roll up. If using bean curd sticks, slit them lengthways and
fill each tube with a teaspoon of the mixture. Wrap the bean
curd rolls in a cotton or muslin cloth and arrange in a steamer.
Steam for 30 minutes. Eat warm or cold.

豆
花
## Flowery Bean Curd
SERVES 4

Don't be misled by the name of this dish, it is not for the faint-
hearted! The combination of Sichuan pickle, yellow bean paste
and soy make it very salty and only possible to eat in small
doses. Perhaps we can compare it to ready-salted crisps and
peanuts. Vendors still roam around the teahouses of Chengdu
hawking ready-cooked bean curd in wooden buckets which
swing on the end of a shoulder pole. Numerous sauces are served
as dips in different bowls. The vendors are well-liked by
children, who follow them around and eat the curd on the street
corners. In this recipe we have used croûtons, although to be
absolutely authentic it should be a kind of deep-fried and
crushed wheat dough.

1 tablespoon vegetable oil
1 teaspoon yellow bean paste
25 g (1 oz) Sichuan pickle, finely chopped
225 g (8 oz) silken bean curd, cut into cubes
4 tablespoons mild stock
1 tablespoon light soy sauce
1 teaspoon chilli oil
2 tablespoons rice vinegar (Zhenjiang vinegar if available)
1½ teaspoons ground Sichuan pepper
2 spring onions, finely chopped
124 g (4 oz) croûtons

Heat the oil in a wok until it just begins to smoke, then add the
yellow bean paste and stir-fry over a high heat for about a
minute until it congeals. Add the pickle and stir for a few
seconds, then remove the wok from the heat and reserve.

Place the bean curd in a pan with the stock over a low heat
until it is heated through. Mix the soy sauce, chilli oil and
vinegar into the pickle mixture and pour into a dish. Add the
bean curd and sprinkle the pepper, spring onions and croûtons
on top.

## 醋溜白菜 Sautéed Sour Chinese Leaves

SERVES 2–3

I have included this dish because it is Zhou Xun's father's favourite. It is very light, and a great appetizer which is said to 'open the stomach'. It will go with almost any combination of dishes. White cabbage can be substituted for the Chinese leaves, although this makes a slightly heavier, crunchy dish, and it will have to be simmered for a little longer before adding the cornflour mixture.

$1\frac{1}{2}$ tablespoons rice vinegar
$1\frac{1}{2}$ tablespoons soy sauce
$\frac{1}{2}$ teaspoon salt
2 teaspoons sugar
2 teaspoons cornflour, blended with a little water
3 tablespoons vegetable oil
30 Sichuan peppercorns
300 g (10 oz) Chinese leaves, cut into 3 cm ($1\frac{1}{2}$ inch) squares
3 teaspoons sesame oil

Mix together the vinegar, soy sauce, salt, sugar and cornflour. Heat the oil in a wok until smoking. Add the peppercorns and fry until black, to flavour the oil, then scoop them out and discard. Add the Chinese leaves and stir quickly for 30 seconds. Pour in the mixed ingredients and bring to the boil. Simmer for 1 minute, stirring, then finally add the sesame oil and serve immediately.

# Snacks

酥
皮
蔥
餃

## Crispy Onion Patties

MAKES 15–20

This is a traditional Muslim dish which can be served as a light
snack with salad, as a side dish, or simply to go with drinks.
There have been Muslims in China since the eighth century,
and a flourishing, prolific and literate community since the
sixteenth century. The addition of dried shrimps would strictly
not be allowed in Islamic law but Chinese Muslims tend to be a
little liberal, especially when it comes to food.

50 g (2 oz) dried shrimps, chopped
225 g (8 oz) bean sprouts, blanched for 1 minute, drained and
chopped
125 g (4 oz) spring onion, white part only, finely chopped
1 teaspoon ground Sichuan pepper
2 teaspoons salt
500 g (1 lb) plain flour
100 g (3½ oz) butter, lard or ghee
200 ml (7 fl oz) water
vegetable oil, for deep-frying

Mix together the dried shrimps, bean sprouts and spring onions,
and stir in the Sichuan pepper and salt.

Rub 350 g (12 oz) of the flour with 75 g (3 oz) of the butter.
Add the water and knead into a dough. Knead the remaining
flour and butter together to make another dry dough. Roll the
moist dough into 2 long sausages, and cut each one into 10
portions. Divide the dry dough into 20 portions. Press 1 piece of
dry dough on top of each piece of the moist dough and press
down. Roll each one out into a round, thin enough to make a
dumpling skin. Place a small portion of filling in the centre of
each round and fold into a half moon. Press the edges together.

Heat the vegetable oil in a wok until it begins to smoke. Turn
down the heat slightly and deep-fry the patties until they are
golden brown. Remove with a slotted spoon and drain on
kitchen paper.

*Tangerine Duck* (p. 51)

新
繁
面
魚

## Xinfan Bread Fish

MAKES 12

In the tradition of making one thing look like another, the Sichuanese of Xinfan, a small town outside Chengdu, have turned bread into fish! Chinese chives are only available seasonally, but we have found that an equal mixture of English chives, coriander and spring onion makes a delicious alternative. Using olive oil is also not authentic, but a delicious variation. Serve as a snack or side dish on a bed of mixed green salad to complete the seascape.

500 g (1 lb) plain flour
400 ml (14 fl oz) water
2 heaped teaspoons salt
1 teaspoon ground Sichuan pepper
225 g (8 oz) Chinese chives, finely chopped
olive oil, for deep-frying

Sift the flour into a bowl and mix with the water, salt, Sichuan pepper and chives. Beat with a wooden spoon until the mixture leaves the sides of the bowl. Roll out on a floured surface into a sheet 1 cm (½ inch) thick and cut out fish shapes about 10 cm (4 inches) long.

Heat the oil in a wok until it begins to smoke. Add the fish one by one and fry until they are golden brown. Remove with a slotted spoon and drain on kitchen paper

*Chilli French Beans* (p. 74)

蛋
烘
糕

## Waffles

MAKES 12

Egg waffles are the classic Chengdu dimsum, comparable to pancakes. They can be eaten at any time of day. For a savoury version replace the sugar with a little salt and fill the waffle with any savoury meat or vegetable filling.

200 g (7 oz) sugar
300 ml (½ pint) warm water
500 g (1 lb) plain flour
6 eggs, beaten
1 teaspoon bicarbonate of soda blended with 1 tablespoon water
vegetable oil, for frying

FILLINGS
black sesame seeds, toasted and finely ground, mixed with sugar
red bean paste
tahini and honey
lotus seed paste

Dissolve the sugar in the warm water. Sieve the flour into a large bowl and make a well in the centre. Pour in the sugar solution, then pour the beaten eggs on top. Stir and mix slowly with a wooden spoon. Add the bicarbonate of soda solution and stir till thoroughly mixed. Leave to stand for 30 minutes. The mixture should pour quite easily. If it is too thick, add a little more water.

Heat an omelette pan and brush with a little oil. Spoon on a thin layer of the mixture as if making a pancake, turning the pan constantly for a minute or so to distribute the heat evenly. When the underside is golden brown turn over and brown on the other side. Transfer to a plate and add one of the sweet fillings, then fold over. Make the remaining waffles in the same way.

# One-Dish Noodle Meals

蟻
蟻
上
樹

## Ants Climbing the Trees

SERVES 1

This is Sichuan's answer to spaghetti bolognaise, but spicier and
without tomatoes. If you double or treble the ingredients it
makes a wonderful family dish. Any more will be difficult to
cook in one go. You can vary the amount of pepper to suit. The
ants are the pieces of mince, scattered in the lightly browned,
tree-like noodles.

125 g (4 oz) fen si noodles, divided into manageable lengths
3 dried Chinese mushrooms, soaked in hot water for 30 minutes
2 tablespoons vegetable oil
125 g (4 oz) minced pork or beef
2 cloves garlic, finely chopped
½ green pepper, cored, seeded and thinly sliced
1 tablespoon chilli bean paste
1 tablespoon Shaoxing wine
1 tablespoon light soy sauce
250 ml (8 fl oz) chicken stock (see page 18)
1 teaspoon ground Sichuan pepper

Soak the fen si noodles in hot water until soft but still al dente,
then drain. Drain the mushrooms, discard the tough stems and
chop the caps finely.

Heat the oil in a wok until it begins to smoke. Add the meat
and stir-fry until it browns. Add the mushrooms, garlic, pepper,
chilli paste and wine and stir-fry for 2 minutes. Add the soy
sauce, noodles and stock and simmer for 5 minutes. Remove
from the heat and sprinkle with Sichuan pepper. Stir and serve
immediately.

牌
坊
麵

## Paifang Noodles

SERVES 2

Paifang noodles can be bought at any noodle shop in Chengdu. Here, this is a workaday convenience meal as most of the ingredients are dried or come straight out of a can. Only the noodles demand a trip to Chinatown, although pre-cooked egg noodles can also be used. Being dried, the shrimps remain pleasantly crunchy, although if you prefer them soft they can be pre-soaked for 20 minutes.

1 tablespoon vegetable oil
1½ tablespoons light soy sauce
1 teaspoon ground black pepper
½ tablespoon Shaoxing wine
1 tablespoon dried shrimps
4 tablespoons sliced bamboo shoots
6 button mushrooms (optional)
2 tablespoons sliced straw mushrooms
225 g (8 oz) oil noodles

Heat the oil in a wok and add the soy sauce, pepper, wine and shrimps, stirring together for 3 minutes. Add the bamboo shoots, mushrooms and the noodles and simmer together for another 2 minutes. Toss to mix thoroughly.

擔
擔
麵

## Dan Dan Noodles

SERVES 2

Both Chengdu and Chongqing have shops and stalls that specialize in this inexpensive and tasty dish. The sauce need not be cooked at all if boiled noodles are used – simply mix the sauce ingredients in each bowl while the noodles are cooking and then assemble at the last minute. This recipe uses fresh white noodles, which need to be heated and tossed in the wok. If you are preparing the meal for a number of people, it is worth enhancing the stock by boiling it for half an hour with star anise, Sichuan pepper, onions, fresh ginger and wine.

½ tablespoon chilli oil
1 tablespoon vegetable oil
2 tablespoons light soy sauce
2 tablespoons beef stock
2 tablespoons tahini
2 cloves garlic, crushed and finely chopped
225 g (8 oz) fresh white or wun tun noodles
3 tablespoons bean sprouts, rinsed and dried
1 tablespoon sesame oil
1 tablespoon Shaoxing wine
2 spring onions, finely chopped
2 teaspoons ground peanuts

Mix together the chilli oil, vegetable oil, soy sauce, stock, tahini and garlic. Blanch the noodles briefly – wun tun noodles will need to be cooked for 2 minutes – and drain

Heat the sauce mixture in a wok. Add the bean sprouts and stir and toss for a couple of minutes until heated through. Add the sesame oil, noodles and wine. Stir to coat well, then turn into 2 bowls. Sprinkle each bowl with the chopped spring onions and ground peanuts.

炒
麵
## Hot-tossed Noodles
SERVES 2

225 g (8 oz) oil noodles
2 tablespoons vegetable oil
200 g (7 oz) bean sprouts, rinsed and dried
150 g (5 oz) lean pork, cut into strips
½ teaspoon salt
½ tablespoon soy sauce
1 teaspoon chilli sauce
½ teaspoon sugar
40 g (1½ oz) Sichuan pickle, finely chopped
1½ tablespoons stock (see page 18)
3 spring onions, finely chopped
1 teaspoon sesame oil
1 tablespoon Shaoxing wine

Boil the noodles for 1 minute, then drain.

Heat 1 tablespoon of the oil in a wok until it begins to smoke. Turn the bean sprouts in the oil for a minute, and remove and drain on kitchen paper. Add the remaining oil to the wok and heat. Add the pork and stir until the meat changes colour. Then add the noodles, salt, soy sauce, chilli sauce, sugar, pickle, stock and spring onions. Stir and mix thoroughly for 4 minutes, then return the bean sprouts to the wok with the sesame oil and wine. Stir-fry for another 2 minutes, then serve.

# Chicken Dishes

怪
味
雞

## Weird Flavour Chicken

SERVES 8

It is said that this dish is so named because not one of the many flavours predominates. However, the hot nutty flavour, commonplace in Sichuan, does characterize this dish. It is certainly one of the most aromatic of Chinese sauces, and very simple to prepare.

500 g (1 lb) cooked, boned chicken, cut into 3 cm (1¼ inch) shreds
1 small cucumber, halved, seeded and cut into 3 cm (1¼ inch) lengths

SAUCE
1 tablespoon sesame seeds
1 teaspoon ground Sichuan pepper
1 cm (½ inch) piece of root ginger, finely chopped
3 cloves garlic, crushed and finely chopped
1 tablespoon tahini
2 teaspoons sugar
1 tablespoon chilli sauce
1½ tablespoons vinegar
1½ tablespoons Shaoxing wine
1 tablespoon sesame oil
2 tablespoons dark soy sauce
chopped parsley, to garnish

Combine the chicken and cucumber on a serving dish. Dry-fry the sesame seeds and Sichuan pepper for a few seconds, then grind with a pestle and mortar. Mix with the rest of the seasonings and pour over the chicken. Garnish with chopped parsley.

麻
辣
雞

## Pepper and Chilli Mala Chicken

SERVES 4

This dish makes a substantial meal when served with rice. It is light and refreshing, combining a hot peppery flavour with the taste of ginger and onion.

225 g (8 oz) chicken breast, cut into 2.5 cm (1 inch) cubes
1 tablespoon Shaoxing wine
1 egg white
4 tablespoons vegetable oil
1 tablespoon cornflour
1 teaspoon Sichuan peppercorns, toasted
½ teaspoon salt
2 tablespoons light soy sauce
½ tablespoon rice vinegar
1 teaspoon sugar
2 teaspoons sesame oil
1 tablespoon hot bean sauce
2.5 cm (1 inch) piece of root ginger, finely chopped
1 medium leek, sliced lengthways, then cut across into 5 mm (¼ inch) slices
125 g (4 oz) button mushrooms, finely sliced
3 cloves garlic, crushed and finely chopped

Place the chicken in a shallow dish with the wine, egg white, 1 tablespoon oil and the cornflour. Turn to coat, then leave to marinate for 10 minutes. Grind the peppercorns, then mix with the salt, soy sauce, vinegar, sugar and sesame oil.

Heat 2 tablespoons of oil in a wok. When it is just beginning to smoke, drain the chicken and place in the wok. Stir continuously until it changes colour. Remove the chicken with a slotted spoon and reserve. Clean the wok with kitchen paper. Heat the remaining oil in the wok and add the hot bean sauce and ginger and stir. Add the leek and mushrooms to the wok and turn together for a minute. Finally add the garlic and the soy mixture. Bring to the boil and simmer for a further minute. Return the chicken to the wok and simmer until the sauce has thickened.

# Beef and Pork

水
煮
牛
肉

## Water Margin Beef

SERVES 2-3

In Sichuan they often say that the name refers to the classic
novel of the same name – but the novel is set in Shandong, to
the east of China, so the idea seems fanciful. Served with rice
this is a meal in itself.

225 g (8 oz) sirloin steak, thinly sliced then cut into 2 x 4 cm (1 x
2 inch) pieces
1 teaspoon salt
2 teaspoons dark soy sauce
2 teaspoons cornflour blended with 3 tablespoons water
2 dried chillies
10 Sichuan peppercorns
6 tablespoons vegetable oil
75 g (3 oz) Chinese cabbage, sliced
2 sticks celery, sliced then cut into 6 cm (2½ inch) chunks
1 leek, sliced lengthways then cut into 6 cm (2½ inch) chunks
2 large spring onions, sliced
1 tablespoon hot bean paste
250 ml (8 fl oz) stock (see page 18)
2 cloves garlic, crushed

Place the beef in a shallow dish with the salt, soy sauce and
cornflour mixture. Turn to coat then leave to marinate for 15
minutes. Meanwhile, toast the chillies and peppercorns under a
hot grill for 1 minute, then grind with a pestle and mortar.

Heat 2 tablespoons of oil in a wok until it begins to smoke,
add the cabbage, celery, leek and spring onion and stir-fry for 2–3
minutes. Push them to the edge of the wok. Add another 2
tablespoons of oil and fry the hot bean paste until the oil
reddens. Stir in the vegetables and add the stock. Bring to the
boil, then add the beef and garlic and stir for a few seconds until
the beef changes colour. Then quickly turn out the beef mixture
on to a serving dish. Sprinkle the toasted chilli and peppercorns
on top. Meanwhile, heat the remaining oil in the wok then pour
over the dish and bring it sizzling to the table.

粉
蒸
牛
肉

## Steamed Rice-flour Beef

SERVES 4

This is a famous Sichuan speciality which is specially designed to improve your head for alcohol. Serve with light dishes, such as stir-fried vegetables, and Chinese wine, or as an appetizer. Because of the rice coating it is not necessary to serve extra rice or noodles.

75 g (3 oz) rice
25 g (1 oz) glutinous rice powder
1 teaspoon five-spice powder
225 g (8 oz) braising beef, thinly sliced across the grain into 3 x 2.5 cm (1½ x 1 inch) strips
1 tablespoon dark soy sauce
1 teaspoon light soy sauce
2 slices root ginger, finely chopped
2 tablespoons Shaoxing wine
2 teaspoons sugar
2 tablespoons vegetable oil
pinch of salt
1 tablespoon sesame oil
1 tablespoon hot bean paste
pinch of ground black pepper
pinch of ground Sichuan pepper
pinch of chilli powder
freshly chopped coriander

Dry-roast the rice in a frying pan or wok, stirring until it is golden brown. Place the rice in a food processor and grind roughly, then remove and roll the rice with a rolling pin. Mix with the glutinous rice powder and five-spice powder.

Place the beef in a shallow dish with the soy sauces, ginger, wine, sugar, oil, salt and sesame oil. Add the rice powder and mix well. Then add the hot bean paste.

Spread out the beef strips on a heatproof plate. Put the plate in a steamer, cover and steam for 30 minutes or until the beef is tender. Turn the beef on to a serving plate, sprinkle with the ground pepper and chilli powder, and coriander to taste.

## 陳麻婆豆腐 Old Pockmarked Mrs Chen's Bean Curd
SERVES 4

Generally known simply as mapo doufu, this is one of the most popular suppers all over China. It is the kind of food you would expect to be served if Chinese students abroad were to invite you for an informal supper. The dish was invented in the last century by the Chen family, who still have a restaurant in Chengdu that serves only mapo doufu. Serve with rice.

400 g (14 oz) bean curd, cut into 1.5cm (¾ inch) cubes
2 tablespoons vegetable oil
125 g (4 oz) minced pork
2 slices root ginger, finely chopped
2 cloves garlic, crushed and finely chopped
2 teaspoons hot bean sauce
150 ml (¼ pint) water
1 tablespoon Shaoxing wine
2 tablespoons light soy sauce
¼ teaspoon pepper
½ spring onion, finely sliced
½ teaspoon sesame oil

Soak the bean curd in boiling water for 3 minutes, then drain. Heat the oil in a wok. When it is just beginning to smoke, add the pork and stir until it changes colour. Add the ginger, garlic and hot bean sauce and stir-fry for about 4 minutes. Pour in the water, wine and soy sauce. Bring to the boil and simmer for 4 minutes. Add the bean curd to the wok and toss gently. Bring to the boil again and simmer for 5 minutes. Scatter on the spring onion and sprinkle with sesame oil. Serve immediately

回
鍋
肉

## Double-cooked Pork

SERVES 4

Double-cooked pork is a popular family dish which takes its
name from the process of boiling and then stir-frying the meat.
It is never served as a banquet dish and is rarely seen on
restaurant menus. Serve with rice or noodles.

225 g (8 oz) boneless pork chops
1 cm (½ inch) piece of root ginger
10 Sichuan peppercorns
2 tablespoons vegetable oil
1 tablespoon chilli bean paste
1 teaspoon yellow bean paste
1 tablespoon hoisin sauce
1 leek, halved lengthways then cut into 2.5 cm (1 inch) pieces
1 tablespoon light soy sauce

Heat enough water to cover the pork in a pan. When the water
boils add the pork, ginger and peppercorns. Bring back to the
boil, skim off the froth and then reduce the heat. Simmer for
about 30 minutes until the pork is tender but not falling apart.
Remove the pork with a slotted spoon and leave to cool.

When they are cool enough to handle, cut the chops into very
fine slices less than 5 mm (¼ inch) wide, each with a piece of
skin on the end. Heat the oil in a wok until it begins to smoke,
then drop in the pork. Stir for a minute and push to one side of
the wok. Mix the chilli bean paste, yellow bean paste and hoisin
sauce into the oil and then stir into the meat for 1 minute. Add
the leek and continue to stir-fry over a high heat until it is all
well cooked. Add the soy sauce, stir and serve.

## 榨菜肉絲 Shredded Pork and Sichuan Pickle

SERVES 2

This dish is very salty and needs to be eaten with rice or
noodles.

200 g (7 oz) lean pork, cut into matchstick-sized pieces
1 tablespoon dark soy sauce
3 tablespoons vegetable oil
1 teaspoon cornflour
125 g (4 oz) Sichuan pickle, finely chopped
1 spring onion, chopped into 5 mm (¼ inch) pieces
75 ml (3 fl oz) light stock

Place the pork in a shallow dish with the soy sauce, 1 tablespoon
of the vegetable oil and the cornflour. Turn to coat, then leave to
marinate for 15 minutes.

Heat the remaining oil in a wok until it begins to smoke. Add
the pork and stir-fry over a high heat for 2 minutes. Pour away
any excess oil. Add the pickle and spring onion and stir for
another 2 minutes. Mix in the stock and bring to the boil before
serving.

# Fish Dishes

重慶魚片

## Chongqing Fish Slice

SERVES 3–4

This dish originated in the town which served as the
Guomindang capital when the Nationalists were driven west
during the Japanese invasion of the late 1930s. It is wonderfully
simple and tasty and only takes about 10 minutes. Perhaps the
best thing about it is that you can use any white fish fillet, fresh
or frozen. Serve with rice.

vegetable oil, for deep-frying
150 g (5 oz) pickled cabbage or Sichuan pickle, thinly sliced
2 red pickled chillies (optional), thinly sliced
400 ml (14 fl oz) water
400 g (14 oz) white fish fillets, such as cod or halibut

Heat the oil in a wok until it begins to smoke. Add the cabbage
and chillies, if using, and deep-fry for 1½ minutes (1 minute if
using pickle). Remove with a slotted spoon and drain on kitchen
paper.
    Bring the water to the boil, add the fillets and simmer until
they turn opaque. Remove the fish with a fish slice and keep
warm. Place the pickles and chilli in the pan and simmer for 5
minutes. Return the fish to the pan, bring back to the boil and
serve.

椒
麻
魚
## Pepper and Sesame Whitebait

Jiao Ma, 'pepper and sesame', is a combination of Sichuan
peppercorns and sesame oil. Nuts – peanuts, sesame, cashew,
walnut and pine – are commonly thrown over the finished
product. This recipe is often used for small-boned fish and we
have chosen whitebait simply because it is readily available. The
tart taste of the onions and the aromatic sesame and peanuts
make a fine contrast with the crispy fish. Serve with a mixed
green salad, rice, bread or mantou (see page 56).

225 g (8 oz) whitebait
1½ tablespoons Shaoxing wine
½ teaspoon salt
50 g (2 oz) peanuts
vegetable oil, for deep-frying
2 tablespoons sesame oil
1 small onion, finely sliced
1 cm (½ inch) piece of root ginger, finely chopped
1 teaspoon ground Sichuan pepper
2 teaspoons sugar
100 ml (3½ fl oz) stock (see page 18)
pinch of salt

Place the whitebait in a shallow dish with 1 tablespoon of wine
and the salt and leave to marinate for 15 minutes. Drain and
leave to dry. Dry-fry the peanuts in a wok until golden brown.
Loosen the skins by rolling a spoon over the top of the peanuts,
then rub off the skins with a tea towel.

Heat the oil in a wok until it begins to smoke. Add the
whitebait and deep-fry until crisp. Remove with a slotted spoon
and drain on kitchen paper. Pour off the oil.

Gently heat the sesame oil in the wok and add the onion,
ginger, Sichuan pepper, sugar, remaining wine, stock and salt.
Bring to the boil and simmer to reduce. Turn the heat up, return
the fish to the wok and toss to heat through. Mix in the peanuts
and stir for another minute. Serve immediately.

宫
爆
蝦
仁

## Gongbao Shrimps
SERVES 2–3

Yet another of Gongbao's dishes (see page 43). The shrimp may
be replaced by pork or chicken, and pine nuts, almonds or
walnuts may be used instead of peanuts. These Gongbao dishes
emanated from a wealthy official's kitchen and not from the
streets of Sichuan, but they are very common now. Ding
Gongbao, the creator of these recipes, was posted as an officer of
the Imperial court to Sichuan from Beijing, where these
Gongbao dishes are equally famous. Serve with rice.

1 teaspoon sugar
2 teaspoons rice vinegar
1 tablespoon light soy sauce
2 teaspoons Shaoxing wine
1 teaspoon cornflour
2 tablespoons vegetable oil
25 g (1 oz) raw peanuts
4 Sichuan peppercorns
2 cloves garlic, crushed and finely chopped
1 teaspoon finely chopped root ginger
1 dried chilli (optional)
225 g (8 oz) peeled, cooked shrimps
1 large spring onion, chopped into 5 mm (¼ inch) pieces

Mix together the sugar, vinegar, soy sauce, Shaoxing wine and
cornflour in a bowl. Heat the oil in a wok until it begins to
smoke, add the peanuts and stir-fry until golden brown. Add the
peppercorns, garlic, ginger and chilli. Stir for 2 seconds over a
high heat. Add the shrimps and stir for 1 minute. Pour in the soy
mixture and stir for another minute, then finally add the spring
onion and serve.

## Fragrant Yuxiang Prawns
SERVES 4

Yet another Yuxiang 'fish fragrance' dish, but this one does indeed contain seafood. The light, sweet and sour effect of the sauce makes a delicious contrast with the crispy batter.

225 g (8 oz) peeled prawns, deveined
¼ teaspoon salt
2 free-range eggs
2 heaped tablespoons cornflour
vegetable oil, for deep-frying
chopped coriander, to garnish

SAUCE
1 teaspoon soy sauce
1 tablespoon vinegar
¼ teaspoon salt
2 teaspoons sugar
1 large spring onion, finely chopped
2 teaspoons cornflour blended with a little water
100 ml (3 ½ fl oz) stock (see page 18)
25 g (1 oz) pickled chilli (optional), grated
1 cm (½ inch) piece of root ginger, finely chopped
3 cloves garlic, crushed and finely chopped

Soak the prawns in salted water for 15 minutes, then remove and pat dry on kitchen paper. Beat the salt with the eggs and the cornflour to make a thick batter. Dip the prawns in the batter to coat well. To make the sauce, mix together the soy sauce, vinegar, salt, sugar and spring onions. Blend the cornflour solution with the stock.

Heat the oil in a wok until it begins to smoke. Put in the prawns and stir until golden brown, gently separating them. Remove with a slotted spoon and drain on kitchen paper. Place on a warm serving dish. Strain off and reserve the oil, clean the wok with kitchen paper and return about 1 tablespoon of the oil to the wok. Quickly stir-fry the chilli, then add the ginger and garlic and stir together. Pour on the soy and stock mixtures and slowly bring to the boil, stirring continuously. Simmer for 30 seconds and then pour over the prawns. Garnish with chopped coriander.

# Desserts

## Pearl Dumplings
珍珠圓子

MAKES 12

Like the Chen family's mapo doufu shop and the Lai family's tong yuan shop, there is one small restaurant exclusively devoted to this delicacy. Pearl dumplings are a variety of steamed dumplings coated with glutinous rice. There are many types of filling – we have provided two options.

50 g (2 oz) uncooked glutinous rice
125 g (4 oz) cornflour
2 eggs, beaten
400 g (14 oz) cooked glutinous rice
300 g (10 oz) red bean paste or black sesame paste
halved walnuts, to decorate
vegetable oil

Soak the uncooked rice in cold water for 20 minutes. Drain and spread it on a plate. Mix the cornflour and egg together, then stir into the cooked glutinous rice while the rice is still warm. Take a heaped tablespoon of the glutinous rice mixture, roll it into a ball and press into a flat round. This is a very sticky process and takes a little practice. Take a heaped teaspoon of red bean paste and place in the centre of the round. Fold the edges around the paste, pinching the opening closed. Roll the mixture between the palms into a round dumpling. Roll the dumpling over the uncooked rice so that the rice sticks to the surface. Press half a walnut in the centre. Repeat this process with the remaining mixture.

Place the dumplings on a lightly oiled plate, leaving plenty of room between each one to allow the rice to expand. Steam over rapidly boiling water for about 20 minutes until the rice is transparent. Alternatively, the dumplings can be deep-fried in hot oil for 3 minutes on each side until golden brown, then dusted with icing sugar. In this case do not roll the dumpling in uncooked rice.

ALTERNATIVE FILLING
1 slice root ginger, finely chopped
1 spring onion, finely chopped
75 g (3 oz) peeled shrimps
125 g (4 oz) lean pork, finely minced
½ teaspoon salt
½ tablespoon light soy sauce
½ teaspoon sugar
pinch of pepper
2 tablespoons vegetable oil

Mix the ginger, spring onion and shrimps evenly into the pork.
Add all the remaining ingredients. Proceed as in the recipe
above, but increase the steaming time to 30 minutes to ensure
that the dumplings are cooked through.

豆
沙
涼
茲
粑

## Sticky Red Bean Cake

MAKES 10

These cakes are often eaten at the spring or moon festival. In May they are thrown into the river to commemorate the story of the exiled scholar and official Qu Yuan who, believing that his king had been beguiled by corrupt advisers, committed suicide by jumping into the Miluo River in grief and protest. The fish, having eaten the cakes, will leave the body of Qu Yuan. Some of our friends who have tried these cakes think that the river is the appropriate place for them, but if you like your sweets sticky and wheat-free, this is for you!

500 g (1 lb) glutinous rice, soaked in 450 ml (¾ pint) cold water for 2 hours
150 g (5 oz) sesame powder or ground sesame seeds
70 g (2½ oz) caster sugar
225 g (8 oz) red bean paste

Place the rice in a heatproof dish in a pan of water. Cover and steam for about an hour until well cooked and sticky. Pound the cooked rice with a pestle for 5 minutes until it becomes doughy. Mix together the sesame powder and sugar and dust a work surface with half the mixture. Roll and press out the rice dough into a 30 x 20 cm (12 x 8 inch) sheet roughly 2.5 cm (1 inch) thick. Roll out the bean paste on top of the dough. Fold in the short sides to meet in the centre, then fold in half along the central join, taking care not to break the rice layer. Sprinkle the remaining sesame mixture all over the folded dough. Cut the envelope into 10 pieces roughly 2.5 cm (1 inch) wide.

黑芝麻湯

## Sweet Black Sesame Soup

SERVES 6

Black sesame is said to be very cooling and nourishing. Have a small bowl of this to finish your meal.

150 g (5 oz) black sesame seeds
50 g (2 oz) peanuts
25 g (1 oz) glutinous rice powder or plain ground rice
1½ litres (2½ pints) water
sugar, to taste

Dry-fry the sesame seeds and peanuts in a wok. When they begin to brown, remove and grind to a fine powder. Combine them with the rice powder in a food processor and with the motor running slowly add the water until mixed well. Pour the mixture into a pan and add sugar to taste. Bring to the boil. When the liquid boils turn down the heat and simmer for 10 minutes, stirring to prevent it sticking. Add more water if the mixture thickens too much.

湯
圓

## Sweet Soup Balls

MAKES 30

The sweet soup balls symbolize good fortune and are
traditionally eaten at New Year. It is one of the fun preparations
that children are allowed to participate in before the festival.
You can find them with all kinds of filling, but those below are
the most usual. Be sure to put 5 balls in each bowl – 4 are
inauspicious as the word for 4 in Chinese is similar to a
homonym for death.

350 g (12 oz) glutinous rice flour
300 ml (½ pint) water
125 g (4 oz) red bean paste or black sesame paste
2 tablespoons brown or rock sugar
3 slices root ginger
1½ litres (2½ pints) water

Place the flour in a bowl, make a well in the centre and pour in
the water slowly, mixing well. Knead until the mixture forms a
smooth malleable dough that does not break when squeezed.
Roll the dough into a sausage. Nip off a cherry-sized piece of
dough and roll it between the palms into a ball. Flatten it
slightly. Make a deep indentation in the middle of the ball and
place a teaspoon of paste inside. The paste should amount to
about one-third of the quantity of dough in the ball. Fold the
edges of the dough ball round the filling, completely enveloping
the paste. Seal the edges carefully and shape the dough into a
ball once more, rolling it between the palms until it is perfectly
round. Repeat this process until all the dough and paste has been
used up.

Place the sugar and ginger in a pan with the water. Bring to the
boil and simmer for 2 minutes. Carefully drop all the balls into
the pan and simmer gently for about 5 minutes, by which time
the balls should have floated up to the surface. Place 5 balls in
each bowl with some of the ginger soup.

# 3   Recipes from the Southern Teahouse

Café society has always been a vibrant feature of traditional Cantonese life. From places where you simply drink wine and tea and eat nuts and dried snacks to the dimsum restaurants with their stacked bamboo baskets full of dumplings and steamed buns there is a venue for every occasion. The main aim is to while away the time in congenial company. As most Chinese in the West originate from South China and, in particular, the province of Guangdong where Guangzhou (Canton) is the capital, the snacks served in the great western Chinatowns of San Francisco, New York and London are naturally Cantonese. Westerners are therefore inclined to associate teahouse food with recipes from the southern teahouse.

The few blocks tightly bordering on Gerrard Street in London look like any other Chinatown anywhere in the West. Crates of sweet potatoes, bak choy and winter melon spill out over the pavements and gaudy restaurant frontages declare their Happy Friendly Joy King Lupsup message and wink at you with neon lights. An unidentifiable savoury sweetness hangs in the air and bags of rubbish block the basement stairs. On the street and in the Chinese supermarkets everyone moves with singular purpose, even if their object is simply shopping for the next meal. The only loitering seems to happen in secret, behind closed doors, with the clatter of majong, the flash of a Kungfu kit and the certainty of triad authority.

All overseas Chinese return to Chinatown again and again as if it were an umbilical cord to a homeland that by now may only be a distant memory. With so many Hong Kong and Cantonese Chinese still employed in the restaurant trade, Sunday is the occasion for the family outing to Gerrard Street for dimsum, the collection of steamed and deep-fried snacks that form the basis of light lunch and teahouse society. Unlike ordinary Cantonese restaurant food the lunch-time snacking traditions serve dishes that are not eaten with rice, and therefore tend to be less greasy. As a general impression they may have a gooey consistency, an unknown, sometimes alarming quality, which may explain why dimsum took a while to catch on in the West. But for Chinese, Sunday lunch in Chinatown is a regular ritual, no less than roast beef and Yorkshire pudding, except that it is an affirmation of identity enacted by the family as part of the community, rather than in the private sanctuary of the Englishman's castle.

A typical Sunday lunch-time spread might include bao zi, the steamed stuffed buns which are generally rather sweet, but can be stuffed with savoury fillings such as cha shao or sweet red bean paste, the ubiquitous spring roll, steamed rice wrapped in lotus leaves, sticky rice pancakes stuffed with all kinds of wonders, turnip cakes, chickens' feet, steamed pork and seafood dumplings delicately wrapped and presented in the steaming baskets. With the relative prosperity of Guangdong province the Cantonese menu is very varied. Food from the hinterland arrives via the great rivers, and there are well-stocked lakes as well as thousands of miles of coastline to fish.

The purpose of my own forays into Chinatown have changed over the years. As a child, the New Year celebrations were filled with dimsum and screechy Chinese singers at the New World Restaurant in Newport Place. Then on our outings to the cinema father would take us first for the classic crispy Cantonese deep-fried noodles with various seafood and meat toppings. These are very fine egg noodles which are first boiled and then pressed against the bottom of the frying-pan until slightly brown and turned over like a pancake until both sides are crispy. Any topping, typically mixed meats or seafoods glazed in brown gravy is then scattered over the top. This is a gourmet's nightmare, but it tastes pretty good to the average child.

More lately, as my palate is becoming increasingly Chinese, I have begun to appreciate the finer qualities of congee – a soft rice porridge which is often served at breakfast. Most congees are a little bland for the western palate, although anyone with a love of plain oatmeal should take to it well. It is fortifying and easy to digest for the young, the elderly and the infirm. Chinese herbs can also be added to the basic stew. In fact, the basic rice gruel can be supplied with as many ingredients as you choose, both dried, pickled and fresh.

As a teenager starting a night out on the town in central London I would frequently be driven into Soho by a craving for wun tun noodle soup – the minced pork, prawn and spring onions, wrapped in a soft dough skin and served in chicken broth. Then there was a time when I would test the mettle of my friends by presenting them with chicken's feet, a much-loved picnic speciality which demands noisy sucking to liberate skin from bone in one clean movement. As there are more and more vegetarians among my acquaintances, I am now denied this indulgence.

Chinese cuisine is not noted for its baking and, in general, that is fair judgement. Nor are the patisseries themselves very sophisticated. However, there are one or two gems that should not be overlooked. First, there is an excellent Cantonese egg tart which is more delicate and less sickly than the English counterpart and has a delicious pastry. Sweet red beans (aduki) make the stuffing for many substantial cakes and desserts, some covered in a sticky rice dough, others with pastry. Tea-time is all day, every day, so the cafés that sell tea, sweets, cakes and soya milk drinks tend to be open from mid-morning to mid-evening.

The vast majority of Cantonese teahouse snacks and foods form the basis of most of the Chinese cookbooks available in the West. Their authors fail to tell you that good dimsum are almost impossible to cook. Even top-class restaurants will employ a very expensive specialized chef to produce dimsum of quality. We have, therefore, limited the number of dimsum recipes here to the simplest, and added the basic Cantonese noodle and congee dishes. Instead of going over well-trodden and infertile ground we have chosen to represent the food from another lively teahouse tradition found in Southern China. Attached to the Buddhist temples there will be a canteen that serves its own monks, but will also provide cheap and wholesome vegetarian fare to the traveller or pilgrim who has made the journey to the temple in order to burn incense and beseech the gods for help in family or business matters or in their forthcoming exams.

The quality of the food served in the temple teahouses is as various as in any other kind of restaurants. The vegetarian recipes below come from the Cantonese Buddhist repertoire. To make a vegetarian stock savoury the quickest way is to throw in the MSG, and Chinese monks are no exception to this practice. However, a good Buddhist teahouse can provide colourful and creative vegetarian fare. The simulation of meat dishes with soy bean and gluten products puts vegetarian sausages and burgers to shame, but I have always felt that this tradition, both in China and the West, was founded on a hankering for meat, and rather missed the point of celebrating the vegetable itself.

Amongst Buddhist prohibitions are the Wuxin 'Five Bitternesses', strong-tasting foods that are thought to upset. The Five Bitternesses usually include spring onions, garlic, Chinese chives, Sichuan pepper and Chinese cinnamon. It is said that if the ghosts smell the strong flavours on your breath they will come and lick your lips. To ward off evil spirits gentler dishes are prepared with ginger and Chinese mushrooms to leave you with a freshness more attractive to the gracious shades of the nether world. I celebrated my thirtieth birthday in the canteen of a monastery on Lion Head Mountain. At dusk, a light supper and fresh green tea in the mountains of mid-Taiwan was enough to convince me that we had won the good intentions of the local spirits!

# Soups and Snacks

鹽
酥
蝦

## Crispy Salted Prawns

SERVES 4

Serve this as a starter with wine or cocktails. Unusually, it is
quite traditional to chew the shell and spit it out after extracting
the flavours.

275 g (9 oz) tiger prawns in their shells, heads and tails removed
½ tablespoon Shaoxing wine
vegetable oil, for deep-frying
2 cloves garlic, crushed and finely chopped
1 red chilli, seeded and finely sliced
1 large spring onion, chopped
pinch of salt
pinch of pepper

Place the prawns in a dish with the wine and leave to marinate
for 10 minutes.

Heat the oil in a wok until it just begins to smoke. Add the
prawns and deep-fry for 2 minutes. Remove the prawns with a
slotted spoon and drain on kitchen paper. Pour off the oil.
Return the prawns to the wok with the garlic, chilli and spring
onion. Toss together for a minute. Sprinkle with salt and pepper
and turn together once more.

## Fillet of Fish Congee
SERVES 4–6

This is a warm soup with a cooling effect: the saltiness of the pickle has the effect of taking the heat inwards.

225 g (8 oz) long-grain rice
2.5 litres (4 pints) strong chicken or fish stock (see page 18)
10 dried Chinese mushrooms, soaked in hot water for 30 minutes
3 tablespoons vegetable oil
1 onion, sliced
3 tablespoons Sichuan pickle, finely shredded
1 cm (½ inch) piece of root ginger, very thinly sliced
2 tablespoons soy sauce
1 tablespoon sesame oil
225 g (8 oz) cooked shrimps, chopped
225 g (8 oz) cod or haddock fillet, thinly sliced lengthways
lettuce and coriander leaves, to serve

Rinse the rice thoroughly and put it into a heavy casserole with the stock. Bring to the boil. Turn down the heat to medium and boil for 5 minutes. Stir well and cover. Turn to the lowest heat possible and simmer for about 1 hour. Add water if the rice begins to stick to the pan. The final consistency should be a little like porridge.

Meanwhile, drain the mushrooms, reserving the soaking liquid, and discard the hard stems. Slice the caps finely. Heat the oil in a wok until it begins to smoke, then add the onion and toss for 30 seconds. Add the mushrooms, pickle and ginger and stir for about 1 minute. Mix in the soy sauce and mushroom soaking water. Bring to the boil, then reduce the heat and simmer until the mushrooms have absorbed most of the liquid. Finally turn up the heat and mix in the sesame oil.

When the rice is ready add the fish, shrimps and mushroom mixture to the casserole and mix together. Stir gently until the fish is cooked. Serve with lettuce and coriander leaves.

羅
宋
湯

## Luosong Soup

SERVES 4

It is said that eating figs is the best way to sustain a youthful complexion and shining eyes.

1½ tablespoons vegetable oil
1 cm (½ inch) root ginger, thinly sliced
1 carrot, cut into 5 mm (¼ inch) slices
2 sweet potatoes, peeled and cut into 5 mm (¼ inch) slices
2 tomatoes, cut into 5 mm (¼ inch) slices
1 litre (1¾ pints) water
4 dried figs
150 g (5 oz) cauliflower, divided into small florets
salt and pepper to taste.

Heat the oil in a pan, add the ginger and stir until the fragrance is released. Add the carrot and sweet potatoes. After a few minutes put in the tomatoes. Add the water and figs and bring to the boil. Turn down the heat and simmer for 1 hour. Add the cauliflower, bring back to the boil and simmer for 15 minutes. Season with salt and pepper to taste.

醒
胃
菠
菜
湯

## Spinach Soup to Stimulate the Stomach

SERVES 4

This is one of those soups designed to get the digestive juices
flowing. It can be served as a starter or between heavier courses.

4 dried Chinese mushrooms, soaked in hot water for 30 minutes
vegetable oil, for deep-frying
125 g (4 oz) Sichuan pickle, cut into matchstick strips
1½ tablespoons vegetable oil
1 cm (½ inch) piece of root ginger, finely sliced
750 ml (1¼ pints) water
2 tomatoes, cut into 5 mm (¼ inch) slices
50 g (2 oz) pickled cabbage, sliced
50 g (2 oz) fen si noodles
2 teaspoons cornflour
salt, pepper and sesame oil to taste
150 g (5 oz) young spinach, roughly torn

Drain the mushrooms, discard the tough stems and slice the
caps finely. Heat the oil in a wok until it just begins to smoke.
Add the Sichuan pickle and fry for 30 seconds. Remove and
drain on kitchen paper.

Heat the 1½ tablespoons of oil in a pan. Add the ginger and
stir. Add the mushrooms and stir to coat with oil. Pour in the
water and bring to the boil. Add the tomatoes and pickled
cabbage. After 2 minutes add the Sichuan pickle and noodles.
Blend the cornflour with a little water and pour into the pan,
stirring thoroughly. Season with salt, pepper and a little sesame
oil. Finally add the spinach and bring back to the boil. Give the
soup a good stir and serve immediately.

鮮
素
湯

## Fresh Vegetarian Soup

SERVES 4

This is a delicate summer soup flavoured with fresh herbs. For those who like a stronger-tasting soup use vegetarian stock (see page 19) or add a little bouillon powder.

5 dried Chinese mushrooms, soaked in hot water for 30 minutes
1½ tablespoons vegetable oil
1 cm (½ inch) piece of root ginger, finely sliced
1 litre (1¾ pints) water
2 tomatoes, cut into 5 mm (¼ inch) slices
2 large sticks of celery, halved lengthways and cut into 4 cm (1¾ inch) segments
1 cake bean curd, about 12 cm (5 inch) square, cut into cubes
1 teaspoon salt
pepper, to taste
1 handful fresh chopped coriander and fennel, or fresh herbs to taste

Drain the mushrooms, reserving the soaking water. Discard the hard stems and slice the caps finely. Heat the oil in a wok. When it is hot add the ginger and stir around to flavour the oil. Add the mushrooms and toss for a few seconds. Pour in the water and reserved soaking water. Skim off any scum. When it boils add the remaining ingredients. Bring back to the boil, then turn down the heat and simmer for 3 minutes.

# Vegetables and Vegetarian Dishes

護
國
菜

## The Patriotic Vegetable
SERVES 4
When Zhao Bing, the last Emperor of the Song dynasty, was
fleeing for his life he was looked after by a monk in a temple
near Chaozhou. The monk prepared the following dish for him.
It is good to eat with noodles.

500 g (1 lb) spinach
3 tablespoons vegetable oil
125 g (4 oz) sliced straw mushrooms
50 g (2 oz) sliced smoked ham
1 teaspoon salt
500 ml (17 fl oz) chicken stock (see page 18)
1 teaspoon cornflour blended with water
1 teaspoon sesame oil

Blanch the spinach for 2 minutes, then drain. Heat 2 tablespoons
of oil in a wok and add the mushrooms, ham, salt and stock and
simmer for 10 minutes. Meanwhile, quickly stir-fry the spinach
in the remaining oil. Add the spinach and the cornflour solution
to the stock and simmer until thickened. Serve sprinkled with
the sesame oil.

蘿
蔔
酥
餅

## Flaky Radish Fritters

MAKES 20

500 g (1 lb) self-raising flour
8 tablespoons cold water
4 tablespoons vegetable oil

STUFFING
400 g (14 oz) Chinese radish, grated
salt, to sprinkle
200 g (7 oz) pickled cabbage, finely chopped
3 spring onions, finely chopped
½ teaspoon salt
2 teaspoons five-spice powder
pepper, to taste
vegetable oil, for shallow-frying

Sift 325 g (11 oz) of the flour into a bowl and slowly mix in the water until you have a sticky dough. Cover and set aside for 30 minutes.

Meanwhile, sieve 160 g (5½ oz) of the flour into another bowl and make a well in the centre. Heat the oil in a pan gently then pour it slowly into the well. Work the oil into the flour, pushing and squeezing the dough with the fingertips.

To make the stuffing, sprinkle the radish with a little salt and leave for 20 minutes. Squeeze out excess water then mix the radish with the other stuffing ingredients.

Dust the work surface with a little of the remaining flour and shape the first dough into 2 sausages. Cut each one into 10 sections. Press each section flat and roll out into 10 cm (4 inch) thin rounds with a rolling pin. The round should be thinner at the edges, so roll around the edges again.

Shape the oiled dough into another sausage and divide into 20 pieces. Place each piece at the centre of a pastry round and press down with the fingers, flattening it so that it makes a smaller, yellow round on top of the original round.

Place a teaspoon of stuffing in the centre of each round. Draw the sides up and gather together the edge as if making tiny pleats. When you have what looks like a tiny drawstring purse press the opening together. Then turn the bun in the palm of one hand alternatively nipping and pressing down on what remains of the opening until it can no longer be seen. Press as flat as possible, without making the bottom layer of dough so thin that you can see through it.

Heat the oil in a wok, add the buns and fry in batches for about 5 minutes over the lowest heat possible until the underside browns, pressing down with a spatula. Turn and brown the other side. If the heat is too high the outside of the fritters will burn while the inside will not be cooked.

韭
菜
薄
餅

## Chinese Chive Crepes

MAKES ABOUT 20

This is a dish for a hot summer's day, best eaten with cold green
beans or corn congee.

300 g (10 oz) plain flour
400 ml (14 fl oz) water
150 g (5 oz) Chinese chives, finely chopped
2 teaspoons salt
vegetable oil, for frying

Mix the flour with the water to a smooth batter. Add the chives
and salt and mix well. Heat 1 teaspoon of oil in an omelette pan.
Pour in a large tablespoon of batter and spread into a thin layer.
Cook until brown on one side, then turn to brown on the other.
Continue until the batter is finished, adding more oil as
necessary.

炒
腐
竹

## Tossed Bean Curd Skin

SERVES 2

200 g (7 oz) dried bean curd skins, soaked in hot water for 30
minutes until soft
3 dried Chinese mushrooms, soaked in hot water for 30 minutes
1½ tablespoons vegetable oil
salt and light soy sauce, to taste
2 sticks of celery, diced
1 green pepper,cored, seeded and diced

Drain the bean curd skins and pat dry on kitchen paper. Cut into
4 cm (1¾ inch) squares. Drain the mushrooms, discard the tough
stems and slice the caps.

Heat the oil in a wok. When it just begins to smoke add the
bean curd skins. After 1 minute add salt and soy sauce to taste
and stir for a further 30 seconds. Finally add the mushrooms and
remaining vegetables and stir together for a minute before
serving.

炸
豆
腐
丸

## Deep-fried Bean Curd Balls
SERVES 4

4 dried Chinese mushrooms, soaked in hot water for 30 minutes
3 tablespoons flour
2 cakes of bean curd, about 12 cm (5 inch) square
150 g (5 oz) carrots, finely chopped
3 whole water chestnuts, finely chopped
1 teaspoon salt
1 teaspoon sugar
vegetable oil, for deep-frying
150 g (5 oz) shelled raw peanuts

Drain the mushrooms, reserving the soaking water, discard the
tough stems and chop the caps finely. Place the flour in a bowl
and add the bean curd, breaking it up with chopsticks. Mix in
the carrots, water chestnuts, salt and sugar. Use enough of the
mushroom soaking water to make a thick doughy mixture
which is neither dry nor wet.

Heat the oil in a wok, but do not let it smoke. Use a
dessertspoon to scoop up balls of the dough. Press a peanut into
the top of each one, then carefully drop into the oil. Fry for about
5 minutes, or until they turn golden brown. Remove with a
slotted spoon and drain on kitchen paper.

老
少
平
安

## Peace and Comfort for Old and Young

SERVES 4

We have no idea how this dish got its name. In fact, it is quite
spicy, so be careful how much soy sauce is used, and eat it with
a plain dish, or with rice.

50 g (2 oz) dried Chinese mushrooms, soaked in hot water for 30
minutes
vegetable oil, for deep-frying
25 g (1 oz) fen si noodles
2 cakes of silken bean curd, about 12 cm (5 inches) square
50 g (2 oz) Sichuan pickle, finely chopped
a little apple, orange and pear peel, diced
soy sauce, to taste
1 teaspoon sesame oil
25 g (1 oz) chopped coriander

Drain the mushrooms, discard the tough stems and dice the
caps. Heat the oil in a wok until almost smoking, add the
noodles and deep-fry until golden brown and crisp. Remove with
a slotted spoon and drain on kitchen paper. Pour off the oil
leaving about a teaspoon in the wok. Add the mushrooms and
turn for 30 seconds in the oil. Stir in the bean curd, breaking it
up with chopsticks, the noodles, pickle and peel. Finally add the
soy sauce.

Turn the mixture into a heatproof dish. Place the dish in a
steamer, cover and steam for 15 minutes. Drizzle on the sesame
oil and garnish with coriander.

## 炊 枝 竹　Braised Bean Curd Sticks
SERVES 4

50 g (2 oz) dried Chinese mushrooms, soaked in hot water for 30 minutes
vegetable oil, for deep-frying
125 g (4 oz) peanuts, skins removed
200 g (7 oz) bean curd sticks, broken into 4 cm (1¾ inch) pieces
500 ml (16 fl oz) water
2 tablespoons vegetable oil
salt, sugar, light soy sauce and sesame oil, to taste

Drain the mushrooms, discard the tough stems and chop the caps. Heat the oil in a wok until it begins to smoke. Add the peanuts and deep-fry until golden brown. Remove with a slotted spoon and drain on kitchen paper. Roll with a rolling pin to slightly break up the nuts. Pour off the oil leaving 1½ tablespoons.

Scatter in the bean curd sticks and stir-fry until they turn golden brown. Remove with a slotted spoon and place in a pan. Cover with the water and leave for 10 minutes. Bring the water to the boil and simmer until the bean curd sticks are just soft and the water has almost evaporated. Turn off the heat, cover and leave.

Heat the 2 tablespoons of oil in the wok and add the mushrooms, peanuts and bean curd sticks. Season with a dash of salt, sugar, soy and sesame oil. Stir-fry for a few minutes, then serve.

酥
炸
芽
菜
餅

## Bean Sprout Fritters

SERVES 4

200 g (7 oz) plain flour
1 small carrot, grated
1 green pepper, cored, seeded and thinly sliced
1 red pepper, cored, seeded and thinly sliced
15 g (½ oz) Sichuan pickle, finely chopped
225 g (8 oz) bean sprouts
salt and sugar, to taste
vegetable oil, for frying
125 g (4 oz) cashew nuts

Sift the flour into a bowl and add enough water to make a soft
dough. Stir in the vegetables and add a little salt and sugar. Heat
a little oil in an omelette pan. Place 2 tablespoons of the dough
in the pan. Place 3 cashew nuts on top and press down to make a
fritter. Cook until brown underneath, then turn and brown the
other side. Repeat with the remaining dough, adding more oil as
necessary. Serve with chilli oil or hot bean sauce.

腐
乳
燴
茄
子

## Steamed Aubergine with Bean Curd Dressing
SERVES 4

3 pieces of fermented bean curd, red or white
1 teaspoon sugar
2 tablespoons water
2 aubergines, cut into 2 x 4 cm (1 x 1¾ inch) chunks
1 tablespoon vegetable oil
chopped coriander, to garnish

Squash the bean curd and sprinkle with sugar, then mix with the
water.
    Place the aubergine on a plate in a steamer and steam, for
about 20 minutes, until soft. When the aubergine is nearly done
heat the oil in a pan and add the bean curd sauce. Stir together
well. When heated through, place the aubergine on a serving
dish and pour on the sauce. Sprinkle with coriander and serve.

# One-dish noodle meals

海
鮮
炒
面

## Slow-braised Seafood Noodle
SERVES 6

50 g (2 oz) squid
½ tablespoon vegetable oil
50 g (2 oz) sliced bamboo shoots
750 ml (1¼ pints) warm fish stock
10 g (½ oz) dried shrimp, soaked in cold water
1 tablespoon salt
1 teaspoon pepper
50 g (2 oz) cooked shrimps
50 g (2 oz) cooked shelled mussels
500 g (1 lb) oil noodles
1 tablespoon sherry
4 tablespoons chopped spring onions

Cut the squid in half and score with diagonal lines on the inside
to make a diamond pattern. Then cut into 3 cm (1¼ inch)
squares.

Heat the oil in a wok, add the bamboo shoots and stir-fry very
quickly. Remove from the wok with a slotted spoon and place in
a pan with the stock, soaked shrimps, salt and pepper. Bring to
the boil, then reduce the heat and simmer for 5 minutes. Add
the squid, shrimps and mussels to the pan and simmer gently.
Add the noodles and heat through. Finally add the sherry and
spring onions, stir well and serve.

## 什 肉 脆 面 Shallow-fried Noodles or Two Sides Brown

SERVES 4

Shallow-fried noodles are best made using fresh egg noodles. If unavailable, the finest quality dried egg noodles will do.

400 g (14 oz) fresh egg noodles or 200 g (7 oz) dried noodles
1 egg white
½ tablespoon cornflour
2 teaspoons Shaoxing wine
2 teaspoons salt
125 g (4 oz) boned, skinned chicken breast, thinly sliced
125 g (4 oz) fresh prawns, shelled and deveined
6 dried Chinese mushrooms, soaked in hot water for 30 minutes
2 tablespoons chicken stock (see page 18)
1 tablespoon light soy sauce
pinch of sugar
pinch of pepper
6 tablespoons vegetable oil
1 cm (½ inch) piece of root ginger, finely chopped
125 g (4 oz) sliced bamboo shoots
1 small carrot, finely sliced
50 g (2 oz) French beans, halved and blanched
2 spring onions, sliced
2 teaspoons sesame oil

Bring a large pan of water to a rolling boil. Add the fresh noodles and bring back to the boil, then immediately drain, rinse under cold water and drain again. Alternatively, soak the dried noodles in boiling water for 10 minutes, then drain, rinse under cold water and drain again. Spread the cooked noodles on a flat surface and leave for at least 30 minutes until they dry. Meanwhile, prepare the topping.

Mix the egg white with 1 teaspoon of cornflour, the wine and the salt. Place the chicken and prawns in separate bowls, stir half the egg white mixture into each bowl and leave to marinate for 30 minutes. Drain the mushrooms, discard the tough stems and quarter. Combine the stock, soy sauce, sugar and pepper.

Blend the remaining cornflour with a little water.

Heat the oil in a wok over high heat. When hot, deep-fry the noodles quickly for a few seconds, then pour off half the oil. Reduce the heat to medium and coil and press the noodles into the bottom of the wok. Continue to fry for a few minutes until browned. Turn the crisp noodles over and repeat on the other side, adding more oil if necessary to prevent them sticking. Lift out the noodles with a fish slice and reserve.

Reheat the oil in the wok until it just begins to smoke. Add the chicken and prawns and stir-fry quickly. As soon as they change colour, remove with a slotted spoon. Drain off and reserve the oil and wipe out the wok with kitchen paper. Reheat 1 tablespoon of oil in the wok. Add the ginger and turn in the oil, then add all the vegetables and toss together for 30 seconds. Add the stock mixture and bring to the boil, stirring constantly. Add the prawns and chicken and stir together for a few minutes. Finally, add the cornflour mixture and stir gently to thicken, then sprinkle with sesame oil. Place the noodles on a warm serving dish, pile the mixture on top and serve.

## Cantonese River Noodles with Beef in Black Bean Sauce

豆
豉
牛
河

SERVES 4–5

This should be a familiar dish, since it is often served by
Cantonese chefs in restaurants and takeaways. The difference is
that we have used fresh river noodles or hofun (see page 266),
which are generally saved for the staff alone. They are best fresh,
but are also available dried, in which case they should be pre-
cooked.

375 g (12 oz) fresh hofun or 175 g (6 oz) dried
400 g (14 oz) lean beef, cut into thin 4 cm (1½ inch) strips
1½ teaspoons salt
1 egg white
1½ tablespoons cornflour
4 tablespoons vegetable oil
1 Spanish onion, thinly sliced
2 slices root ginger, finely sliced
2 cloves garlic, crushed and finely chopped
2 tablespoons salted black beans, soaked for 3 minutes, drained
and chopped
1 tablespoon light soy sauce
1½ tablespoons oyster sauce
1 tablespoon chilli sauce
4 tablespoons stock
1 red pepper, cored, seeded and cut into thin strips
3 spring onions, cut into 3 cm (1¼ inch) sections

If using dried hofun parboil for 7–8 minutes, or according to
packet instructions, and drain. Leave to soak in cold water to
prevent them sticking until ready to use. In the restaurant fresh
hofun are cooked in the microwave for 2 minutes at the lowest
(defrost) setting: then they can be added to the wok at the last
minute for the final assembly. Rub the beef with the salt, dip in
egg white and dredge with cornflour.

Heat the oil in a wok until it just begins to smoke. Add the
beef and stir-fry quickly until it changes colour. Remove the

beef with a slotted spoon and reserve. Drain off and reserve the oil and wipe out the wok with kitchen paper. Reheat 2 tablespoons of the oil in the wok. Add the onion and ginger and stir-fry for 1 minute. Add the garlic, black beans, soy sauce, oyster sauce, chilli sauce and stock. Bring to the boil then add the beef and peppers, stirring constantly.

Add the hofun and spring onions. Turn up the heat as high as possible, turning together for 1 minute (longer if the hofun have not been microwaved). The hofun will tend to stick together, so keep the mixture moving, but not too vigorously, as the hofun may break. If the mixture is too dry and keeps sticking, add a litle more oil.

東
江
鹽
焗
雞

## Eastern River Salt-baked Chicken

SERVES 6

Eastern River is a region of the province of Canton. Because they have plenty of sea salt they are famous for their salt-baked chicken.

1 cornfed chicken, about 1.5 kg (3 lb)
3 teaspoons salt
3 tablespoons groundnut oil
3 slices root ginger
2 teaspoons five-spice powder
2 tablespoons sliced spring onions
1 teaspoon sesame oil
1 teaspoon ground ginger
1 kg (2 lb) sea salt
2 tablespoons chopped coriander

Dry the chicken and rub the cavity with 1 teaspoon of salt. Cut 2 pieces of muslin, about 8 cm (3½ inch) square. Brush one piece of muslin with groundnut oil. Use the other to wrap the ginger, five-spice powder and spring onions into a parcel. Wrap the parcel again with the oiled muslin. Push the parcel inside the chicken. Mix together the sesame oil, remaining plain salt and ground ginger.

Preheat the oven to 180°C, 350°F, Gas 4. Heat the sea salt in a pan until it browns. Spoon one-quarter of the salt into the bottom of a casserole and place the chicken on top. Cover the chicken with the rest of the sea salt. Cover and roast in the preheated oven for 1½ hours, or until cooked. Remove the chicken from the casserole and discard the salt. Remove the skin, take the chicken off the bone and cut into strips. Sprinkle with the sesame oil mixture and garnish with coriander.

# Desserts

香蕉薄餅

## Banana Fritters
SERVES 4–6

2 bananas
125 g (4 oz) self-raising flour
2 tablespoons milk
1 tablespoon soft margarine
1–2 tablespoons vegetable oil
1 tablespoon honey (optional)

Mash the bananas. Sift the flour into a bowl. Slowly add the milk, margarine and the mashed banana and mix well to form a dough.

Heat a little of the oil in a frying pan and place 1 tablespoon of the dough in the pan. Press down with a spatula to form a fritter. Brown on each side over medium heat. Repeat with the remaining dough, adding more oil as necessary. If you like your fritters sweet, serve with honey.

## Big Steamer Cake
SERVES 20

500 g (1 lb) glutinous rice powder
125 g (4 oz) honey, or more to taste
4 tablespoons vegetable oil
50 g (2 oz) dried red dates, stoned and chopped
25 g (1 oz) dried apricots, chopped
2 tablespoons shelled sunflower seeds
vegetable oil, for deep-frying
2 tablespoons toasted white sesame seeds

Mix the rice powder with enough water to make a sticky thick dough. Stir the honey into the rice dough and gradually pour in the oil and mix well. Mix in the dates, apricots and sunflower seeds. Turn the dough into a square heatproof dish and steam for 2 hours. Remove the cake and leave to cool, then chill for 30 minutes to 1 hour.

Take a dessertspoon of the cake dough and dust with rice powder, forming it into a ball. Repeat with the remaining dough. Heat the oil in a wok until just smoking and deep-fry the balls until golden brown. Remove with a slotted spoon, drain on kitchen paper and sprinkle with sesame seeds.

# 4 Therapeutic Recipes from the Teahouse

Now in the practice of medicine you must first understand the source of the illness and where it is invading, then use food to treat it. If there is no recovery with dietary therapy, only then prescribe medicine.
*Beiji Qianjin Yaofang (Sun Simiao, c. 650)*

In one short chapter it is not possible to explain all the nuances of oriental dietary therapy (some of the basic terms are introduced in the Appendix, page 277). In the classification of foodstuffs and pharmaceuticals the mixing of correlative magic, associations with Yin and Yang and the Five Phases, empirical observations about the nature and effects of foods are all tossed together in a fabulous stir-fry and it would be misleading to propose a single coherent theory. This chapter simply aims to illustrate the inseparable link between food and medicine, a link which we can explore with a few creative flourishes of our own.

My first experience of watching therapeutic food served up was in a street café in Snake Alley, Taibei where the snakes were being squeezed and tormented into giving up their bile for the sake of male virility. Snake meat is indeed very tasty, but this is the gross end of the market. Many commercial remedies are geared towards male fears about impotence and these, like rhino horn, are often the practices that have, in recent years, brought oriental dietary and medical practice into sharp conflict with the animal rights movement. Tiger bone is supposed to be good for arthritis, probably because there are few arthritic tigers. Unless astronomically expensive, tiger bone is always fake, and contrary to the belief of the government agency that raided the Chinatown herbalist, there is no tiger in tiger balm. Then there are those products that might cause offence, such as bat's droppings, an effective cure for bleeding, or dog and donkey penises, which are believed to be a remedy for male neuroses

The famous therapeutic teahouses of Chengdu and Hangzhou, formerly state-owned, are now popular tourist haunts. They also serve foods that may be unacceptable. Terrapins may be good for the kidneys, but this is the specialist end of the market. They also serve home-style remedies to aid digestion. Black rice congee or ginseng tea are as common as terrapin dishes. Chinese angelica and other mild medicinal herbs are classic additives to stock or stew. Sweet soups made of white fungus and rock sugar tone the lungs. The menus are also extremely tasty. There may be someone on hand to advise customers about how they should eat if they are actually ill, but this is not how the establishments are generally used. For local families they provide an inexpensive venue for a special night out, a curiosity where they can publicly affirm and participate in their tradition of food as medicine.

Most Chinese grannies know a great deal about the different actions and qualities of very ordinary food, and are often only too happy to tell you what you should and shouldn't eat. These days their explanations are likely to be influenced by western medical thought as they add recommendations about how green tea reduces cholesterol in the blood or how white chrysanthemum lowers high blood pressure. Cantonese culinary culture, in particular, is steeped in an understanding of how different herbs can be used in ordinary stews and soups. For women recovering from childbirth and the elderly with their weak digestive systems there are well-known food remedies to restore and strengthen. Understanding the action of different foods is a living part of the tradition which is still in evidence on the shelves in Chinatown where selections of restorative herbs are sold for adding to the stockpot.

Often the most immediate observations about how, for example, ginger heats the body and promotes an upward move-ment that counteracts colds, or cucumber cools and has a downward calming movement, can be the most instructive and useful in preparing foods that complement one another. With time and attention we can educate ourselves into a bodily awareness of what kinds of foods induce strength and vitality. Learning to listen to the responses of your body does not usually mean following the desires of the mouth. What the mouth desires may be the key to a dietary deficiency, but over-indulgence in the desired flavour will not make you feel better. We are generally aware of the sluggish sleepiness that overcomes us after a heavy meal, but how many of us know how invigorating a good bowl of chicken soup laced with ginger can be? Our own grandmothers certainly used to know about chicken soup, whether they were Jewish, West Indian, French or Chinese.

The secret lies mainly in eating a varied diet that combines a range of flavours and ingredients, and that adapts to changes in the environment and in our health. To begin with we must pay attention to seemingly superficial aspects. Unattractive food immediately destroys the appetite, and pleasure is a primary key to developing the relationship with your food. A good aroma is instantly engaging. In Yuan Mei's (1715–1797) famous cookbook he reminds us that:

The eyes and nose are the mouth's neighbours and the matchmakers for the mouth. Fine dishes fill the eyes with colour and the nose with their aromas. Each is unique, some pure like autumn clouds, others as exquisite as amber . . .

In addition, we should start to get to know the underlying nature of our own bodies and then match the condition with foods that nourish and strengthen. If an illness is acute then it is important to consult a skilled practitioner because ordinary food may not be appropriate. But with minor symptoms we may be able to help ourselves. Where discomfort ends and illness begins can be an entirely subjective matter. But even when we are not suffering from a specific debilitating condition our experience of health is variable and can be influenced by the food we eat. We can be more or less energetic, sleep deeply or lightly, digest efficiently or have better or worse periods, feel muzzy or clear-headed and it is these variations that determine the quality of our lives.

For a general introduction to body types and food classifications study the Appendix (page 277) and read the discussion of some of the basic terms and theories of the Chinese medical traditions. Of course we can only skim the surface, and references to some of the better books on the subject are also given on page 274. Quite apart from finding tonic foods for the individual there is a lively tradition of foods for specific conditions, such as asthma, indigestion and debility arising from childbirth. But rather than arrange this chapter by condition, which would have emphasized the curative power of food, we have chosen to concentrate on its ability to strengthen and fortify the body against illness.

## A Banquet for Four Seasons
In the spring generate, in the summer grow, in the autumn harvest, in the winter preserve, this is the way of ancestor Peng.
*Zhangjiashan Yinshu (c.200 BC)*

Tradition associates ancestor Peng with longevity. Benefiting from a health regimen of therapeutic exercises, breath cultivation and regulated sexual practice he is reputed to have lived seven hundred years. Here in a quotation from a therapeutic exercise manual he is associated with modes of behaviour that are closely attuned to the season as if in a rural or agricultural life. Activity begins in the spring, reaches its zenith in the summer and autumn months and subsides into virtual hibernation when daylight is at its shortest. Health care – hygiene, breathing and exercise, diet and sexual activity – should also change according to the season in order to cultivate and refine the body and prepare for the next season.

What is meant by attuning the body to the season and eating in accordance with the movement of the year? Eating only locally grown food might be the first step, but it is not a practical proposition for most urban dwellers. Besides, supermarkets have transformed our eating habits and spoiled us with the joy of clean, brightly coloured vegetables from all over the world all year round. In our time-conscious lives it is hard to re-adjust to preparing and living with only seasonal fare. Following the season can also mean following the ambience and movement of that season, in other words, the Qi of that season in the way we cook.

In one of its earliest known appearances the word Qi was used to describe conditions of light and weather. The six Qi were sunshine, shade, wind and rain, dark and light, the changing moods of the environment. Developing an awareness of the season in the dishes that we eat can mean being guided by the availability of the produce, right down to matching the mood of the season with the quality of the food, or considering specific foods and flavours to support the physical functions and organs that are associated with the season. The stomach, for example, is associated with late summer, the sweet flavour and a gentle upward movement; the kidneys are thought to have an affinity with winter, the salt flavour and therefore an inward movement; and the heart is associated with summer and heat. Human moods and emotions also correspond to the physiology of the organ system. The liver is associated with anger, the heart with joy. See the Appendix for an extended list of associations.

Each of the seasonal banquets described in this chapter is preceded by a representation of the mood of the season and our interpretation of how to follow it in the choice of foods. Then every recipe begins with a simple analysis of its therapeutic value. There are a number of different ways in which food is thought to complement the season and classical texts often propose different theories. We have been quite eclectic in our approach in order to give the reader a broad introduction to oriental dietary therapy. First, we can follow the movement of the season. When the weather is hot, sweet, spicy warming foods will help the body adapt to the climate. We can choose to harmonize rather than counter-balance. Apart from using spices to preserve, hot and pungent foods tend to promote sweating, which in turn cools the body. My father would pride himself on being able to play tennis through the scorching midday hours in Fuzhou. Normally he would never sweat, but after exerting himself under the fierce sun he would find the cooling sweat so effective that he could play on until his partner dropped from exhaustion.

Alternatively, we may choose to counterbalance the movement of the season. In extreme heat, or for those who tend to be constitutionally hot, cooling foods are naturally beneficial. The same paradox can be found in winter. Winter Qi is sinking and cooling and food should be found to follow its movement. Yet cooling foods are not cold foods that chill the body. They are bitter, salty and sour foods in the form of warm savoury soups and stews which carry the heat inwards and downwards as if simulating hibernation. Heat is conserved within.

When an extreme is reached it transforms into its opposite, that is the simplest dynamic represented in the theory of Yang and Yin. Yang and Yin are not anything in themselves, but simply a way to describe how the same phenomenon can be constantly changing. Light becomes dark, day becomes night, the sun is replaced by the moon. As the seasons reach their zenith they too can be described in terms of the movement of Yang and Yin. Extreme Yin is reached on the coldest darkest days and Yang is born as the days begin to lengthen again. The zenith of Yang is in the long hot summer days. Medical books are full of references to the balance of Yin and Yang Qi. Yang Qi, like summer heat, rises in the body while Yin Qi cools and descends. With the rising of Yang Qi commonly implicated in such symptoms as dryness, flushing, fever, drunkeness or anger, many therapeutic techniques emphasize the cooling, calming effect of cultivating Yin through diet, exercise and meditation.

The recipes in this chapter have been specially selected to reflect a well-balanced way to eat throughout the year. They pay attention to the mood of the season by co-ordinating details of flavour, effect on the body's temperature, organ systems and suitability for body type. Our friend and colleague Dr Xu Guang has helped select different herbs and foodstuffs and given advice on the actions and movements of food, while Lily Xiong has been on hand with her instinctive good taste, and to provide recipes and the advice of her mother and her mother's cooks.

Arranging the dishes in the form of seasonal banquets is not a traditional format, but authenticity has not been the only guiding principle in our choices. If we had translated all the menu of the Sichuan therapeutic teahouse it might have been more authentic, but the ingredients would be difficult to find and the rationale behind the dishes opaque. To understand the common language of healthy eating in China it is best to learn a little theory, a few basic dishes, and then to apply it with creativity in choosing and combining different foods. In the background the associations with Yin, Yang and the Five Phases always provide paradigms against which to assess specific choices.

Readers may find themselves inclined towards one or other of the banquets and this may reveal their own constitutional strengths and weaknesses – a point of departure in itself. By paying attention to minute reactions in our bodies it is easy to learn to distinguish between jangling coffee highs, and the clarity of spirit that is combined with a keenness of the senses and that cool, quiet feeling of having boundless resources; between the heaviness of an over-burdened digestive system and the lightness and comfort following a good meal. A second-century BC manual of breathing meditations describes the state of well-being induced by nourishing Yin:

Put the Qi in order with intention and the eye will be bright, the ear keen, the skin will gleam, the one hundred vessels will be full and the Yin will be born. From this you will be able to stand for a long time, go a long way and live for ever.

It may not be coincidental that ideas about nourishing Yin, the quieter, darker, more introspective aspects of life, began to flourish during the Warring States period, when the whole of China was in a state of disintegration and warfare. Visions of an alternative lifestyle lived out in the peace and safety of a rural environment and away from the centres of power and government became fashionable in some elite societies. Perhaps we too can find a parallel in our own troubled times. One response to social and political confusion is often to concentrate on cultivating the body and soul. Diet is an essential part of the maintenance of good health. When combined with good exercise, hygiene, breathing and sex it may well be a recipe for the immortals!

# The Spring Banquet

On spring days, after rising early, pass water, wash and rinse the mouth, wash the teeth, exhale, loosen the hair and ramble around in front of the house, go to meet the purity of the early morning dew, receive the quintessence of Heaven and after drink one cup of water and in this way you may increase your life span. Enter the chamber [indulge in sexual activity] between dusk to the depth of night [when it is time to] cease activity, increasing it will harm the Qi.
*Zhangjiashan Yinshu (c.200 BC)*

Spring is a transitional season. From the depths of winter, the most Yin of the seasons, activity begins, warmth returns and the days become longer. It is a time of issue and the setting of new plans. In early spring food is still scarce, so one should eat a little less and begin to cleanse the body. Instead of heavy meats and nuts choose more vegetables and white meat. The vegetables that are available will tend to be green and tender so our spring banquet is also green and light in colour to celebrate the new colour of the season. From the dark, cold, still months of winter spring will re-kindle the Yang Qi in the environment and it is appropriate to cook lightly and lace the food with slightly warming flavours – pungent, sweet and aromatic flavours which also encourage upward and outward movement.

With growth and change all around, the warm, intoxicating nights of late spring may also be the nights that ferment dissatisfaction. Frustration can easily boil into anger, and it is important to support and calm the function of the liver, the organ system associated with springtime and the mood of anger (see Appendix, page 281). Sour foods guard against the excesses of the liver, while bitter foods tend to support and nourish. Traditional voices will warn not to eat too much warming food for fear that it will agitate the volatile. Cooking with vinegar, which is both sour, bitter and a little warming, and adding a touch of pungent food will complement the expanding mood of the season. Yuxiang dishes cooked with small amounts of Sichuan pepper are perfect spring dishes, especially when combined with the lightly tossed tender green shoots of spinach.

The dishes have been selected to be eaten together as a banquet, but can equally well be served separately in combinations of your choice. Each one is described in terms of its therapeutic value and can be related to the table of food classes and more detailed discussion of Chinese medical ideas and terminology in the Appendix (page 277).

菠
菜
豆
腐
湯

## Spinach and Silken Bean Curd Soup

SERVES 4

This is a light soup that cooks early spring spinach quickly over a high heat to retain its nourishing qualities. It makes a refreshing change from long-cooked winter stews. The dark green spinach and white bean curd make a delightful springtime colour combination.

150 g (5 oz) young spinach
4 dried Chinese mushrooms, soaked in hot water for 30 minutes
225 g (8 oz) silken bean curd, cut into 2.5 cm (1 inch) cubes
1 tablespoon vegetable oil
50 g (2 oz) button mushrooms, finely sliced
1 tablespoon light soy sauce
1 tablespoon Shaoxing wine
500 ml (16 fl oz) strong stock (see page 18)
2 teaspoons cornflour blended with a little water
½ teaspoon salt
pepper, to taste
1 teaspoon sesame oil

Blanch the spinach in boiling water, rinse, squeeze dry and chop finely. Drain the mushsrooms, discard the tough stems and slice the caps finely. Blanch the bean curd in boiling water for 10 minutes. Drain and leave to dry in a sieve.

Heat the oil in a wok over a high heat. Add the fresh and dried mushrooms and turn for a minute. Add the spinach, soy sauce and wine and stir for 30 seconds. Add the stock, cornflour solution, bean curd, salt and pepper. Bring back to the boil and simmer gently for 3–4 minutes. Sprinkle with sesame oil and serve.

魚
香
雞
絲

## Yuxiang Chicken

SERVES 4

The sour flavour of the Sichuan Yuxiang sauce is appropriate in spring. The meat should be leaner as the spring diet demands that you should eat a little less, and more lightly. The hotter, pungent flavours in the combination of hot bean sauce and ginger and garlic are also appropriate to the gentle upward movement that occurs in the environment when the weather is beginning to get warmer.

4 wood ear mushrooms, soaked overnight in warm water
225 g (8 oz) skinned, boned chicken breast, cut into matchstick-sized strips
1 tablespoon cornflour
1 tablespoon Shaoxing wine
pinch of salt
3 tablespoons vegetable oil
2.5 cm (1 inch) piece of root ginger, finely chopped
3 cloves garlic, crushed and finely chopped
1 tablespoon hot bean sauce
2 spring onions,finely chopped
1½ tablespoons light soy sauce
1 teaspoon sugar
1 tablespoon vinegar
2 teaspoons sesame oil

Drain and rinse the wood ears and chop finely. Place the chicken breast strips in a shallow dish with the cornflour, wine and salt, turn to coat and leave to marinate for 15 minutes.

Heat the vegetable oil in a wok until it just begins to smoke. Put the chicken into the oil and stir and toss until the meat changes colour. Add the ginger, garlic, hot bean sauce, wood ears and spring onion and stir to mix evenly. Pour in the soy sauce, sugar, vinegar and sesame oil. Bring to the boil and simmer for 1 minute, then serve.

## 爆炒豬肝 Flame-fried Pig's Liver

SERVES 2–3

Liver, whether pork, beef or lamb, is said to support the liver. It is one of those magical things – like resonates with like. Pork liver, with its bitter flavour, is particularly good. The leek is also thought to benefit the liver. Its pungency, when combined with the warmth and pungency of the ginger, garlic and coriander and the tossing over a high heat, also encourages the upward and outward movement appropriate to springtime.

2 tablespoons vegetable oil
1 large leek, halved lengthways and finely sliced on the diagonal into thin strips
pinch of salt
½ tablespoon fermented black beans, soaked in hot water for 10 minutes
1 cm (½ inch) piece of root ginger, finely chopped
225 g (8 oz) pig's liver, cut into thin 3 x 2.5 cm (1¼ x 1 inch) slices
2 cloves garlic, crushed and finely chopped
1 tablespoon dark soy sauce
1 tablespoon Shaoxing wine
pinch of sugar
4 tablespoons stock (see page 18)
2 teaspoons sesame oil
coriander leaves, to garnish

Heat 1 tablespoon of oil in a wok until it begins to smoke. Add the leek and toss to coat. Sprinkle in the salt and continue to toss for 1 minute, then remove with a slotted spoon and set aside.

Add the remaining oil and heat until it begins to smoke. Strain the black beans and mash roughly. Add to the wok with the ginger, turning constantly. Add the liver, garlic, soy sauce, wine, sugar and stock and stir-fry until the liver is cooked and well coated. Give the contents of the wok a final thorough stir and add the sesame oil. Serve garnished with coriander.

炒　**Stir-fried Prawns and Asparagus**
蘆　SERVES 4
筍　This is the perfect spring dish. Asparagus taken straight from the
蝦　ground barely needs cooking, and when stir-fried its colour
deepens to a rich green. It is classified as bitter in flavour with a
slight pungency and nourishes the liver. Prawns are warming
and sweet, and also gently nourish the liver.

12 tiger prawns, shelled and deveined
pinch of salt
1 teaspoon Shaoxing wine
2 teaspoons cornflour
2 teaspoons vegetable oil
vegetable oil, for deep-frying
225 g (8 oz) asparagus, trimmed and cut on the diagonal into 2.5
cm (1 inch) pieces
100 ml (3½ fl oz) stock (see page 18)
pinch of sugar
1 tablespoon light soy sauce
2 teaspoons sesame oil
chopped coriander, to garnish

Place the prawns in a shallow dish with the salt, wine, cornflour
and 2 teaspoons of oil. Turn to coat, then leave in the refrigerator
to marinate for 30 minutes.

Heat the oil for deep-frying in a wok until it just begins to
smoke. Add the prawns and cook until they change colour, then
remove with a slotted spoon and set aside. Pour off the oil
leaving about 2 tablespoons in the wok. Add the asparagus and
toss in the oil until it changes colour. Add the stock and sugar.
Bring to the boil and simmer for 1 minute to reduce the stock.
Return the prawns to the pan with the soy sauce and sesame oil.
Toss together for another 30 seconds and serve garnished with
coriander.

醋
餾
雙
絲

## Sour Splashed White Cabbage and Carrots

SERVES 4

The sour flavour of the vinegar in this dish is moderated by a
pungent hot sauce, making it perfect to match the expansive
movement of the season without causing agitation.

2 tablespoons vegetable oil
2 teaspoons hot bean sauce
2 carrots, thinly sliced
125 g (4 oz) white cabbage, thinly sliced
½ teaspoon salt
2 tablespoons Zhenjiang vinegar
1 tablespoon light soy sauce
2 tablespoons stock (see page 18)
coriander leaves, to garnish

Heat the oil in a wok until it begins to smoke. When it is hot
add the hot bean sauce and stir together. Then add the
vegetables and toss together until well coated by the oil.
Continue to turn vigorously for 2 minutes. Add the remaining
ingredients and stir into the vegetables. Turn down the heat and
cook for a further minute. Serve garnished with coriander.

## Stir-fried Broccoli with Garlic and Red Bean Curd

炒
綠
菜
花

SERVES 4–5

This is another lightly cooked dish of fresh green vegetables, gently spiced with fermented bean curd.

2 teaspoons red bean curd
2½ tablespoons vegetarian stock (see page 19)
1 tablespoon light soy sauce
1 tablespoon Shaoxing wine
225 g (8 oz) broccoli, divided into small florets, stems sliced diagonally
2 tablespoons vegetable oil
2 cloves garlic, crushed and finely chopped
1 teaspoon salt
1 teaspoon sugar

Blend the red bean curd with the stock, soy sauce and wine.

Parboil the broccoli for 2 minutes then drain. Heat the oil in a wok until it begins to smoke. Add the broccoli, garlic and salt and stir for 1 minute. Sprinkle the broccoli with the sugar and then pour the red bean mixture over the top. Stir and toss over a high heat until all the broccoli is coated. Turn down the heat and simmer for 3 minutes, then serve.

山
楂
糕

## Hawthorn Jelly

SERVES 4

Hawthorn fruit is slightly tart and warming and supports the liver. It is available in Chinese supermarkets, dried in thin wafers and wrapped in brightly coloured paper to be sold as children's sweets known as 'Haw Flakes'.

200 ml (7 fl oz) water
12 packets of haw flakes
2 litres (3½ pints) water
50 g (2 oz) agar agar
75 g (3 oz) sugar
2 tablespoons lemon juice

Heat the water in a pan, add the haw flakes and stir until melted. Bring the 2 litres (3½ pints) of water to the boil in another pan and add the agar agar. Turn down the heat and simmer for 10 minutes. Add the sugar and lemon juice and return to the boil. Mix the 2 liquids thoroughly and pour into a large serving bowl. Leave to cool and set for 4 hours.

杏
酪
飲

## Almond Milk

MAKES 30 CUPS

125 g (4 oz) sweet almonds
500 g (1 lb) clear honey

Pour boiling water over the almonds and leave to cool. Pour off
the water and repeat 4 times. Grind and mash the almonds.

Heat the honey until it is runny. Leave it to cool for a
moment, then add the almond mash and mix well. To serve, add
one dessertspoon of the mixture to a mug for each person and
pour on boiling water. Mix thoroughly.

白
菊
花
茶

Chrysanthemum tea is commonly available in tea-bags at any good health food shop. However, it is not so good as white chrysanthemum which is very cooling. White chrysanthemum, like camomile, is good for headaches and the kind of agitation experienced when the Yang Qi of the liver is rising. It is particularly useful in bringing down a raised blood pressure and conditioning the skin. White chrysanthemum is only available from good Chinese herbalists.

Jasmine is thought to stimulate the liver and is good as a digestive, for increasing the appetite and for bloating. Rose tea is warming and also stimulates the liver.

# The Summer Banquet

On summer days wash the hair more frequently, bathe less, do not sleep late, eat more vegetables, get up early and after urinating wash with water, separate the teeth, loosen the hair, pace slowly in front of the house, after a while drink a cup of water. Enter the chamber between dusk and midnight [when it is time to] cease, increasing it will harm the Qi. *Zhangjiashan Yinshu (c.200 BC)*

Summer is the zenith of Yang. In the agricultural year it brings maximum activity, expression and colour. It is the time to make sure that all plans for the year reach maturity and fulfilment. Get up early and be energetic, making the most of the day. There is no need to eat too much heavy food that is difficult to digest. Eat less meat, eggs, milk or nuts. With fruits and vegetables ripening all around it is time to take advantage of the feast on offer.

In extreme heat it is beneficial to find food to cool the body. This is not necessarily cold food and salads, but often more heating and pungent foods that will cool by inducing sweating. Cayenne and red pepper, fresh ginger and black pepper may be the secret to summer cool, so choose dishes from the Sichuan chapter. To find exactly the appropriate method to cool yourself you must be aware of your own inner condition. If you have a tendency to overheat under ordinary circumstances, the heat of summer may be agitating in itself, and you may choose foods which cool immediately, like mint tea or cucumber, courgette and bean curd, apple or mung beans.

For the person who tends to insomnia and agitation, foods to calm the function of the heart, the organ associated with summer, are essential. The spirit is thought to reside in the heart. Heart, mind and spirit are not differentiated in the western way: if the spirit is not properly anchored in the heart it may wander and result in a distracted mental state. To rediscover inner peace all stimulants should be avoided, and the blander, calming, less pungent foods should be chosen from this banquet.

Our summer banquet combines foods that cool both by heating and by cooling directly. The contrasts between dishes are most extreme. Both plain steamed foods and hot flame-fried foods have been included as well as dishes that are chilli hot and cucumber cool.

The dishes have been selected to be eaten together as a banquet, but can equally well be served separately in combinations of your choice. Each one is described in terms of its therapeutic value and can be related to the table of food classes and more detailed discussion of Chinese medical ideas and terminology in the Appendix (page 277).

北
京
辣
魚
湯

## Beijing Pepperpot Fish

SERVES 3–4

This is a soup to make you sweat! The fish is light and easy to digest, but when combined with the chilli and ginger it should start the banquet with a bang.

225 g (8 oz) white fish fillets, cut across the grain into 4 x 2.5 cm (1¾ x 1 inch) pieces
salt
1 tablespoon cornflour
1 egg white, beaten
vegetable oil, for deep-frying
1 tablespoon Sichuan pickle, chopped
2 teaspoons hot bean paste
500 ml (16 fl oz) chicken stock (see page 18)
2.5 cm (1 inch) piece of root ginger, finely chopped
1 clove garlic, crushed and finely chopped
2 tablespoons vinegar
½ teaspoon pepper
1 spring onion, chopped

Dust the fish with salt and cornflour and turn in the egg white. Heat the oil in a wok until almost smoking. Add the coated fish and cook for 1 minute then remove with a slotted spoon and drain on kitchen paper. Keep warm. Add the pickle to the wok and cook for 1 minute, then remove with a slotted spoon and drain on kitchen paper. Pour off the oil. Put the hot bean paste into the wok and stir it around. Add the stock and bring to the boil with the pickle. Add the ginger and garlic and bring back to the boil for 1 minute. Add the fish, vinegar and pepper and simmer for 3–4 minutes. Pour into a heated tureen, sprinkle with spring onion and serve.

紅
油
雞

## Hot-tossed Shredded Chicken in Red Chilli Oil

SERVES 4

This is a cold dish that is designed to heat you up and make you sweat. Serve this soon after the soup as they will have a similar action.

1 small cucumber or ½ cucumber, halved lengthways and cut into thin 4 cm (1¾ inch) strips
225 g (8 oz) cooked chicken, cut into thin 4 cm (1¾ inch) strips
1 spring onion, finely chopped
1 tablespoon red chilli oil
2 cloves garlic, crushed and finely chopped
1 cm (½ inch) piece of root ginger, finely chopped
1 tablespoon sesame oil
1 tablespoon rice vinegar
1 tablespoon soy sauce
2 tablespoons stock (see page 18)
½ teaspoon ground Sichuan pepper

Spread out the cucumber strips on a serving dish. Arrange the chicken strips on top. Mix the remaining ingredients together and pour over the top. Serve immediately.

凉
拌
芹
菜

## Cold-tossed Celery

SERVES 4–6

Celery and kelp are some of the most cooling vegetables used to clear summer heat. Together, they make a delicious salad which can accompany any set of dishes, but the combination should not be eaten regularly by those who tend to be constitutionally cold. The tomatoes provide the essential colour contrast to match the season. Celery is specifically used to lower high blood pressure and reduce high cholesterol. Kelp has many therapeutic uses in both eastern and western dietary lore. Most are of a cooling nature with an inward, downward movement. It tends to reduce swelling and improve the blood flow. Black wood ears are classified as sweet and neutral, and so serve to provide a little balance to this dish.

50 g (2 oz) kelp, soaked in warm water overnight
50 g (2 oz) black wood ears, soaked in warm water overnight
200 g (7 oz) celery, cut into 3 cm (1¼ inch) lengths
2 tomatoes, skinned
1 tablespoon light soy sauce
1 tablespoon sesame oil
⅓ teaspoon salt
½ teaspoon sugar
1 teaspoon vinegar

Drain the kelp, place in a pan of boiling water and simmer for 4 hours. Drain and slice finely.

Meanwhile, drain the wood ears, rinse under cold water, drain again and slice finely. Blanch the celery. Slice the tomatoes, then shred them. Place the kelp, wood ears, celery and tomatoes in a bowl. Mix together the soy sauce, sesame oil, salt, sugar and vinegar. Pour over the vegetables and toss well.

## Garlic Aubergine
SERVES 4–6
In this recipe the cooling summer aubergine is matched with plenty of garlic and ginger. The pungent and aromatic tastes promote upward and outward movement in the body which harmonizes with the movement of summer. The aubergine is steamed to ensure a light flavour and texture to contrast with the strong sauce.

2 medium aubergines
3 cloves garlic, crushed and finely chopped
1 tablespoon vegetable oil
2 slices root ginger, finely chopped
2 tablespoons Zhenjiang vinegar
2 tablespoons light soy sauce
1 tablespoon sugar
1 tablespoon sesame oil

Cut the aubergines in half and score through the skin diagonally to make a diamond pattern, making deep cuts into the flesh to ensure that it cooks. Work the garlic with a pestle until it is pulpy.

Steam the aubergines on a heatproof dish for 30 minutes. Pour off any fluid and set aside in a warm place. Heat the oil in a wok and add all the remaining ingredients, stirring in the garlic and ginger first. Bring to the boil and simmer for 1 minute. Pour the sauce over the steamed aubergine and serve immediately.

小
蔥
拌
豆
腐

## Cold-tossed Chinese Chives and Bean Curd

SERVES 4

Bean curd is a neutral flavour, while the chives are pungent. When combined with the saltiness of the pickle, the dish is instantly cooling on a hot day.

1½ tablespoons Sichuan pickle, chopped
1½ tablespoons pickled cabbage, chopped
125 g (4 oz) Chinese chives, or a mixture of coriander, spring onions and English chives, chopped
2½ tablespoons vegetable oil
2½ tablespoons sesame oil
2 tablespoons dark soy sauce
3 tablespoons rice vinegar
2 teaspoons sugar
2 cloves garlic, crushed and finely chopped
2 tablespoons rice wine
200 g (7 oz) silken bean curd, cut into 2.5 cm (1 inch) cubes

Mix the pickle, cabbage and chives with the oils, soy sauce, vinegar, sugar, garlic and wine. Leave to stand for 30 minutes. Arrange the bean curd on a serving dish. Spoon the sauce over the bean curd and serve.

五
香
蠶
豆

## Five-spice Broad Beans

SERVES 4

Broad beans are fairly neutral in flavour, but the addition of the aniseed and red peppers makes a pungent warming dish with vibrant colour to match the season. The red peppers support the heart, the organ associated with summer.

300 ml (½ pint) stock (see page 18)
225 g (8 oz) broad beans
2 star anise
1 tablespoon dark soy sauce
1 teaspoon brown sugar
1 tablespoon vegetable oil
125 g (4 oz) red pepper, cored, seeded and cut into squares the same size as the beans

Heat the stock in a pan and add the beans, star anise, soy sauce and sugar. Simmer until the beans are soft and tender and the liquid has reduced. Heat the oil in a wok until it begins to smoke. Add the red pepper and stir-fry for a few minutes until they soften. Add the beans and the reduced liquid. Bring to the boil and simmer for 5 minutes.

清蒸鯉魚

## Clear Steamed Carp
SERVES 2–3

Steaming is one of the simplest, healthiest and most popular ways of cooking fish. The carp is particularly good for dispersing heat in summer, but other river fish such as trout will do just as well and be less bony. Being classified as neutral and sweet it naturally acts on the stomach and spleen, the organs associated with late summer. It is very easy to digest. The Yellow River produces the most delicious carp in all of China. Carp is not readily available in ordinary fish shops, but most fishmongers will order it overnight, or you can choose from a selection of live carp in Chinatown. The method can be applied to any white fish of a similar size and is particularly good for cooking sea bass. It is most important not to over-steam as the white flesh will become soggy. On the other hand, to prevent under-cooking red-hot oil can be poured over the filleted fish to 'drum' the flavours into the flesh.

1 carp, about 1 kg (2 lb), gutted and scaled, with head left on
3½ teaspoons salt
3 dried Chinese mushrooms, soaked in hot water for 30 minutes
2 spring onions, halved lengthways and cut into 5 cm (2 inch) pieces
5 thin slices root ginger
2 tablespoons Shaoxing wine
½ tablespoon sugar
125 ml (4 fl oz) water
2½ tablespoons light soy sauce
4 tablespoons vegetable oil
finely sliced bamboo shoots, red pepper, carrot and chilli, to garnish

Pat the fish dry and rub inside and out with 2 teaspoons of salt. Place in a heatproof dish. Drain the mushrooms, discard the hard stems and slice the caps thinly. Arrange the onions, ginger and mushrooms inside and around the carp. Mix the wine, sugar, remaining salt and water and pour over the carp.

Place the dish in a steamer, cover and steam over water at a rolling boil for 15–20 minutes, until the flesh has turned white. Remove the fish from the steamer and carefully remove the bones. Pour the soy sauce over the length of the fish. Meanwhile, heat the oil in a wok until it begins to smoke, stir-fry the garnishing vegetables in the oil for 1 minute, then pour over the fish.

## 辣 Hot Pepper Pork
## 子
## 肉 SERVES 3
## 丁
To counterbalance the cooling fish and bean curd a little hot
chilli with the only main meat dish will do the trick.

225 g (8 oz) lean pork, cut into 1 cm (½ inch) cubes
2 teaspoons cornflour
1 egg white, beaten
pinch of salt
1 tablespoon vegetable oil

SAUCE
2 teaspoons hot bean sauce
125 g (4 oz) green peppers, cored, seeded and cut into 1 cm (½
inch) squares
3–4 red chillies, finely sliced
1 spring onion, finely sliced
1 cm (½ inch) piece of root ginger, chopped
1 tablespoon sliced bamboo shoots
1 teaspoon Shaoxing wine
1 teaspoon light soy sauce
½ teaspoon sugar
2 teaspoons cornflour, blended with a little water
1 tsp sesame oil

Mix the pork in a shallow dish with the cornflour, a little water,
the egg white and salt, and leave to marinate for 15 minutes.
   Heat the oil in a wok until it just begins to smoke. Drain the
pork and add it to the wok, turning until it changes colour.
Remove with a slotted spoon and reserve. Wipe out the wok
with kitchen paper. Heat the hot bean sauce in the wok, then
add the peppers, chillies, spring onion, ginger and bamboo shoots
to the wok. Toss together until they are well coated and then
return the meat to the pan, adding the wine, light soy sauce and
the sugar. Finally add the cornflour mixture. Turn together until
the sauce has thickened and then pour on the sesame oil.

糖
水
綠
豆

## Mung Bean Dessert

SERVES 6

Mung beans are valued very highly for their therapeutic qualities. They are said to be cooling, good for the genito-urinary system and able to counteract food-poisoning. When eaten regularly they are thought to aid development in children, reduce high blood pressure and benefit the stomach. The tangerine provides a tangy quality while the coconut milk is a Malaysian variation. This dessert is pleasant combined with stewed fruit.

200 g (7 oz) mung beans, rinsed
1.5 litres (2½ pints) water
1 piece dried tangerine peel
1 can of coconut milk
honey or rock sugar, to taste

Place the beans and water in a pan and bring to the boil. Turn down the heat, cover and simmer for 30 minutes. Add the tangerine peel and coconut milk and simmer for another 15 minutes. Add honey or sugar to taste. Serve hot or cold with stewed apples or pears or leave to cool and add 2–3 canned lychees.

椰
味
水
果
羹

## Fruit and Coconut Compote

SERVES 6

If you love school puddings, this is for you. Father and his brothers would always order bread and butter pudding or trifle whenever they could. This is a delightful refinement of the tapioca-type version of school pud, especially rich in summer fruit.

200 g (7 oz) dried pears, peaches, pineapple or apples, or a combination of these, soaked for 30 minutes
125 g (4 oz) green sago pearls
200 ml (7 fl oz) water
2 cans coconut milk
sugar or honey, to taste

Drain the dried fruit and cut into small pieces. Place in a pan with all the other ingredients. Bring to the boil and simmer for 15 minutes. Leave to cool, then chill in the refrigerator. Serve with lychees or fresh fruit salad.

薄荷茶

## Mint Tea

There are many ways of making mint tea, but none can beat the mixture of a good quality afternoon tea and fresh spearmint. Gunpowder green has a delicate straw-coloured liquor and has the lowest caffeine content of all teas, so it will invigorate you but still let you sleep. Fresh mint is also good as a digestive. If you like your tea stronger use kemun tea, the traditional black tea of China. Rinse the pot with hot water and spoon in 1 teaspoon per person plus '1 for the pot'. Pour in the boiling water and leave to brew for 3 minutes. Meanwhile, put a handful of fresh mint into a heatproof glass beaker with a separate metal handle. Add sugar to taste. Pour on the tea.

# The Autumn Banquet

On autumn days bathe and wash the hair frequently. In eating and drinking your fill indulge the body's desires. Enter the chamber whenever the body is nourished and derives comfort from it – this is the way of benefit.    *Zhangjiashan Yinshu (c.200 BC)*

Autumn brings a gathering in and cleansing in preparation for winter. The Qi of the season begins to be contained and turn inwards again. Although the environment can still be bright and warm there is often a delicate stillness in the air. The warm wet months between the end of summer and the beginning of autumn are associated with the earth phase and the function of the stomach and spleen or pancreas. A mild, sweet flavour enters and strengthens these organ systems. They are best supported with foods that have a mildly sweet nature and no artificial additives, such as grains and fruit – the foods readily available at this time of year.

Grief is the emotion appropriate to autumn – as we review things past and let go of old attachments to happier times a melancholy mood seems to complement the wide skies, yellowing leaves and paling light. Grief is often held in the chest and throat and this is the area which we constrict to hold back tears. Through strengthening the lungs, the organ associated with autumn, we can prepare for the onslaught of the cold weather and fortify the body against colds and flu. While it is still time to enjoy the abundance of the harvest, great preparations should be made for winter. Just as the ditches need to be cleared of leaves, so the colon must also be strengthened to stimulate its cleansing function in the body.

For autumn, the abundance of food is matched with a greater choice in cooking. Flavours can be fuller, with hot, spicy, aromatic flavours dominating, drying excess mucus from the lungs. Pungent is the flavour associated with this season, so plenty of spices and peppers can be used. At the same time plain pure food to cleanse the body and the colon can be chosen to complete the contrast. Plenty of grains and more meat and nuts can be re-introduced. To follow the downward and inward turn of the seasonal movement choose more salty, bitter and sour foods to balance both the blandness and the spice. Foods should be cooked a little longer than before. In our autumn banquet we have chosen slightly more sombre colours – warm, earthy colours for late summer and white for early autumn.

The dishes have been selected to be eaten together as a banquet, but can equally well be served separately in combinations of your choice. Each one is described in terms of its therapeutic value and can be related to the table of food classes and more detailed discussion of Chinese medical ideas and terminology in the Appendix (page 277).

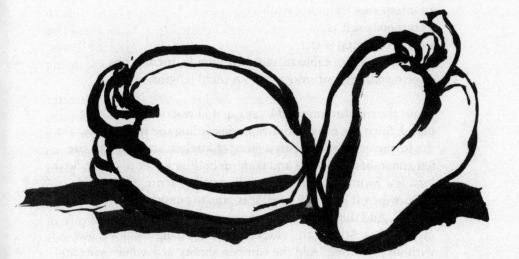

黃
耆
雞
湯

## Huang Qi Chicken Soup

SERVES 10

Chicken is classified as warm and sweet-flavoured, which is good for the functions of the stomach and spleen, the organs associated with late summer. Being gentle on the digestive system, the soup is good for convalescence and should also be very invigorating. Huang qi gently strengthens the yang, the qi and the spleen. It also nourishes the blood, especially during periods of weakness following giving birth. Most Cantonese-style supermarkets will recognize and sell you huang qi if you show them the Chinese characters, otherwise take the recipe to a herbal supplier (see page 272).

6 dried Chinese mushrooms, soaked in hot water for 30 minutes
100 g (3½ oz) radix astragali (huang qi), soaked in warm water for 30 minutes
125 g (4 oz) fen si noodles
1 tablespoon vegetable oil
6 cm (2½ inch) piece of root ginger, finely sliced
1 kg (2 lb) chicken drumsticks, each chopped into 3 pieces
125 g (4 oz) bamboo shoots
2 tablespoons soy sauce
3 tablespoons Shaoxing wine
2 teaspoons salt
1 litre (1¾ pints) water
½ Chinese white cabbage, cut into 3 cm (¼ inch) strips
3 spring onions, cut into 3 cm (1¼ inch) lengths

Drain the mushrooms and huang qi and reserve the soaking liquid. Slice the mushroom caps, discarding the hard stalks. Tie the huang qi together with a piece of kitchen string. Place the fen si noodles in a bowl and pour on boiling water to cover. Soak for a few minutes until just soft but still al dente, then drain.

Heat the oil in a wok until it begins to smoke, swirling the oil around. Add the ginger, turn and then add the chicken and mushrooms. Stir-fry the chicken until it changes colour, but without browning. Add the bamboo shoots, soy sauce, wine and salt and turn to coat thoroughly. Transfer the contents of the wok to a casserole.

Heat the reserved soaking liquid with the water and add to the casserole. Place the bundle of huang qi in the casserole. Bring to the boil and skim off any froth. Cover and simmer gently for 40 minutes.

Remove the huang qi bundle. Move the chicken to one side of the casserole and slide the fen si noodles down the side to the bottom. Add the cabbage, carefully keeping it to one side. Simmer gently for another 5 minutes. To serve, scatter the spring onions over the top.

宮
爆
肉
丁

## Gongbao's Pork Chunks

SERVES 3–4

This dish is perfect for autumn. The combination of pork with almonds clears phlegm and supports the lung and colon. The pungency of the ginger and hot chilli help to dry mucus.

350 g (12 oz) lean pork, cut into 2.5cm (1 inch) cubes
2 tablespoons dark soy sauce
1 teaspoon cornflour
1 tablespoon Shaoxing wine
2 teaspoons sugar
pinch of salt
3 tablespoons vegetable oil
75 ml (3 fl oz) hot chicken stock (see page 18)
4 dried chillies
1 tablespoon finely chopped root ginger
124 g (4 oz) green pepper, cored, seeded and cut into 2.5 cm (1 inch) squares
2 teaspoons Zhenjiang vinegar
50 g (2 oz) toasted slivered almonds
1 teaspoon sesame oil

Place the pork in a shallow dish with 1 tablespoon of the soy sauce and leave to marinate for 30 minutes. Blend the cornflour with the wine, the remaining soy sauce, sugar and salt.

Heat 2 tablespoons of the oil in a wok until it just begins to smoke. Add the pork and stir-fry until it changes colour. Add the stock and stir-fry for 1 minute. Pour into a bowl and set aside. Wipe out the wok with kitchen paper.

Add the remaining oil to the wok over a high heat and swirl it around until it begins to smoke. Add the chillies, stirring and pressing them into the oil until they darken. Add the ginger and green pepper and stir-fry for another minute. Return the meat to the wok with the green peppers and stir-fry together for 1 minute. Stir the vinegar into the cornflour mixture and pour it over the meat and peppers. Add the almonds and stir until well covered with the sauce. Sprinkle with sesame oil and serve.

涼
拌
红
绿

## Madam Fei's Spinach and Radish Salad

SERVES 5

This colourful dish emphasizes the sweet pungent flavour of the
radishes which also nourish and dry the lungs.

1 bunch large red radishes
2 teaspoons salt
900 g (1 lb 14 oz) young spinach, stalks removed
2 teaspoons light soy sauce
1½ teaspoons caster sugar
3 teaspoons sesame oil
pinch of pepper
radish roses, to garnish

Flatten the radishes with the side of a cleaver or meat tenderizer.
Sprinkle with one teaspoon of salt. Place the spinach in a pan
and pour a kettleful of boiling water over it. Drain immediately
and rinse with cold water. Drain and dry thoroughly. Chop the
spinach, then sprinkle with the remaining salt, soy sauce, sugar,
oil and pepper and mix well. Arrange on a large serving dish and
place the salted radishes on the top. Garnish with radish roses.

涼
拌
銀
耳
黃
瓜

## Cold-tossed White Fungus and Cucumber

SERVES 4

White fungus is widely used as a food to nourish the lungs. It has a fairly neutral, inoffensive taste, so it needs to be dressed with pungent and aromatic flavours, or sweetened as in White Fungus Soup (see page 174).

50 g (2 oz) white fungus, soaked overnight
1 cucumber
½ teaspoon salt
3 cloves garlic, crushed and finely chopped
2 teaspoons vinegar
½ tablespoon sesame oil

Drain the white fungus, cut out the hard brown-yellow stem and discard. Tear the fungus into small pieces. Pound the cucumber all along its length with the side of a chopper until it is distorted and half flattened. Cut it across into 1.5 cm (¾ inch) sections. Sprinkle with salt and leave to drain in a colander for 10 minutes. Toss the white fungus with the cucumber. Mix with the remaining ingredients and toss well.

清蒸木樨蝦

## Clear-steamed Egg and Prawns

SERVES 6

2 eggs
300 ml (½ pint) stock (see page 18)
salt and pepper, to taste
12 raw peeled prawns, deveined
2 tablespoons cooked peas
1 tablespoon soy sauce
1 spring onion, finely chopped

Beat the eggs and mix in the stock. Add salt and pepper to taste.
Stir in 10 prawns and the peas and put in an attractive, heatproof
dish. Place in a steamer, cover and steam for 15 minutes.
Arrange the remaining 2 prawns on top and pour on the soy
sauce. Steam again for 4 minutes. Sprinkle spring onion over the
top and serve.

三
鍾
香
菇
粥

## Congee with Three Mushrooms
SERVES 4

Rice is classified as neutral (neither hot nor cold), sweet and
good for the stomach and spleen, which are associated with late
summer and early autumn. Congee, which is the staple of many
people's diets in the East, has never caught on in the West. It is
probably the bland and gooey quality of the over-cooked rice
combined with strong pickles that puts westerners off. However
it is no more gooey than risotto or more bland than porridge. To
make it more acceptable to the western palate we have made a
drier congee so that it can be eaten from a plate, and boiled the
rice in stock to make it savoury. You can vary the stock to your
taste. A beef stock will make a very substantial meal, while a
lighter vegetable stock will make a staple to accompany dishes
of a stronger flavour. The mushrooms are also classified as
neutral, sweet and good for the stomach. Button mushrooms
may also support the lungs by helping to clear mucus in the
respiratory system. It is altogether a tremendous, hearty dish for
early autumn. When served with salad or French beans this dish
can be eaten as a vegetarian main course, or serve it simply as
the staple accompaniment to meat.

10 dried Chinese mushrooms, soaked in hot water for 30 minutes
225 g (8 oz) long-grain rice, rinsed
2 litres (3½ pints) stock (see page 18)
5 tablespoons vegetable oil
1 onion, sliced
200 g (7 oz) button mushrooms, sliced
½ large can straw mushrooms, drained
1 tablespoon Sichuan pickle, finely shredded
2 tablespoons dark soy sauce
1 tablespoon crushed rock sugar
salt, to taste
1 tablespoon sesame oil

Drain the Chinese mushrooms, reserving the soaking water,
discard the hard stalks and slice the caps finely.

Place the rice in a heavy casserole with the stock. Bring to the boil. Reduce the heat to medium and boil for 5 minutes. Stir well and cover. Turn to the lowest heat possible and simmer for about 1 hour. Add water if the rice begins to stick to the pan. The final consistency should be sticky, but thicker than porridge, so that it can be served on a plate rather than in a bowl.

Heat the oil in a wok until it begins to smoke and add the onion. Toss to coat with oil for 30 seconds. Add all the mushrooms and the pickle and stir-fry rapidly for about 2 minutes. Mix in the soy sauce, reserved soaking water, sugar and salt to taste. Bring to the boil then turn down the heat and simmer until the mushrooms have absorbed most of the liquid. Finally increase the heat and mix in the sesame oil. Pour the contents of the wok into the casserole with the rice and mix well together.

紅
棗
南
瓜
湯

## Red Date and Pumpkin Soup

SERVES 6–8

Red dates are the dried, prune-like fruit of the jujube tree, which is famed for its therapeutic uses. The seeds are used to calm the heart, but the fruits, combined with pumpkin, which is classified as pungent, are good for chronic chest complaints – coughs and bronchitis. This is also one of the traditional soups for toning the blood after childbirth.

30 red dates, stoned
500 g (1 lb) pumpkin, cut into chunks
1½ litres (2½ pints) water

Place the dates, pumpkin and water in a large pan and bring to the boil. Turn the heat down and simmer for 45 minutes. Mash the pumpkin into the soup and serve.

一
品
香
蕉
糕

### No 1 Banana Pancake

SERVES 3

This is a delicious way of serving banana, which is a well-known laxative. It is said to clear heat and nourish both lungs and colon. Traditionally, it is accompanied by a sticky sauce, but it is quite sweet enough on its own.

4 medium bananas
150 g (5 oz) plain flour
25 g (1 oz) chopped walnuts
50 g (2 oz) raisins

SAUCE (OPTIONAL)
2 tablespoons honey
50 g (2 oz) sugar
20 g (¾ oz) cornflour blended with a little water

Mash the bananas in a bowl and work in the flour until it is all well mixed. Shape the mixture into a big round cake on a flat heatproof dish. Scatter the walnuts and raisins on top. Place the dish in a steamer and steam for 20 minutes. To make the sauce, mix the honey and sugar into the cornflour. Heat gently in a pan until it thickens and dribble over the cooked pancake.

銀
耳
湯

## White Fungus Soup

SERVES 4

Both white fungus and ginko nuts are widely used as a food to
nourish the lungs.

50 g (2 oz) white fungus, soaked in hot water for 2–3 hours until
soft
1½ litres (2½ pints) water
10 ginko nuts
50 g (2 oz) rock sugar

Drain the fungus and rinse well. Cut out and discard the hard
brown stems. Place the fungus in a pan with the water, nuts and
sugar and simmer for 1 hour until sticky. Serve warm or cold.

## Autumn Purifying Tea

MAKES 4

This tea is designed to tone the Qi and calm the nerves whilst also reducing cholesterol. It is gently cleansing to the liver and kidneys. See page 273 for advice on buying the herbs. The quantities are so tiny it is not possible to give accurate imperial equivalents.

14 g Lotus leaf (He Ye)
3 g Licorice (Gan Cao)
2 g Mint (Bo He)
21 g Hawthorn (Shan Zha)
12 g Henon bamboo (Dan Zhu Ye)
2 litres (3½ pints) water

Soak the herbs in half the water for 30 minutes. Using a non-metal enamel or heatproof glass saucepan bring the herbs and water to the boil. Turn down the heat and simmer for 30 minutes. Strain and reserve the liquid. Return the herbs to the pan with the remaining water and bring to the boil. Turn down the heat and simmer for another 30 minutes. Strain and mix the 2 liquids together. Drink a warm cup morning and night. This recipe should do for 1 person for 2 days. The tea can be kept in the refrigerator for up to 3 days and re-heated.

Almond Tea (see page 28) would also be a good autumn drink. It eases both phlegmy coughs and constipation.

姜
汁
蜜
奶

## Ginger Milk

Ginger milk is warming to the lungs and the stomach and is
especially good for stomach-ache, nausea and vomiting caused
by eating too many cold foods. For simplicity, off-the-shelf
ginger cordials made only with ginger and sugar make a
convenient substitute for the ginger juice and honey.

300 ml (½ pint) milk
3 teaspoons ginger juice
honey, to taste

Warm the milk and add the ginger juice and honey.

# The Winter Banquet

On winter days, bathe and wash the hair frequently, keep the hands cold, keep the feet warm, keep the face cold, keep the body warm. In resting get up late and while lying down and stretching you must be straight. Enter the chamber between dusk and just before midnight [when it is time to] cease activity – increasing it will harm the Qi.
*Zhangjiashan Yinshu (c.200 BC)*

Life in winter emphasizes containment and conservation of resources. Like the seed in the frozen ground it is important to be still. The wise are said to sleep a lot and keep warm (without having too much sex). It is important not to strain the Yang Qi by being too active, because this will jeopardize resources left for spring and summer when they are most needed. Contract and enrich the inner world, sleep, dream and restore the body. During the short hours of daylight all activity should be vigorous to maintain the body's heat.

Winter food is often deep-coloured and preserved, so it is best incorporated into stews and stocks and cooked for a long while to release its flavours. Dried foods need pre-soaking and long cooking. Salty and bitter food is appropriate to promote a sinking quality which will carry the body heat inward. Too much salt, as too much of any food, will be detrimental to health, but for a reasonably well person, the salt flavour will guide the nourishment to enter the kidneys, the organ system associated with winter. While the food may be served warm, the cooling nature of the ingredients and flavours will have the effect of carrying warmth and nourishment inward and storing and conserving it in the lower body.

The kidneys are often associated with ageing. The organs themselves are thought to store the finest, quintessential Qi which determines the resources available to us to fend off illness and live for a long time. If we have lived a dissolute lifestyle then the kidney stores will be diminished and ageing will come prematurely. Unlike the Qi of other organs this fine Qi is difficult to replace, and only long-term life-style changes – rest, diet, exercise and meditation – will make much difference. Our winter banquet provides some herbs to strengthen the Qi and savoury stews to batten down the body's hatches and conserve all the strength needed for spring.

The dishes have been selected to be eaten together as a banquet, but can equally well be served separately in combinations of your choice. Each one is described in terms of its therapeutic value and can be related to the table of food classes and more detailed discussion of Chinese medical ideas and terminology in the Appendix (page 277).

## Duck Soup

SERVES 10

This is a savoury tonic to begin the winter banquet. Duck
supports the lungs and kidneys and the flavour carries the
warmth of the soup inwards.

1.75 kg (3½ lb) duck
2 litres (3½ pints) stock (see page 18)
3 cm (1¼ inch) piece of root ginger
4–5 pieces dried tangerine peel
3 teaspoons salt
2 tablespoons ginko nuts
1 Chinese leaf cabbage, sliced lengthways into broad strips
2 tablespoons light soy sauce
4 tablespoons Shaoxing wine
2 spring onions, chopped

Cut away the parson's nose and surrounding fat from the duck.
Place the whole duck in a casserole with the stock and bring to
the boil. Simmer for 20 minutes.

Skim off the scum and any fat on the surface. Add the ginger,
tangerine peel and salt to the stock and reduce the heat. Simmer
gently for 1 hour, turning the duck carefully every now and
then. Add the ginko nuts and simmer for another 30 minutes.
Remove the duck and carefully take the meat off the bones,
cutting it into strips. Skim off any fat on the surface of the soup.
Add the cabbage, soy sauce, wine and spring onions. Replace the
duck meat and bring back to the boil.

當
歸
燉
羊
肉

## Angelica Lamb Stew

SERVES 4–6

Chinese angelica is a very commonly used herb in Chinese medicine. Its primary function is to nourish the blood and regulate menstruation, promote blood circulation and to relieve abdominal pains, especially after childbirth. It is important to use the 'head' of the root rather than the 'tail', which is sold separately. Tangerine peel has a warming quality and a pungent, bitter flavour. It is good for eliminating phlegm. Together with the lamb, a warming meat that tones the kidneys, the organ associated with winter-time, this stew is perfect for keeping out the cold. Chestnuts also reinforce the benefit to the kidneys. The salt flavour of the soy and yellow bean also guide the nourishment downward and inward towards the kidneys where warmth and Qi can be properly conserved.

40 g (1½ oz) Chinese angelica (dang gui: see page 263), soaked in cold water for 30 minutes
10 dried Chinese mushrooms, soaked in hot water for 30 minutes
2 large pieces of dried tangerine peel, soaked in hot water for 30 minutes
750 g (1½ lb) boned shoulder or leg of lamb, cut into 3 cm (1¼ inch) cubes
3 tablespoons vegetable oil
2.5 cm (1 inch) piece of root ginger, finely sliced
600 ml (1 pint) stock (see page 18)
5 tablespoons dark soy sauce
1 teaspoon sugar
1 tablespoon yellow bean paste
4 tablespoons Shaoxing wine
175 g (6 oz) cooked chestnuts, or dried chestnuts, soaked and pre-boiled (see page 262)

Drain and squeeze the Chinese angelica. Place in a muslin bag and secure with some thin string. Drain the mushrooms and tangerine peel. Discard the hard mushroom stems and slice the caps in half. Parboil the lamb for 3 minutes and drain.

Heat the oil in a casserole. When it begins to smoke add the ginger and stir in the oil. Add the lamb and stir-fry together for a further 3–4 minutes. Add the tangerine peel, Chinese mushrooms, stock, soy sauce, sugar, yellow bean paste, wine, angelica and chestnuts. Bring to the boil and simmer gently for 2 hours, stirring occasionally.

西
門
慶
核
桃
炒
韭
菜

## Xi Menqing's Stir-fried Walnut and Chinese Chives

This is a well-known, warming dish for increasing or sustaining virility, especially in old age. Walnut stimulates the yang aspect of the kidney, which is thought to be involved in the production of seminal essence and which also deteriorates in old age. The shape of the walnut is also thought to resemble the kidneys themselves. The warm drying quality of the pungent Chinese chive is good for the digestion and also stimulates kidney yang. Xi Menqing was a famous philanderer from the *Water Margin* who came to a sticky end after ill-advisably having an affair with Golden Lotus, sister-in-law of stalwart hero Wu Song. Lili, who gave me this recipe, is also a devout Buddhist and is now doing penance for promoting unacceptable behaviour!

2 tablespoons vegetable oil
125 g (4 oz) walnuts
40 g (1½ oz) Chinese chives, chopped into 2.5 cm (1 inch) pieces
½ teaspoon salt
1 teaspoon sesame oil

Heat the oil in a wok and add the walnuts. Turn the heat down and fry until the walnuts have a yellow colour, being careful not to burn them. Pour off one half of the oil. Add the Chinese chives and the salt and stir-fry quickly. Sprinkle with the sesame oil and serve.

炒
雙
冬

## Hot-tossed Two Winters with Courgette
SERVES 3–4

6 large dried Chinese mushrooms, soaked in hot water for 30
minutes
225 g (8 oz) courgettes, cut into 2.5 cm (1 inch) lengths
½ teaspoon salt
3 tablespoons vegetable oil
1 cm (½ inch) piece of root ginger, finely chopped
125 g (4 oz) sliced bamboo shoots
1 teaspoon sugar
1 tablespoon light soy sauce
1 tablespoon Shaoxing wine
sesame oil, to taste

Drain the mushrooms, reserving the soaking water. Discard the
hard stems and slice the caps. Sprinkle the sliced courgettes
with the salt.

Heat the oil in a wok until it just begins to smoke. Add the
ginger and mushrooms and toss together for 1 minute. Add the
remaining ingredients, except the sesame oil, with 3 tablespoons
of the mushroom water. Toss together for 1 minute, then cover
the wok and turn down the heat. Simmer for 4 minutes then
sprinkle with sesame oil and serve.

蘿
蔔
絲
餅

## White Radish Fritters

MAKES 4

As winter progressed and there were only root vegetables left at the bottom of the ice holes, cooking had to become more creative. These fritters are quick and easy to make, as well as tasty.

200 g (7 oz) white Chinese radishes, grated
225 g (8 oz) self-raising flour
1 tablespoon chopped coriander
1 spring onion, chopped
1 teaspoon five-spice powder
2 teaspoons salt
vegetable oil, for shallow-frying

Mix the radish with the flour in a bowl. Add enough water to make a thick pancake mixture. Add the coriander, spring onion, five-spice powder and salt and mix thoroughly.

Lightly oil a small omelette pan, heat gently and pour in enough batter to make a small pancake. Fry over a gentle heat until brown on one side. Turn over and cook until brown on the other side. Repeat with the remaining batter.

## Eight Treasure Pudding

SERVES 6

This is the classic party pudding. We serve it at the New Year festival. Prepare well in advance as the un-steamed pudding will mature for up to 4 days in the refrigerator. Many of the dried fruits, like angelica, have therapeutic qualities. The red bean paste is a tonic which nourishes the heart. Being well steamed, the pudding is easy to digest, so you can also serve this to the old and sick as restorative food.

500 g (1 lb) glutinous rice, rinsed
4 tablespoons vegetable oil
3 tablespoons sugar
400 g (14 oz) sweet red bean paste
25 g (1 oz) walnuts or ginko nuts
6 tablespoons candied and dried fruit, such as angelica, cherries, lychees, loquat and dates, plus extra to decorate

Place the rice in a pan and pour in enough water to cover to a depth of 1 cm (½ inch). Bring to the boil and simmer gently for 30 minutes, adding more water if it seems to be sticking. Add the oil and sugar and stir until well mixed. Meanwhile, soften the red bean paste by placing it in a bowl over a pan of hot water for 30 minutes. Heavily grease the sides of a large heatproof basin or bowl. Stick the nuts and candied or dried fruits in a pattern on the sides and bottom of the bowl. Divide the rice into 4 portions and the bean paste into 3 portions. Place a portion of rice in the bowl, then spread a layer of bean paste on top of the rice. Repeat the layers, finishing with a rice layer and packing the mixture down into the bowl. Cover the bowl and refrigerate.

When ready to cook, place the bowl in a steamer, cover and steam steadily for at least 1½ hours, topping up the water in the steamer as necessary. Invert the basin on to a large round heated serving dish to turn out the pudding. Decorate with extra candied fruit.

荔
枝
姜
湯

## Sweet Ginger Soup with Dried Lychees
SERVES 4

750 ml (1¼ pints) water
4 cm (1¾ inch) piece of root ginger, finely chopped
225 g (8 oz) dried lychees
4–5 tablespoons crystallized ginger, chopped
rock sugar or honey, to taste

Heat the water in a casserole. Add the fresh ginger and bring to
the boil. Add the dried lychees, reduce the heat and simmer for
30 minutes. Add the crystallized ginger and rock sugar to taste
and simmer for 10 minutes.

## Long-life Tea

MAKES 4 SERVINGS

Taken every day for a couple of weeks this recipe is a mild tonic. It is said to stimulate Qi, strengthen the kidneys and detoxify the blood. Dan shen invigorates and moves the blood and calms the spirit. See page 273 for advice on how to purchase the herbs.

10 g Red Root Salvia (Dan shen)
12 g Licorice (Gan Cao)
30 g Wolfberry (Gou Qi Zi)
2 litres (3½ pints) water

Soak the herbs in half the water for 30 minutes. Using a non-metal enamel or heatproof glass saucepan bring the herbs and water to the boil. Turn down the heat and simmer for 30 minutes. Strain and reserve the liquid. Return the herbs to the pan with the remaining water. Bring to the boil, then reduce the heat and simmer for another 30 minutes. Strain and mix the 2 liquids together. Drink a warm cup morning and night. This recipe should do for 1 person for 2 days. The tea can be kept in the refrigerator for up to 3 days and re-heated.

# 5  Recipes from the Japanese Teahouse

On tea drinking:

> The first bowl is so soothing to the throat,
> The second bowl disperses loneliness,
> With the third bowl I search my soul for five thousand ancient
>   volumes,
> The fourth bowl brings on a gentle sweat which washes away all
>   unhappiness,
> The fifth bowl purifies bones and muscle,
> With the sixth bowl I get through to a radiance of the spirit.
> *Lu Dong (Tang dynasty)*

## Zen and the Tea Ceremony

The Japanese teahouse or chashitsu is the temple of the teahouses
and best illustrated by the four guiding principles in its design –
harmony, reverence, purity and silence. Sen-no-Rikyu (1521–
1591), a Buddhist priest, is said to have adapted the principles to
architecture after the classic tea ceremony that still forms the
heart of religious practice in Buddhist temples in Japan. All the
other styles of Chinese teahouse described in these chapters are
also represented in Japanese society, but the chashitsu is
exclusively Japanese. As both dwelling of the priest and temple
in one, it is a place where preoccupation with form and ceremony
has raised the Chinese tea ritual into new realms.

To watch the tea ceremony, the heart of religious ritual in Zen
Buddhist temples, is to watch the ritualization of secular life, the
elevation of the simplest daily function into an elusive spiritual
experience. Every movement is prescribed, from the sitting
position of the men and women to the priest who walks
backwards into the teahouse through a side door. In some
teahouses the tea water is boiled in a tea kettle over a brazier
sunk into the floor. In others, there is a separate room where the
tea is prepared by servants before it is brought to the participants
who await in the main room, women kneeling and men in the
lotus position.

Minute attention is paid to the style of teaware and accessories.
Once the tea bowl is offered it must be taken in two hands and
turned – a number of times to the left and then again to the right –

in order to appreciate the special quality of the bowl. Each bowl is deliberately imperfect: somewhere there will be a blemish or a crack, or the shape will not quite achieve a full round. Its flaw serves to emphasize individuality and to mirror the imperfections of life. The tea is then sipped, savoured and appreciated, the bowl is wiped and passed to the next participant.

Both Zen and the tea ceremony are the end product of a long process of religious and philosophic transformation that came about as Buddhism migrated eastward and came into contact with new cultures. Beginning in the Han dynasty (second century), Buddhism took root in China and by the Tang dynasty (seventh century to tenth century) Buddhist organizations had received imperial patronage and simultaneously amassed great fortunes. Tea cultivation was introduced to Japan in the eighth century, when Japanese monks returned from China and Chinese temples inspired by contact with the Chinese Chan sect of Buddhism, as well as with the ancient written language and learning.

The monks may also have brought home roughly glazed tea bowls and simple tea lore based on the literature created for tea devotees, detailing recommendations for tea utensils and tea-making as well as fascinating stories about legendary tea masters. Lu Yu's famous work, the *Tea Classic* (780), exhaustively explained proper tea drinking. He particularly emphasized details such as the importance of the purity of water. Water from mountain springs was most highly prized, and Buddhist monasteries in the mountains probably had the best access. River water was next best, and well water was least sought after. Another source places melted snow in twentieth place, and yet another eulogizes the water from the snow especially collected from plum blossoms.

Together with a concern for the purity of the water some of the finest elements of all three great civilizations are preserved within the philosophies and ceremonies of Zen Buddhism. From Indian Mahayana Buddhism came the knowledge of the Buddha nature said to be immanent in everyone, the practice of meditation and introspection, and a belief in instant enlightenment. Chinese Daoism contributed its humour and love of paradox, a distrust of words and human society. To a distillation of all of these traditions Japanese culture added its own highly developed forms of ceremonial etiquette.

It was not until the thirteenth century that the tea ceremony in

Japan began to reach maturity, and the Japanese adopted any of the ritual etiquette associated today with tea-drinking. By the fifteenth century a tea cult was so well-established that a tea-room within the Silver Pavilion was designed for the Shogun Yoshimasu in Kyoto, and in the seventeenth century the military dictator, Hideyoshi, invited the entire population of Kyoto to participate in his tea ceremony. Eventually it became unnecessary to differentiate between the sacred and the secular elements of the ceremony.

The extravagance of the medieval tea ceremony and teaware soon led to a call for a return to religious austerity. In the Buddhist temples many architects were both craftsmen and Zen priests in one, and could design the temple teahouse to reflect their concern with infusing daily life with spirit. The teahouse was reduced to what was aesthetically and structurally indispensable – a bare, white paper structure, about 10 feet by 4 feet, supported by posts and beams, perhaps with windows randomly placed in every side.

As in Chinese ink drawings, the black boundaries of the beams and supports only serve to emphasize the empty surfaces of the paper. It is not the black alone that is important, but rather the expanse of white, not the three dimensions, but the contrast with the empty space that suggests freedom while simultaneously containing and gathering the spirit. Very few objects break the emptiness. Those that do only serve to emphasize it – a single bloom, an ink landscape, rush matting. Care is taken that no theme is repeated. In the *Book of Tea* Okakura Kakuzo states:

With a fresh flower, a painting of flowers is not permitted. With a round kettle, the water carrier should be faceted. A black glazed cup should not be used with a black lacquer tea-caddy. To position a vase or an incense burner on the tokonoma, be careful not to put it exactly in the centre, to avoid dividing the space equally.

Apart from religious teahouses, there are also many secular teahouses which form an integral part of the dwellings of wealthy families and provide both an aesthetic and religious dimension to the home. The path to such a teahouse often leads through a walled tea garden. Along the way a hidden spring might gush into a deep stone basin, or autumn leaves fall in drifts across the path. Here and there grotesque rocks suggesting mountains, clouds or animals jut out from the shrubbery, robed in thick green moss and lichen. Before the entrance a sheltered bench provides a convenient place for guests to pause and await the ceremony, or to take a moment to recover afterwards. On one side are a stone lantern and a wash basin, on the other a rack to hang up your sword and suspend all thoughts of conflict.

Nowadays, because of its lengthy nature and demanding etiquette, the tea ceremony is largely performed by women of wealthy families who can afford to spare three years to dedicate themselves to the learning of the art, considered an integral part of a traditional classical education. But everyone, priests, elders, housewives and business men alike, can participate and enjoy the qualities derived from Indian Buddhism and Chinese Daoism that remain embodied in the tea ceremony ritual. Even for those devoted to the pursuit of earthly wealth, the tea ceremony offers an opportunity to become completely immersed in a ritual sequence as if, voluntarily surrendering independence, he or she can momentarily become one with a greater movement in the universe.

## Japanese Tea

Japanese tea ceremony is much larger than the tea itself, but care is taken that each element be brought as close as possible to perfection. Macha Gyokuro is the best quality tea, green and foamy and reserved especially for the ceremonies in the temples or in the special houses of tea-growing areas. The cup is only filled half-full, for any more than three sips will leave you feeling light-headed. Each sip is savoured and criticized for its fragrance, its vivacity and aroma, not drunk to quench the thirst.

There are many grades of tea to be found in Japan and each has its own special place. The roughest is Bancha which, being made from the stalks of the tea plant, looks brown in colour. Bancha is served with a hot towel and a glass of water as an appetizer before any ordinary meal. It is often used in macrobiotic diets. Sencha, the next grade up, is taken during and after meals. Although the leaves are not of the top quality it has become popular in the West. On the other hand Gyokuro is really the finest of the ordinary teas. It is made from the tips of the tea bush and produces a tea that is a jade green colour.

Apart from these three main grades there are some speciality teas, such as the dry-fried brown Hojicha which has a wonderfully pervasive aromatic aroma, the southern island Sencha that is flavoured with salted plum and served with a plum blossom floating in it, or the Kombucha, a fishy tea garnished with some salted seaweed. In summer Mugicha, which is really a tea made from barley, is often taken cold at breakfast-time.

## Teahouses and Noodle Bars

Pilgrimages to Japanese tea ceremony houses should not be made in search of good quality, nourishing food. Alongside the rough-textured bowl of tea the tea master may serve exquisitely formed models of fruits or sugar impressions of his own chop or personal seal, delicacies to admire rather than to eat. But there are plenty of other Japanese bars that serve our theme of the teahouse as a focus of nourishing cheap food and good society. One where people go to gossip and chat is simply called the Kissaten 'The Teahouse'. Nowadays the Kissaten is fairly modern in design, with marble-topped tables and chairs in the European café tradition. Here they also sell Japanese imitations of western sweets and savoury snacks, advertised outside by those dishes of plastic food that translate the fare to the public on the street.

Another favourite are the wagashi patisseries where customers sit at two-seater tables and eat traditional Japanese cakes, tartlets and other sweetmeats. Some may be shaped like little shortcrust boats with a filling of sweet potato, egg, almond and sugar, glazed with egg yolk, others cut into delicate slices, such as yokan red bean jelly, or fashioned into sweet dumplings made of glutinous rice or sweet bean paste. These cakes are essentially Japanese and many regional specialities exist. Some of these, for example kasutera-cake and dorayaki, bear witness to early maritime connections with the Dutch and Portuguese.

More familiar, and closer to our present theme, are the Chinese egg noodle ramen bars so familiar to Londoners today. In London the ramen bars are designer affairs, but in Japan they may be no more than a basic counter on a station platform with revolving stools. Behind the bar is a vat of boiling water for the egg noodles and a tureen of broth, maintained just under the boil to keep it clear and hot enough for the next customer. When the customer orders, a quick assembly of noodles and stock is decorated with a selection of seaweed, mushroom, pork, fishcakes and oysters. Women are more likely to go to work with a lunch box, so the typical customer at such a ramen bar is the young Japanese businessman. One bizarre and common sight is a line of young men in suits lined up on the revolving chairs, each with a copy of one of the ubiquitous manga cartoon books open in their laps. It is not so much that they have perfected the art of slurping ramen and reading comic strips simultaneously, but rather that the comic book protects their perfectly tailored trousers!

Although many ramen bars style themselves after Chinese noodle bars and make a point of advertising their Chinese noodles, there is much to be learned from the Japanese hybrid. Where most Chinese enterprises will be happy if the customers gulp down their food and look satisfied, the Japanese are driven by an obsession to perfect the product and the process. Chicken noodle soup is available everywhere in China, but it is a homely dish, and no one bothers to write down a recipe. The Japanese have turned it into a fine art. Some small ramen bar owners go to incredible lengths to preserve the secrecy of their broth recipe. Broth, like tea, must have fragrance, vivacity and aroma. Mountain spring water is often imported from famous Chinese spas or a special oil or spice is added according to a closed family tradition.

The Japanese way of eating ramen is also more in harmony with modern western life. Deep-fried or even stir-fried foods can be avoided. Ramen soups certainly suit diets that recommend less saturated fat, less red meat and more carbohydrate. They leave you feeling fresh, light and alive and make a nourishing lunch-time snack. Allergic types should beware of MSG and seafood, both hard to avoid in Japanese cuisine. In Japanese MSG is called aji-no-moto, the origin of taste, which indicates how essential it is considered. Despite its pervasive presence MSG is a fairly recent product, modelled after a substance called flavour powder in Chinese. So far we have not been able to trace the real flavour powder. The recipes that follow avoid MSG, but ours are the exception rather than the rule. These days it is difficult to create an authentic Japanese taste without it.

With the pace of Japanese urban life speed of food preparation is essential. Even the basic broth can be prepared from dried ingredients. Most of the recipes are faster and less fussy than their Chinese counterparts. They can be prepared by simple assembly and without the skill necessary to blend oils and sauces and therefore with a better guarantee of success. The long list of ingredients before the Chinese recipes is avoided and the result is a cleaner, if more bland taste. One of the great virtues for the western clientele is that to get away with less spice and flavouring the raw materials must always be fresh. You can see what you are eating.

The recipes in this chapter are inspired by our contact with friends and mentors at wagamama, but the fine detail comes more directly from Friederike Maeda. Friederike is a graduate in Japanese from the School of Oriental and African Studies and a fount of wisdom about all things Japanese. She has learned all her recipes under pressure from a Japanese husband who is particularly fussy about his food!

# Stocks

本
出
し

## Dashi Broth

Dashi is the broth which forms the basis for almost all soup dishes and is also added to many other dishes. It is quick to prepare and is usually made for immediate use. The fish and seaweed flavour of bonito flakes (ready-made dried tuna flakes called Katsuo-bushi in Japanese) and kombu (kelp) replace those of the predominantly pork, chicken and vegetable stocks used in Chinese cookery. A pinch of MSG, a Japanese flavour powder, is almost always used, although reducing the ratio of water to bonito and kombu is preferable for those who are additive-conscious. Kombu is available as kelp from most good health-food shops, as may be bonito flakes. Some large supermarket chains are beginning to sell these products on their exotic displays. Otherwise, Japanese food generally necessitates a visit to an oriental supermarket.

6–8 tablespoons bonito flakes (any size – hanakatsuo, the fine ones, are also used for decoration)
1 litre (1¾ pints) water
6 x 10 cm (2½ x 4 inch) piece of kombu

Put the flakes in a pan. Bring the water to the boil separately and pour over the flakes. Wipe the kombu with a clean damp cloth to remove excess salt and impurities. Add to the pan and leave to soak for 15 minutes, then remove. It is important not to boil the kombu as this creates an undesirably strong 'seaweedy' odour and cloudiness. Strain the broth through muslin.

VARIATIONS

The fish broth described below is simply a variation of the many kinds of soup which all have Dashi broth as their basis. It would be used, for example, in some of the winter dishes cooked on the table. In general, soups are made by combining the basic broth and whatever addition is required (chicken, beef or mushrooms) in a ratio of 2:7.

FISH BROTH
500 g (1 lb) fish bones, including fish head

1.5 litres (2½ pints) dashi broth
6 tablespoons light soy sauce
3 tablespoons mirin or sweet sherry
½ teaspoon salt
pinch of MSG (optional)

Place the fish bones and broth in a pan and bring to the boil. Skim all the scum from the surface. Turn down the heat and simmer gently for 10 minutes. Strain carefully and then add the remaining ingredients.

月
見
蕎
麦

## Moon Viewing in Buckwheat Noodles [Tsukimi Soba]

This is a basic buckwheat noodle dish that is a perfect lunch-time snack. The moon is the misty egg yolk nestling amongst the clouds of noodles. Adding cold water to bring the water off the boil ensures that the outside of the soba does not become soggy before the inside is cooked. The end result should be al dente. To make the dish more substantial Japanese cooks put tempura on top of the soup. This makes the batter mushy. It can equally well be eaten separately. Serve the soup piping hot. Blowing on the noodles and sucking them in noisily is considered good manners, but watch your clothing if you are not familiar with this technique!

PER SERVING
300 ml (½ pint) dashi broth (see page 195)
dash of light soy sauce
dash of mirin or sweet sherry
small pinch of salt
pinch of sugar
100 g (3½ oz) soba or udon
1 free-range egg

GARNISH
ajitsuke nori (flavoured nori)
spring onion, chopped
3 pieces of tempura (see page 214), including a large Pacific prawn, (optional)

Heat the broth and add the soy sauce, mirin, salt and sugar. Keep it on a low simmer with no bubbling. Meanwhile, bring a large pan of water to the boil and add the soba. Cook for 6–8 minutes or according to instructions. While the broth is simmering add half a cup of cold water and bring back to the boil. Repeat twice. Drain and rinse the noodles under cold running water to arrest the cooking process and remove the foaming scum that has formed on the surface. Re-heat the noodles by dowsing with hot water so that they do not cool the soup, then drain and place in a bowl. Pour on the stock. Make a round well in the noodles and break the whole egg into the noodles. Place the bowl under a grill until the egg is fully cooked. Garnish with the nori snipped into tiny strips with kitchen scissors, the spring onion and tempura.

とりなんばん饂飩（蕎麦）

## Chicken and Shiitake Mushroom on White Wheatflour or Buckwheat Noodles [Torinamban Udon (Soba)]

SERVES 4

Like most of the Japanese soup noodles this dish will be eaten as a midday snack, a form of fast food.

8 dried Shiitake mushrooms, soaked in hot water for 30 minutes
400 g (13 oz) soba or udon
1 litre (1¾ pints) dashi broth (see page 195)
5 tablespoons light soy sauce
3 tablespoons mirin or sweet sherry
½ tablespoon sugar
small pinch of salt
500 g (1 lb) skinned and boned chicken legs, chopped into bite-sized pieces
1 spring onion, finely chopped, to garnish

Drain the mushrooms, discard the hard stems and cut the caps into quarters.

Prepare the chicken and noodles simultaneously. Bring a large pan of water to the boil and add the soba. Cook for 6–8 minutes or according to instructions. During the simmering add half a cup of cold water and bring back to the boil. Repeat two more times. Rinse the noodles under cold running water, then re-heat by dowsing with hot water and drain.

Meanwhile, bring the dashi broth to the boil and add the soy sauce, mirin, sugar and salt. Add the chicken. Bring back to the boil, then reduce to a simmer for 4 minutes. Add the mushrooms and simmer for a further 3 minutes or until the chicken is cooked through. Divide the noodles between 4 bowls. Remove the chicken with a slotted spoon and arrange on top of the noodles. Pour on the broth. Garnish with the chopped spring onion.

焼き豚ラーメン

## Roast Pork Ramen [Cha Su Ramen]

There is a tradition of placing a colourful selection of ingredients over fresh ramen and dashi broth. Ramen simply means Chinese noodles, but instead of either the dried egg noodles so familiar in every supermarket, or the more tasty fresh oil noodles, the egg noodles available in Japanese supermarkets come frozen, and are therefore softer, and well suited to delicate soups. The secret of this soup lies in the last-minute assembly and presentation. Ingredients for topping the soup might be a mixture of sliced chicken, hard-boiled quail's eggs, prawns, Japanese fishcakes, which are often rolled, pressed or brightly coloured with pink colouring, nori seaweed, deep-fried bean curd (see page 261), roasted pork or grilled, sliced teriyaki meats (see page 208) and wakame seaweed or other tender greens such as spinach.

Alternatively, a plain stir-fry of mixed vegetables or seafood and vegetables will make a delicious topping. This recipe is very similar to our own Teahouse honey roast pork recipe (see page 256), but the delicate seafood taste in the dashi broth and the addition of naruto fish cake makes a subtle difference. Naruto means 'spiral' and refers to the pink swirl in the middle of the cake.

PER PORTION
125 g (4 oz) fresh egg noodles or dried ramen
300 ml (½ pint) hot vegetable stock
5 thin slices of honey roast pork (see page 256)
small handful of spinach or bak choy
50 g (2 oz) sliced bamboo shoots
1 slice of naruto fish cake
chopped coriander and spring onion, to garnish

Bring a large pan of water to the boil. Gradually lower the noodles into the water. When the water comes back to the boil, lower the heat. If fresh noodles are used they need only be simmered for a couple of minutes. (They should not be fully soft as they continue to cook in the stock as they are brought to the table.) Frozen noodles should be de-frosted then treated as fresh.

If dried noodles are being used, bring a large pan of water to the boil and add the dried ramen. During the simmering add half a cup of cold water and bring back to the boil. Repeat twice. Rinse the noodles under cold running water then reheat by dowsing with hot water and drain.

To serve, place the noodles in a bowl and pour on the heated stock. Arrange the remaining ingredients on the surface of the soup.

茄子の味噌煮

## Miso Braised Augergine [Nasu no miso-ni]

SERVES 2

Miso soups are often eaten after the starter and before the main meal in a home-style Japanese meal. This soup, however, is quite substantial on its own, served with rice.

1 aubergine, sliced thickly, then each slice cut into 8 pieces
1 tablespoon vegetable oil
1 tablespoon sake
2 teaspoons rice vinegar
400 ml (14 fl oz) boiling water
125 g (4 oz) silken bean curd, cut into 1.5cm (¾ inch) cubes
25 g (1 oz) miso paste, blended with lukewarm water
finely sliced spring onion, to garnish
10 cm (4 inch) strip of wakame

Soak the aubergine in cold salted water for 30 minutes. Drain and leave to dry.

Heat the oil in a wok and add the aubergine. Add the sake and rice vinegar and stir quickly until it is absorbed. Pour in the boiling water. Bring back to the boil then turn down the heat and simmer until the aubergine is softened. Add the bean curd and blended miso and bring back to the boil. Remove from the heat immediately. Pour into a serving bowl and garnish with spring onion and the wakame.

# Summer Noodles

Noodles tend to be most popular as a lunchtime meal, and are Japan's favourite fast food. Hot noodles (in soup) are served in winter and cold noodles in summer. They are regarded as a meal in themselves and, as such, do not require pickles or vegetables. Any extras are eaten only if one is still a bit peckish.

## Chilled Somen

SERVES 6

This makes a good light summer lunch which can be eaten on
its own, with salad or other vegetable dishes. Summer noodles
(and summer salads containing cold noodles) are usually served
in large flat communal glass bowls and decorated with ice cubes
and some fresh cherries or cherry tomatoes for colour. Each
diner has a small, deep pottery or glass bowl containing the
dipping sauce and a small plate holding the condiments (spring
onions, wasabi, grated ginger and some grated Chinese white
radish or mooli, to be added to taste).

1.5 litres (2½ pints) water, plus extra for cooling
500 g (1 lb) somen (thin white noodles or the slightly thicker
hiyamugi)
4 ice cubes

DIPPING SAUCE
500 ml (17 fl oz) concentrated dashi or chicken broth (see pages
195 and 18)
250 ml (8 fl oz) light soy sauce
250 ml (8 fl oz) mirin or sweet cooking sherry

CONDIMENTS
1 spring onion, finely chopped
wasabi (optional)
mixture of grated white Chinese radish and grated root ginger

Bring the water to the boil. Add the noodles and bring back to
the boil. When at a rolling boil add half a cup of cold water and
bring back to the boil. Repeat twice. Drain, rinsing under a cold
tap until the noodles have completely cooled down. Drain again,
place in a wide dish and scatter the ice cubes on top. Serve with
the condiments.

Mix together the broth, soy sauce and mirin and serve as a dip
for the noodles.

## Sieved Buckwheat Noodles [Zaru Soba]

SERVES 2

Cold plain noodles may not be to everyone's taste, but in Japan they are considered a great delicacy. How they are arranged is critical to the pleasure of eating them. This recipe calls for a special bamboo-framed sieve on which the noodles are piled so that they drain fully, leaving them dry and ready to soak up the dip. Some restaurants go to extreme lengths to serve their noodles in an original way. Friederike, who gave us all these Japanese recipes, tells me of one restaurant which owns its own mountainside outside Kyoto. A mountain stream is channelled into a split bamboo pipe, which leads via several branches to the tables. When the noodles are cooked, a chef dashes up the mountain and drops them into the pipe. By the time they have passed through the bamboo they have been refreshed by the freshest, clearest spring water. The tables each have their own reservoir from which each diner can pick up noodles with chopsticks and dip them in the dishes on the table.

200 g (7 oz) soba
ajitsuke nori, to garnish
2 tablespoons concentrated dashi or chicken broth (see pages 195 and 18)
2 teaspoons light soy sauce
2 teaspoons mirin or sweet cooking sherry

CONDIMENTS
finely chopped spring onion
wasabi
mixture of grated white Chinese radish and grated root ginger

Boil the soba for 6–8 minutes (see page 199) and then rinse them under a cold tap until they are completely cooled down. Lay them out over a slatted bamboo sieve so that they do not become mushy underneath or thin the dipping sauce. Garnish with thin strips of Ajitsuke Nori cut with kitchen scissors. Serve with a dipping sauce made from the mixture of dashi, soy sauce and mirin, and a small plate of condiments.

# Meat and Poultry

## Yakitori Skewered Chicken
### SERVES 4

500 g (1 lb) boned chicken legs, cut into bite-sized cubes
1 large Spanish onion, cut into chunks
2 medium green peppers, cored, seeded and cut into chunks the
same size as the onion
1 large piece of root ginger, finely grated
500 ml (17 fl oz) light soy sauce
500 ml (17 fl oz) mirin or sweet cooking sherry
2 tablespoons sugar

Soak 8 bamboo skewers for 30 minutes in cold water to prevent
them burning under the grill. Alternate pieces of chicken, onion
and pepper on each skewer. Squeeze out the juice from the
grated ginger with your fingers until you have 1 teaspoon of
ginger juice.

   Pour some water into the bottom of the grill pan to catch the
drips from the rack. Put all of the skewers under a medium grill.
Meanwhile, place the soy sauce, mirin, ginger juice and sugar in
a pan and warm gently so that the sugar fully dissolves. Pour the
solution into a tall tumbler. When the chicken is almost cooked
dip the whole skewer into the tumbler so that the chicken and
vegetables are fully coated. Replace under the grill, turning the
skewer once to dry the coating. Repeat the dipping and grilling 4
times. This produces a delicate flavouring. For a hearty flavour
prepare the chicken, onions and peppers beforehand and
marinate in the ginger solution in the refrigerator. For the
strongest flavour, leave overnight, but remember that because of
the high sugar content of the sauce the meat needs to be turned
more frequently under the grill to avoid burning.

## Butajiru Pork and Vegetable Stew

SERVES 2–3

This is a popular dish in winter and is eaten as an
accompaniment to other dishes, especially rice.

500 ml (17 fl oz) dashi broth (see page 195)
3 tablespoons light soy sauce
3 tablespoons sake or dry sherry
1 large carrot, cut into thick strips
1 large potato, cut into 3 cm (1¼ inch) cubes
1 onion, cubed
15 cm (6 inch) piece of white Chinese radish (mooli), cut into
thick strips
225 g (8 oz) pork fillet, cut into bite-sized chunks
1 walnut-sized piece of shiro or white miso paste

Bring the dashi, soy sauce and sake to the boil in a pan and
simmer for 10 minutes together with the carrot, potato, onion,
radish and pork. Take out one ladleful of the soup and blend in
the miso paste. Return the mixture to the pan and bring to the
boil. Take off the heat and serve immediately.

鳥
の
照
り
焼
き

## Chicken Teriyaki [Tori no Teriyaki]

SERVES 4

Teryaki sauce can be bought in all major supermarkets and is
perfect for a speedy supper. Any lean cut of meat can be used,
such as sirloin steak or lean pork. Marinate for 30 minutes in
the sauce, then grill like the skewered chicken (see page 206) for
5–10 minutes until cooked through. It is important to baste the
meat regularly.

The recipe below is a superior version of the above and may be
adapted to other meats, such as beef, pork or duck, as well as
fish – salmon, halibut, large scallops, fresh tuna or monkfish.
Chicken teriyaki can be used as a topping for a ramen soup or
eaten as one of a number of dishes with rice and pickles.

1 large piece of root ginger
2 tablespoons vegetable oil
500 g (1 lb) boned breast of chicken or boned chicken thighs
5 tablespoons light soy sauce
3 tablespoons mirin or sweet sherry
2 teaspoons sugar

Grate the ginger as finely as possible, then squeeze out the juice
with your fingers until you have 1 tablespoon of ginger juice.
Heat the oil in a frying pan. Sprinkle the chicken with the ginger
juice, then place in the pan and turn until it changes colour. Add
the remaining ingredients and cook over a low heat for 8
minutes. Turn the chicken and cook on the other side until
cooked through. Cut into bite-sized slices and serve with a
vegetable dish.

*Old Pockmarked Mrs Chen's Beancurd* (p. 91)

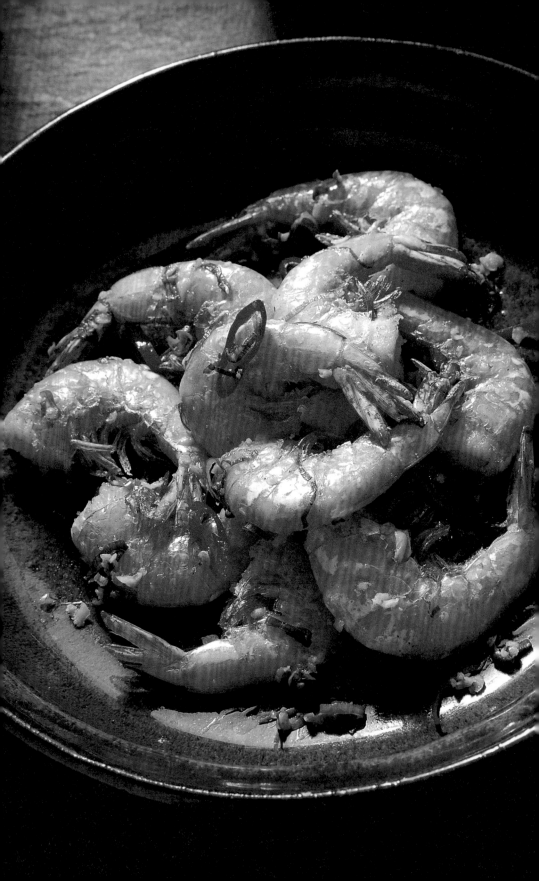

# Fish and Vegetable Dishes

鮭の田楽

## Miso Glazed Salmon [Sake no Dengaku]

SERVES 4

This forms part of a set meal of starter (small fish or vegetable dish, then rice and miso soup or clear soup), several small dishes, one of which will be the main focus of the meal, pickled vegetable dishes and some tofu dishes.

4 salmon steaks
25 g (1 oz) shiro or white miso paste
2 teaspoons mirin or sweet sherry
2 teaspoons dashi broth (see page 195)
1 egg yolk

Poach the salmon steaks gently until almost cooked through. Meanwhile, mix the miso, mirin and dashi in a heatproof bowl and place over gently boiling water. Blend carefully. Add the egg yolk and stir until thoroughly blended. Baste the salmon steaks with the mixture and place under the grill until the topping turns light brown, turning once.

*Crispy Salted Prawns* (p. 108)

豆腐と花鰹

## Silken Bean Curd with Bonito Flakes

SERVES 2

Cold bean curd tends to be eaten in summer towards the beginning of a meal.

200 g (7 oz) silken bean curd, quartered
2 tablespoons dark soy sauce
2 tablespoons bonito flakes (hanakatsuo – the fine variety)
1 spring onion, finely sliced

Drain the bean curd on kitchen paper then pour on the soy sauce. Sprinkle with bonito flakes and spring onion.

VARIATIONS
1. Place a tiny dollop of wasabi on each piece of bean curd and pour on the soy sauce.
2. Pour the soy sauce over the bean curd. Finely grate a piece of peeled white Chinese radish (mooli) and a seeded red chilli and place on top of the bean curd with a shredded, seeded red chilli.
3. Pour the soy sauce over the bean curd. Place a little cone of freshly grated ginger on the bean curd.

散
ら
し
寿
司

## Vinegar-flavoured Rice [Chirashi Zushi]

SERVES 4–5

This is a very substantial, tasty dish made from the slightly
sticky Japanese rice. Do not use glutinous rice as it is not
suitable. Every version of this recipe is slightly different. This
one uses sake, which many sushi chefs consider their top-secret
ingredient – luckily for us they are mistaken!

225 g (8 oz) Japanese short-grain milk rice, risotto rice or English
pudding rice
750 ml (1¼ pints) water
10 cm (4 inch) square piece of kombu
1 tablespoon sake
4 tablespoons rice vinegar
1 tablespoon sugar
pinch of salt

GARNISHES
a little vegetable oil
3 eggs
pinch of salt
4 tablespoons dashi broth (see page 195)
2 teaspoons soy sauce
2 teaspoons mirin or sweet sherry
pinch of salt and sugar
one small carrot, cut into julienne strips
50 g (2 oz) green beans, cut into julienne strips
ajitsuke nori, cut into shreds
4–5 dried Shiitake mushrooms, soaked in hot water for 30
minutes then cut into strips
cooked shrimps and tiger prawns
finely cut smoked trout or salmon
pickled ginger
½ cucumber, cut into julienne strips
freshly cooked peas
crab-sticks, divided into thin strands

Wash the rice under a cold tap until the water runs clear, then
drain. Place the rice in a pan with the water, kombu and sake
and bring to the boil, removing the kombu just before boiling
point is reached. Boil for 5 minutes, then cover and simmer
gently for 20 minutes until the rice has absorbed all the water.
Remove from the heat and leave to stand, covered, for a further
10 minutes (it will continue to cook in the steam). The rice
should be a sticky consistency. Mix the vinegar, sugar and salt
and pour over the rice. Stir gently with a metal spoon – do not
crush the rice or allow it to stick together. When the grains are
sufficiently cooled and evenly coated with the vinegar they
should glisten. Transfer to a round bowl, press gently to shape
the rice, then turn out on to a serving dish.

Meanwhile, to make the omelette, heat a tiny amount of oil in
a frying pan. Beat the eggs with the salt and pour into the pan,
spreading it thinly – the omelette should be about 15 cm (6
inches) in diameter. When cooked on one side, turn and cook the
other side. Transfer to a plate lined with kitchen paper and leave
to cool. Cut into very fine shreds.

Heat the dashi broth, soy sauce, mirin and a pinch each of
sugar and salt in a pan. Add the carrot and beans and cook for 2–
3 minutes, then drain.

To serve, garnish the rice with the omelette strips, carrots,
beans, nori, mushrooms, shrimps and a selection of the other
garnishes to taste.

菠
薐
草
の
お
浸
し

## Spinach Salad [Horenso no Ohitashi]

SERVES 2

This recipe is also good with young asparagus and watercress.

500 g (1 lb) young spinach
2 tablespoons concentrated dashi or chicken broth (see pages 195 and 18)
2 teaspoons light soy sauce
2 teaspoons mirin or sweet cooking sherry
2 teaspoons sesame seeds, toasted

Wash the spinach then place the wet leaves in a pan and cook for 1 minute until it has just wilted. Strain through a sieve, leaving it to drain. Place a small plate on top and press down to squeeze out any excess water. Lay the spinach on a board and cut it into even lengths, then arrange on 2 serving dishes. Mix together the dashi, soy sauce and mirin and pour on the spinach. Sprinkle with sesame seeds.

## Vegetable Tempura

野菜天麩羅

SERVES 4

Tempura cooking is simply a way of deep-frying small pieces of vegetables, fish or prawns coated in a special batter. Each bite-sized piece of vegetable or fish is dipped in a soy-mirin sauce just before eating. The secret of crisp tempura is to make sure that the ingredients are very cold. It is not possible to prepare this dish in advance because the vegetables must be freshly cooked then served immediately. Almost any ingredient can be used, as long as it is not very watery, and can be cut into large bite-sized pieces. We suggest canned or soaked Shiitake mushrooms, ordinary and sweet potatoes, carrots or beans, courgettes, onions, aubergines, pre-cooked ginko nuts, ajitsuke nori, and even basil or maple leaves. Harder ingredients such as potatoes and carrots will naturally take longer to cook.

625 g (1¼ lb) mixed vegetables (see above)
vegetable oil, for deep-frying

BATTER
1 egg
300 ml (½ pint) iced water
215 g (7½ oz) plain flour

DIPPING SAUCE
500 ml (17 fl oz) dashi broth (see page 195)
125 ml (4 fl oz) soy sauce
3 tablespoons mirin or sweet sherry
125 g (4 oz) white Chinese radish
grated root ginger (optional)

To make the batter, beat the egg with the iced water. Sift the flour into the egg mixture. Mix gently, but do not blend thoroughly. Cut the vegetables into thinnish chunks or slices. Pierce the ginko nuts, if using, and place on skewers. To make the dip, bring the dashi, soy sauce and mirin to the boil, then remove from the heat.

Heat the oil for deep-frying in a large pan, but do not let it smoke. To test if the oil is at the right temperature, throw a bamboo skew into the oil: it should bubble and start to foam and rise to the surface immediately. Dip the vegetable pieces into the batter, one at a time, then place in the oil in batches. Cook until golden brown then remove with a slotted spoon and drain on kitchen paper. Serve immediately with the dip. If frying many pieces of tempura, you will need to clean the oil by removing the little broken pieces of batter before they blacken the oil and speckle the batter. (There is an oriental flat metal sieve on a handle specifically for this purpose, but a metal tea strainer will do.)

Just before serving, finely grate the white radish. Squeeze out some of the excess liquid from the radish and ginger, then form the pulp into little cone shapes. Place them on the side of the tempura serving dish. The diners can then add as much radish or ginger to the dipping sauce as they require.

萌
し
の
胡
麻
酢
和
え

## Bean Sprout Salad [Moyashi no Gomazu-ae]

SERVES 4

It is most important that the bean sprouts are fresh, white and hard. Tired bean sprouts will completely spoil the effect of this wonderful salad.

500 ml (17 fl oz) dashi broth (see page 195)
125 ml (4 fl oz) soy sauce
3 tablespoons mirin or sweet sherry
124 g (4 oz) turnip, cut into fine julienne strips
125 g (4 oz) carrots, cut into fine julienne strips
225 g (8 oz) bean sprouts
125 g (4 oz) cucumber, cut into fine julienne strips
2 tablespoons sesame seeds, toasted

DRESSING
2 tablespoons mirin
5 tablespoons rice vinegar
5 tablespoons soy sauce
1 teaspoon sugar

Mix together the dressing ingredients. Bring the dashi, soy sauce and mirin to the boil in a pan. Add the turnip and carrots and boil for 1 minute. Add the bean sprouts. Bring back to the boil and simmer for 1 more minute. Drain and leave to cool. Mix in the cucumber then toss in the dressing and sprinkle with sesame seeds.

胡瓜の一夜漬け

## Friederike's Quick and Easy Japanese Pickle [Kyuri no Ichiya Zuke]

SERVES 4

Everyone has their own recipe for pickle, particularly as many of the proprietary pickles contain potentially harmful colourings. This is Friederike's own recipe.

1 cucumber
1 teaspoon salt
1 teaspoon sugar
3 tablespoons rice vinegar

Score the cucumber along its length on each side with a potato peeler, then slice as finely as possible. Sprinkle with salt and leave for 30 minutes. Combine the sugar and vinegar and pour on the cucumber, mixing thoroughly. Set aside for 5 minutes. Squeeze the cucumber between your hands to wring out excess water. If the salt and sugar are too strong, simply add some cold water and squeeze again.

オクラ・サラダ

## Simple Okra Salad [Okura Sarada]

SERVES 4

The important thing about this dish is that the okra must be as fresh as possible and very firm, with no blemishes or black spots on the skin.

24 okra pods
bonito flakes (the fine variety: hanakatsuo), to taste
1½ tablespoons soy sauce

Boil the okra in salted water for 5 minutes. Rinse under cold running water until cool, then drain. Cut the okra diagonally into thick slices and sprinkle with bonito flakes and soy sauce. Serve immediately.

# Desserts

Like the Chinese, the Japanese rarely serve desserts after a meal, except for finely-sliced fruits. Cakes and desserts tend to be eaten separately, perhaps at tea or mid-morning.

### Red Bean Cake [Yokan]
This cake is often served alone with tea in the Wagashi patisseries.

30 g (1¼ oz) agar agar
100 ml (3½ fl oz) water
75 g (3 oz) sugar
pinch of salt
500 g (1 lb) sweet red bean paste
1 egg white
40 g (1½ oz) gelatine

Place the agar agar in a small pan with the water and bring to the boil. Add the sugar and allow to melt, then strain carefully. Heat the solution again and add the salt, sweet bean paste, egg white and gelatine. Stir carefully. Bring to the boil once again, then pour the mixture into a square metal mould and allow to cool. When firm, cut into rectangles about 5 cm (2 inches) long and 2.5 cm (1 inch) wide.

### Red Bean Pancakes [Dorayaki]
SERVES 5

5 eggs
150 g (5 oz) sugar
75 g (3 oz) honcy
75 g (3 oz) plain flour
¾ teaspoon baking powder
vegetable oil, for brushing

FILLING
5 teaspoons sweet red bean paste
3–4 marrons glacés, chopped

Mix the eggs, sugar, honey, flour and baking powder to a smooth batter in a bowl. Lightly brush a frying pan with oil. Pour enough batter into the pan to make a small pancake, about 9 cm (3¾ inches) in diameter. Cook until light brown, turning once to brown the other side. Drain on kitchen paper and make the remaining pancakes in the same way (there should be 10 pancakes). When all the pancakes are ready, spread a little bean paste in the centre of 5 pancakes, top with a piece of marron glacé, and cover with a second pancake.

## Cheat's Macha Ice-cream
SERVES 4

This ought to be a heresy. Top-quality Japanese green tea powder, normally used exclusively for the tea ceremony, is co-opted for flavouring ice-cream.

2 tablespoons macha powder
a few drops of hot water
500 ml (17 fl oz) vanilla ice-cream

Stir the macha powder into a pasty consistency with the hot water. Partially defrost the ice-cream and mix in the macha until all the ice-cream is light green in colour. Return to the freezer until the mixture reaches normal ice-cream consistency, then serve immediately. Do not re-freeze for later, as the quality deteriorates.

# 6 Recipes from Jenny Lo's Teahouse

Ever since observing my parents opening the Ebury Street
Memories of China in the late 1970s, I have vowed never to have
anything to do with the hard labour of the Chinese restaurant
business. In 1995 Jenny had retired from a decade of running the
Memories restaurants in order to play the piano, play tennis and
dabble in Chinese therapeutic massage. I was in mid-thesis, lost
in medical manuscripts recently excavated from a Western Han
dynasty tomb, still practising a little acupuncture and raising
three children. Everything was swimming along nicely. Then
wagamama blew into our lives.

Wagamama was a phenomenon not to be missed. Bright, fast
and philanthropic, with a message that was lean, green and
successful, it seemed that wagamama was an idea whose time
had come. Outside the Japanese-style canteen in Bloomsbury,
customers were queuing to pay their respects. My parents had
been introduced to Alan Yau, the young Chinese entrepreneur
who is the brains behind wagamama, and they sought his advice
about an old property in Eccleston Street. For some years my
mother had been planning to open a noodle bar on the site of what
had been Ken Lo's Kitchen, the cookery school and shop, but
couldn't put all the pieces in place. Alan generously offered to put
the wagamama team at our disposal and his enthusiasm was
infectious. Next to my father, who had just celebrated his
eightieth birthday, it was obvious what we were missing: the
strength and certainty of youth. Father was heard muttering
Confucius: 'The youth are to be feared!'

Alan listened to our stories, our fantasies of how our own
noodle bar would be. We spoke of a soup kitchen inspired as
much by my father's love of the Confucian philosopher Mencius
as by any serious understanding of the London restaurant market.
Mencius believed in the essential goodness of humanity – a
goodness that grew in the heart and linked each person directly to
heaven. Given the right kind of nourishment people grow into
virtuous citizens. With education, good example and self-cultivation in proper measure, everyone could take their place in a
peaceful society and have confidence in being able to earn a liveli-
hood and find comfort in old age. At its most basic level father's

philosophy was founded on good, healthy, tasty food for all.

In style, we envisaged an interior that would emulate the original Memories of China restaurant in Ebury Street – a style that had popularized the early 1980s look in Chinese restaurants – whitewashed walls, grey quarry tiles and prints of Tang dynasty horses. While reducing the decoration to a minimum, our aim would be to add just enough to create a bright, elegant and welcoming atmosphere. Added to tables in the bench style pioneered by wagamama we imagined simple lattice-work wooden screens, to simulate privacy in the manner of the gaming-houses and teahouses of the early century. My mother-in-law Hilary would provide exquisite hand-thrown bowls in a natural glaze, dripped with midnight blue in the style that was current during the Tang dynasty. A new logo based on the family name in an elegant calligraphy would be our main design feature. Our waiters would be dressed simply in dark trousers and white T shirts sporting the family's old red seal.

We submitted our brief, intrigued with what they might come up with. Within a few weeks the wagamama creative crew worked up a feasibility study, bristling with designs, costings, equipment schedules, analysis of the concept, the market, the food, the development – the whole thing, including a scaled-down model of the shop complete with miniature tables and chairs and battery-operated lights. It was breathtaking. We were to be called the Teahouse, acknowledging a tradition that catered for morning and afternoon snacks, a place where the traveller could pick up a light meal including dimsum, noodles or light rice dishes.

The wagamama shock troops turned out to be six young professionals, who delivered their presentation with the efficiency and conviction of the converted. They were promoting 'post-modern consumerism', a philosophy for the consumer with integrity and a concern for people and their environment – a philosophy that would put a human face on corporate culture, a face that didn't belong to Ronald MacDonald or Colonel Saunders. Fast food was a concept to be appropriated by Zen. We were asked to shift into another dimension where food production would happen with effortless speed and grace.

Enlightenment, however, often comes with a sharp rap on the head. By the end of our meeting we were shown how grace could not be achieved without the most minute attention to detail. We were told about the project determinants, the critical path analysis, the corporate identity, the relationship of staff to turnover, the design, menu mats, the till . . . To be compatible with a fast-food operation our menu was to be standardized and limited, and there would be no booking, no smoking and value for money. No stone was left unturned. We were told we should seize the day.

The verve of the wagamama presentation filled me with a faint sense of unease. For some reason I was assailed by visions of the mounds of washing-up that habitually fill my kitchen sink, the heaps of toys, clothes and piles of books that submerge my life. Lo households are all like that. Indeed most Chinese households I know are cluttered and chaotic with the debris of life. Life itself unfolds haphazardly and business plans are conceived of in dreams and never on paper. Could we really aspire to such clarity of purpose, such perfection and attention to detail? The only thing that Jenny was ready to seize was her tennis racquet.

At times like these a higher authority should be consulted. Father, who could never cope with cash flow projections, was snoring gently in his chair. It was clear that he was not going to seize any day. In times of trouble he had always had Confucius whispering in his ear to guide him. We had never explicitly been asked to acknowledge Confucius and the implicit assumption that children are reared to look after parents. But with middle-age around the corner I had begun to feel just how great the pressure of history could be. Jenny, who was the youngest and who had lived at home for much longer than I, was more naturally prone to the whisperings of Confucius. Yet even she had broken free to develop and express her own talents. Should we return to the fold?

We could, on the other hand, be seduced by efficiency and certain success. After all, the spirit of our brief closely converged with the way proposed by wagamama. Their optimistic business plan predicted that we would do fabulously well, something we would never dare to imagine. We were sure of our own abilities. Jenny and I had eaten well and so extensively throughout our lives that we were well placed to create a simple menu distilled from the best of all of the Chinese communities.

We put the word out that we needed a chef. By Chinese standards we were not paying a magnificent salary, but it was adequate for the kind of cheap canteen style that we envisaged, and it was enough to attract young chefs who wanted to move from the floor into a management position. It was, in any case, better to find a malleable young person rather than an older chef who was resistant to interference. In general, an experienced head chef will take full charge of the kitchen and be resentful about unnecessary intrusions. We needed to develop a creative and responsive relationship. Inevitably, to achieve our purposes, there were many prejudices that had to be challenged.

The head chef at Memories sent us a twenty-three-year-old fresh-faced Vietnamese boy named Tim Diep. He had been working in a very successful Chinese buffet restaurant on the outskirts of town. It was hard to know how to evaluate him, apart from by recommendation. We gave him a try. At the wok he moved with speed, strength and confidence. Most of all he had a willing smile. Unlike the Cantonese chefs that we had been accustomed to, it seemed as if a bad Chinese word never passed his lips. He was a graduate in business studies from Imperial College and spent his spare time rearing goldfish and going to karaoke bars. Like many chefs he was over-educated, but could not match the wages of a fire chef in his field. Tim was the perfect partner for Jenny and they set about testing recipes.

We unashamedly hand-picked recipes that from experience we liked the best. For me, that meant northern family dishes: guo tie, griddled dumplings, wun tun soup, lamb and spring onions and, best of all, long-cooked pork and chestnuts. Jenny leaned towards the seafood and spicy laksa, a singaporean seafood soup available in the best Thai restaurants. Our aim was to create a menu that was broad-based, drawing inspiration from North and South China as well as South-east Asian dishes. While popularizing lesser-known dishes, such as the spicy laksa or braised bean curd with mushrooms, we would not spurn the tried and tested family favourites.

Using a mixture of classic stir-fry and soup noodles with griddled toppings we could ensure that the food would be sealed to preserve its flavour. With minimal fat and plenty of vegetables and seafood we could create a clean taste. The soup meals are also warming in the winter and cooling in the summer. They provide a substantial, filling lunch that assuages the appetite, but will still leave you fresh to go back to an afternoon's work. For more healthy appetites the wok-fried dishes provide a well-balanced and sizeable dish.

Naturally, between sisters, there were many areas of dispute. Despite wanting to be accessible to everyone we were determined not to produce any of the slop served up in the average takeaway – no sweet and sour, no MSG, no lemon curd chicken. Yet people like to recognize what they are eating and, despite decades of Chinese food, the takeaways are still in charge of educating the public. We settled on spare ribs and spring rolls to keep the children happy, although we haven't included the recipes for these here. Like seaweed, they seem to us to have all the virtue of ready-salted crisps. Singapore noodles proved more problematic. I took the view that if people really wanted curry they would chose Indian food. Jenny insisted that it made commercial sense and we agreed to disagree. Jenny and Tim came up with a recipe.

Of the many brands of noodles available in Chinatown Jenny and Tim selected five (two types of fresh egg and rice noodles and a wun tun noodle) and three rice dishes created from authentic Chinese recipes but re-interpreted to suit a contemporary London environment. Of the two fresh egg noodles, delicate Japanese ramen are served in the soup noodle, while the thicker Chinese hand-pulled noodles are wok-fried with seasonal vegetables or seafood in a black bean sauce. River noodles, the broad, flat, rice noodle normally only served to the discerning Chinese staff, are tossed with beef or chicken, peppers and sesame to create an unforgettable dish. The rice stick noodles are reserved for the Singapore dishes and the fresh wun tun noodles for the wun tun soup.

We were to be one of a handful of establishments which does not add MSG. Tim raised his eyebrows but looked compliant. The sensibilities of the migraine or allergy societies are a mystery to oriental chefs. Regardless of whether it is takeaway or Chinese haute cuisine, MSG is the taste of Chinese food. To our mind, apart from doubling the harmful effects of the salt and inducing all kinds of allergic response, MSG gives Chinese food that awful sameness, like the brown sludge. When it is not there people notice immediately – the food is quite likely to taste bland. But that is precisely the challenge. The most immediate response is to increase the salt and sugar, but we were determined to be more creative. Instead of using artificial substitutes Tim could select traditional ingredients to make the stocks savoury, and prepare a fresh vegetarian stock daily from Chinese radish. Basing our interpretations on an understanding of ancient Chinese food combinations the Teahouse could carefully balance Yin and Yang in the variety of foods offered on the menu. From the light and cooling nun's vegetable soup to the rich and succulent long-cooked pork with chestnuts, a purposefully short and simple menu could cater for every taste.

Accompanying the dishes we decided to serve a range of green and red teas, including the famous 'Iron Goddess of Mercy' Wulong, best served hot and black on warm afternoons or after an evening meal. All the Teahouse teas come from around Fujian province, the ancestral home of the Lo family. Jasmine, our most famous, is a fragrant tea, light in colour and best drunk weak without milk or lemon. It is low in caffeine and therefore suitable as an evening drink. Jasmine is a green tea flavoured with the freshly picked jasmine flowers that the mountain women of Fujian wear in their hair in springtime. It is famous as a digestive after a large meal, lunch or dinner. The *British Medical Journal* recently published a Japanese study suggesting that green tea might help prevent cardiovascular disease, liver disorders and possibly cancer. Chinese green is a more delicate tea than Japanese green teas, with the lowest caffeine content of all teas. It comes from the neighbouring province, Zhejiang. The straw-coloured liquor with its thirst-quenching properties make it an ideal tea for a hot day. It is good after an evening meal and will never keep you awake.

We specially commissioned a qualified Chinese herbalist, my friend and colleague, Xu Guang, to design teas to fortify and cleanse the body. Our long-life tea has special properties to revitalize the elderly and weary. It is blended from wolfberry, red root salvia and liquorice which will stimulate your Qi (see page 187), strengthen the kidneys and detoxify the blood. Long-life is the tea most frequently chosen by men. Perhaps they are sensitive to the fact that their life span is shorter than women's. Women choose Guang's cleansing tea which is blended from lotus leaf, hawthorn berries and liquorice. This combination is said to tone the Qi and calm the nerves, while also reducing cholesterol. We also offer a tisane of chrysanthemum which is light and cooling and particularly good for conditioning the skin. Fresh mint steeped in China tea is famous as an invigorating digestive tea. We have created a tea for every taste!

Within a month or so we had had many favourable reviews. Some of them were glowing in their appraisal. It was a great accolade for Jenny and Tim's preparation. They were particularly praised for the laksa, which was a very individual adaptation of the Singapore soup. Gourmets tended to appreciate the long-cooked pork and chestnuts, and everyone raved about the black bean seafood. Ironically, we sold more Singapore noodles than anything else. Jenny and Tim were triumphant. The only criticism made was that we had cashed-in on the ramen craze and copied wagamama! True, we do like Chinese egg noodles!

It was Tim who gave me the idea of fish. I had been unsuccessfully looking for an image of the Kitchen God. It had occurred to me that the Lo incompetence at business might have more to do with failing to satisfy the gods rather than cash flow forecasts. Fish, the chefs said, were necessary to get the fengshui right. The skill of fengshui, literally wind and water, determines how auspicious the layout of a building is, and can indicate whether any design feature interrupts the flow of Qi and therefore the success of the enterprise. Fish, five fish to be precise, would be good for business. Tim and I spent a very pleasant Sunday with the children buying the fish tank and all the necessary accoutrements to make the fengshui work. The next day I bought five glorious goldfish, some with fins, some more golden, some more white than gold, and one prize one with flourishing fins which we called Jenny. The minor fish we called after the chefs and the waiting staff. They looked beautiful and brought a tranquil lazy kind of movement to the empty space.

Both Jenny and I were keen to learn how to toss the wok and to do so fast enough to be useful in the kitchen. Core activity in the restaurant revolves around the fire. We wanted to share the thrill when the oil catches light and the flame leaps high and licks the canopy, but were soon to find out that the space in front of the wok is reserved for the boys. A real chef will have three or four rings and a turbo-fired jet to enhance his speed and performance. I have only known two women who dared to invade that space, but they are the rare kind that tend to be labelled dragon queens.

The wok stands in a ring beneath which the gas jets pump a flame that is never equalled in domestic cookers. By tipping the wok and drawing it towards the body and then thrusting it forward again, all the contents of the wok spin into the air and fold over on themselves. In the other hand a heavy iron spoon completes the action, flipping the food over. It works the left bicep and the forearm in a way never experienced before. Jenny and I pride ourselves on how many boxes of wine we can carry down the stairs to the cellars, but the combination of strength and movement soon defeated us. And then it's not easy to get a second try. Even the sweetest Vietnamese chef will stand by, patronizingly ready to snatch the wok from your hands and demonstrate the smooth action that you will never master.

You have to watch carefully from the sidelines and attempt to embody the movement in your imagination. Then wait for a rogue order and slip into the space in front of the fire while the chef is looking for something in the cellar. That way you have time to practise in peace. It isn't simply controlling the fire and the wrist action, so that the food cooks quickly and does not burn. It is also important to gain an understanding of how to mix the many flavours at great speed in order not to produce 'brown sludge' in every dish. On a shelf above the wok cooker the essential ingredients for stir-frying are lined up in stainless steel bowls: light and dark soy, sugar, salt, oyster sauce, chilli, hoisin, sesame, flour, crushed ginger and garlic. It takes time and a intuitive memory to get the right combinations for each dish.

Now we have had some time to practise stir-frying we are both doing very well, although the chefs, always keen to fan family feuds, say that Jenny is by far the best at it. We continue to learn new tricks every day. Thanks to wagamama Jenny and I have a beautiful teahouse, one which we have grown into and continue to mould and shape to reflect our perception of the best of the teahouse tradition. For our regular customers who describe our food as 'comfort food' we are developing a menu of the kind of therapeutic foods described in Chapter 4. We hope to bring them an even greater sense of well-being. In this chapter we have adapted the recipes from our original menu for the domestic kitchen and trust that they will bring delight and comfort to our readers as well.

# Vegetable and Vegetarian Dishes

酸
菜
## Pickle
SERVES 4

This pickle can be served as a starter, but it can equally well be eaten along with a main dish.

500 g (1 lb) carrots, very thinly sliced into rounds
500 g (1 lb) Chinese radish, very thinly sliced into rounds
2 teaspoons salt
1 clove garlic, crushed and finely chopped
1 red chilli, finely chopped
25 ml (1 fl oz) fish sauce (optional)
200 ml (7 fl oz) rice vinegar or malt vinegar
100 g (3½ oz) sugar
800 ml (1¼ pints) water

Sprinkle the carrots and radish with the salt and leave for 30 minutes until the vegetables become soft. Rinse thoroughly, then pat dry on kitchen paper. Mix all the pickling ingredients together and pour over the vegetables. Leave to pickle for 1 hour. The pickle will keep for up to 1 week in the refrigerator.

## Seaweed

干
貝
鬆

SERVES 5–6

This dish, as you are about to find out, is one of the most
popular swindles in Chinese restaurants in England! Seaweed
does not feature in Chinese cookery so much as it does in Japan,
and the name disguises the fact that the dark green clump on the
plate is actually cabbage. We have included it on account of its
popularity and low cost. It is also ecological: you can use all the
outer leaves of greens and cabbage that are normally discarded.
There is something compulsive about eating this seaweed, like
crisps or peanuts. Watch out, the children soon become
addicted! In most Chinese restaurants the dish is liberally
sprinkled with MSG, which gives it the characteristic dry and
savoury taste. We prefer to use dried fish wool (ground dried
fish), which is available in good Chinese supermarkets, but as all
but one brand of the wool also contain MSG, we have included a
recipe for nut topping that our chef often uses.

1 kg (2 lb) spring greens.
vegetable oil, for deep-frying
1½ teaspoons caster sugar
½ teaspoon salt

ALTERNATIVE TOPPING
1 tablespoon roasted peanuts
1 tablespoon roasted soya beans
sesame seeds, to taste
sugar, to taste

Pull apart all the outer leaves of the spring greens and wash
thoroughly. Take 1 leaf and lay another on top of it with the
stalks over-laid. Repeat until there are about 4 leaves piled up
with the ends of the stalks slightly staggered. Make 2 slanting
cuts through the pile on either side of the light-coloured, thick
stalk of the leaves. Discard the stalks. Make sure not to leave
thick veins – only the dark green soft leaf is required. Fold the
remaining pile of greens in half lengthways and roll tightly from

one end. Shave one end off the roll so that it is cut evenly. Now cut as finely as possible with a very sharp knife, so that the leaf falls away in long, fine shreds. Repeat with the remaining leaves. Place in a colander and leave until completely dry. If there is any liquid left on the leaf it will sizzle and spit in the oil.

Heat the oil in a wok until smoking, then remove from the heat and add the greens in small batches. Stir and return the wok to the heat. Stir for 2½ minutes, or until the greens become dark and crispy. Because the greens are so fine they burn easily, so be careful not to cook them for too long. Remove and drain in a colander to remove excess oil.

Scatter the sugar and salt on top. To make the alternative topping, grind together the roast peanuts and soya beans. Add sesame seeds and sugar to taste, and sprinkle over the seaweed.

茶
葉
蛋

## Tea Eggs

SERVES 6

Tea eggs are the perfect convenience food. They are sold all over
China and often can be seen on street corners floating in vats
full of tea. They turn the plain hard-boiled egg into a delicacy.
The tea will lightly flavour the egg. You can vary the brand, but
it is advisable to choose a fairly strong tasting tea. Eat them
alone, sliced as a garnish, or as a starter on a mixed platter with,
for example, pickles and jellyfish.

6 free-range eggs or 12 quails' eggs
2 tablespoons of any black tea
500 ml (17 fl oz) water

Hard-boil the eggs for 10 minutes. Lightly crack the shells
between the backs of 2 spoons, but do not remove the shell. Boil
the tea leaves in the water and simmer for 5 minutes until it is
strong and dark. Immerse the eggs in the tea until the tea cools.
When the shell is removed the surface of the egg will be marbled
.where the tea has seeped through the cracks.

## 髮菜腐竹 Hair Vegetable and Bean Curd Skins

SERVES 4

Facai (literally 'hair vegetable') is often served as an auspicious dish at the New Year festival. Facai, which also can mean 'make a fortune', is one of those homonyms which Chinese love to amuse themselves with. We made a lot of this dish for our vegetarian friends last New Year in the hope that it would also bring us prosperity! Begin the day before, as the bean curd skins have to be soaked overnight after deep-frying.

vegetable oil, for deep-frying
4 bean curd skins or sticks
8 dried Chinese mushrooms, soaked in hot water for 30 minutes
2 slices root ginger, finely chopped
1 clove garlic, crushed and finely chopped
2 tablespoons oyster sauce
2 tablespoons mushroom soy sauce
1 tablespoon light soy sauce
1 tablespoon Shaoxing wine
1 teaspoon sugar
2 teaspoons sesame oil
250 ml (8 fl oz) stock (see page 18)
25 g (1 oz) facai hair vegetable, rinsed and drained

Heat the oil in a wok until it is almost smoking. Deep-fry the bean curd skins for 15 seconds until they expand. Be careful not to burn them. The deep frying seals the bean curds so that they do not over-cook or fall apart. Remove with a slotted spoon, then place in a bowl of water and leave to soak overnight.

Drain the mushrooms, discard the hard stems and slice each cap into 3 pieces. Mix the ginger with the garlic, oyster sauce, mushroom soy, light soy, wine, sugar and sesame oil.

Heat a tablespoon of the oil in a casserole and stir-fry the mushrooms for 30 seconds. Add garlic, ginger and soy mixture and the stock. Bring to the boil and then simmer for 10 minutes. Add the bean curd and facai and continue to simmer for 5 minutes, stirring gently. If the sauce dries quickly add a little stock.

## Nun's Vegetable Soup

僧
女
菜
麵
湯

SERVES 4

Light and cooling, this soup is both refreshing and easy on the digestion. As the stock is a dominant feature of the dish, it is essential that you prepare it yourself (see pages 18–19). Although this dish essentially employs the chop suey method of cooking, it is as well to know how to do it. You can apply this widely used and versatile method to any vegetables that are left at the end of the week. Avoid over-cooking.

2 tablespoons vegetable oil
2 cloves garlic, crushed and finely chopped
1 cm (½ inch) piece of root ginger, finely chopped
50 g (2 oz) carrot, sliced lengthways
50 g (2 oz) onion, sliced
75 g (3 oz) mangetout
½ red pepper, cored, seeded and finely sliced
½ green pepper, cored, seeded and finely sliced
125 g (4 oz) bean sprouts
25 g (1 oz) sliced bamboo shoots
25 g (1 oz) sliced water chestnuts
400 ml (14 fl oz) vegetable stock (see page 19) per person
pinch of salt
½ teaspoon white pepper
pinch of sugar
1 tablespoon light soy sauce
1 tablespoon vegetarian oyster sauce (see page 267)
1 tablespoon sesame oil
1 tablespoon Shaoxing wine
125 g (4 oz) fresh egg noodles or ramen per person
chopped coriander, to garnish

Heat the oil in a wide heavy frying pan. When it begins to smoke add the garlic, ginger and all the vegetables and turn in the oil for 30 seconds. Add 2 tablespoons of the stock, the salt, pepper, sugar, light soy sauce and vegetarian oyster sauce and stir-fry together for a couple of minutes. Finally add the sesame oil and wine. Turn together for another 30 seconds.

Meanwhile, heat the stock and cook the egg noodles for 1 minute. Drain and rinse the the noodles under cold running water. Return to the boiling stock for a few seconds, then drain. Divide the noodles between large soup bowls. Pour on the stock. Arrange the vegetables on the surface of the soup. Garnish with coriander.

鼓
山
菜
炒
麵

## Drum Mountain Vegetable Noodles

SERVES 2

Drum Mountain towers above the city of Fuzhou. On the summit is the famous Drum Mountain Buddhist monastery, and nearby is the Lo summerhouse where our father would spend the summers of his youth playing tennis. His step-granny, on the other hand, was to be found gold-leafing the Buddha in the temple. Our dish celebrates their memories of Drum Mountain.

1 tablespoon vegetable oil
2 cloves garlic, crushed
1 cm (½ inch) piece of root ginger, finely chopped
50 g (2 oz) carrot, sliced lengthways
½ Spanish onion, sliced
50 g (2 oz) mangetout
50 g (2 oz) red pepper, cored, seeded and thinly sliced
50 g (2 oz) green pepper, cored, seeded and thinly sliced
1 handful of bean sprouts
25 g (1 oz) sliced bamboo shoots
25 g (1 oz) sliced water chestnuts
2 tablespoons vegetable or chicken stock (see pages 18–19)
pinch of salt
pinch of pepper
pinch of sugar
½ tablespoon light soy sauce
1 tablespoon vegetarian oyster sauce (see page 267)
500 g (1 lb) oil noodles
½ tablespoon sesame oil
½ tablespoon Shaoxing wine

Heat the oil, swirling it around in a wide heavy frying pan. When it begins to smoke add the garlic, ginger and all the vegetables and turn in the oil for 30 seconds. Add the stock, salt, pepper, sugar, light soy sauce, vegetarian oyster sauce and the noodles and stir-fry together for a couple of minutes. Finally add the sesame oil and Shaoxing wine. Turn together for another 30 seconds and serve.

## 紅燒冬菇豆腐　Braised Bean Curd and Mushrooms

SERVES 4–5

This is a really substantial, savoury dish. Deep-frying the bean curd makes it crispy, a quality it retains throughout the cooking. The carrot and mangetout are optional, but do make the dish more attractive.

vegetable oil, for deep-frying
20 pieces of bean curd 2.5 cm (1 inch) square
10 large dried Chinese mushrooms, soaked in hot water for 30 minutes
3 tablespoons vegetable oil
6 cloves garlic, crushed and finely chopped
½ medium Spanish onion, finely sliced
1 small carrot, finely sliced
50 g (2 oz) mangetout
200 ml (7 fl oz) hot vegetarian stock (see page 19)
1 tablespoon dark soy sauce
1 tablespoon vegetarian oyster sauce (see page 267)
pinch of pepper
1 tablespoon Shaoxing wine
1 teaspoon sesame oil
1 teaspoon cornflour blended with water

Heat the oil for deep-frying in a pan until it begins to smoke. Add the bean curd and deep-fry for about 10 minutes, or until it turns golden brown. Remove with a slotted spoon and set aside. Drain the Chinese mushrooms, discard the tough stalks then slice the caps roughly.

Heat the 3 tablespoons of vegetable oil in a wok until it begins to smoke. Add the garlic, onion, mushrooms and vegetables. Add the stock and put in the bean curd. Flavour with the soy and oyster sauces. Bring to the boil, turning continuously, and then simmer and reduce for 2 minutes until the sauce thickens a little. Add the pepper, wine and sesame oil and turn for a few more seconds. Stir in the blended cornflour to thicken the sauce. Serve with rice.

# Meat Dishes and Seafood Dishes

雞
片
榨
菜
麵
湯

## Chicken Soup Noodles

Judging by the sales at the Teahouse this is certainly our customers' favourite clear soup. It exudes the lean, clean and green philosophy without being insipid. The strong flavours of the pickle contrast with the plain whiteness of the chicken. It is light and easy to digest while still providing a substantial meal.

PER PORTION
3 dried Chinese mushrooms, soaked in hot water for 30 minutes
125 g (4 oz) boned chicken breast, cut across the grain into strips 2.5cm (1 inch) long
400 ml (14 fl oz) chicken stock (see page 18)
½ tablespoon vegetable oil
handful of pickled cabbage
white pepper, to taste
125 g (4 oz) fresh egg noodles

MARINADE
1 teaspoon sesame oil
½ teaspoon cornflour
½ teaspoon sugar
1 teaspoon Shaoxing wine
pinch of pepper
pinch of salt

Drain the mushrooms, discard the hard stalks and cut the cap into thin slices. Rub the chicken with the marinade ingredients and leave for 15 minutes. Heat the stock.

Heat the oil in a wide heavy frying pan. Add the chicken and press down with a spatula. Cook until golden brown then turn and repeat. Make sure the chicken is cooked in the centre. Meanwhile, put the mushrooms and cabbage on the other side of the pan to cook. Keep turning to heat every side. Sprinkle liberally with pepper. Boil the egg noodles for 1 minute, then drain and rinse under cold water. Return to the boiling water for a few seconds and drain. Place the noodles in a large soup bowl and pour on the hot stock. Arrange the chicken, mushroom and pickle on the top of the soup.

雲
吞
湯
麵

## Wun Tun Noodle Soup

This dish got off to a slow start, but our customers are getting to know it, slowly but surely. So long as you buy the wun tun skins, which are widely available in Chinese supermarkets, it is not difficult to make at home. Then you can put the family to work filling them: it is worth making a large quantity, and keeping any extra wun tuns in the freezer. As teenagers, starting a night out on the town in central London, we would frequently be driven into Soho by a craving for wun tun soup. It would warm and fill the belly just enough to sustain us through the film or the club until the last stop in Brick Lane for hot bagels in the early hours of Sunday morning. The quality of wun tun varies from chef to chef, but once you get the wun tun noodle soup bug nothing else will do.

PER PORTION
125 g (4 oz) fresh wun tun noodles
small handful of spinach or bak choy
400 ml (14 fl oz) chicken stock (see page 18)
chopped spring onions and coriander leaves, to garnish
chilli sauce, to serve

FILLING FOR 100 WUN TUN SKINS (ALLOW 5 PER PERSON)
4–5 dried Chinese mushrooms, soaked in hot water for 30 minutes
5 wood ears, soaked in hot water for 30 minutes
6 water chestnuts, finely chopped
6 strips of bamboo shoots, finely chopped
2 tablespoons chopped Chinese chives or spring onion
500 g (1 lb) minced pork, not too lean
200 g (7 oz) roughly chopped prawns
3 teaspoons sesame oil
1 tablespoon Shaoxing wine
½ teaspoon sugar
2 teaspoons salt
2 teaspoons pepper
2 teaspoons cornflour
1 beaten egg white

*Laksa* (p. 257)

Drain the mushrooms and wood ears, discard the tough stalks, then finely chop the mushroom caps and wood ears. Place in a bowl with the water chestnuts, bamboo shoots, chives, pork and prawns. Add the sesame oil, wine, sugar, salt, pepper, cornflour and egg white and mix thoroughly.

Place a teaspoon of the stuffing in the centre of the wun tun skin. Wet the edges and press together making a triangle. Take the 2 corners of the fold and bring them together again, pressing and sticking them with a little water. If you have made extra wun tuns these can be frozen. Allow 5 wun tun for each person and simmer in boiling water for 10 minutes, then drain.

Meanwhile, boil a pan of water and simmer the wun tun noodles for 2 minutes, then drain. Blanch the spinach or bak choy. Heat the stock. Put the noodles in the bottom of a large soup bowl and pour over the stock. Arrange the spinach and wun tun on top. Garnish to taste with spring onions and coriander and serve with a dip of chilli sauce.

Optional: Add a drop of sesame oil, red vinegar and a pinch of pepper just before serving.

烤
鴨
麵
湯

## Duck Soup

SERVES 4

A duck stock will often be served as the final touch to a meal of Peking duck, when every other part of the duck has been consumed. Our duck soup is more substantial and combines all the best ingredients of the banquet in one dish!

2 boned duck breasts
½ teaspoon salt
1 teaspoon five-spice powder
2 cloves garlic, finely chopped
4 cm (1¾ inch) piece of root ginger, finely chopped
1.5 litres (2½ pints) chicken or duck stock (see page 18)
4 handfuls spinach or bak choy
500 g (1 lb) fresh egg noodles
finely chopped spring onions, to garnish

Place the duck in a shallow dish and sprinkle with the salt, five-spice powder, garlic and ginger. Turn to coat then leave to marinate overnight. Preheat the oven to 120°C, 250°F, Gas 1.

Roast the duck in the preheated oven for 30–40 minutes, until the skin has browned. Slice the breasts thinly.

Meanwhile, heat the stock and blanch the spinach. Boil the egg noodles for 1 minute, remove and rinse under cold running water, then replace in the boiling water for a few seconds. Drain and place in large soup bowls. Pour on the hot stock. Arrange the spinach and duck on top of the soup. Garnish with spring onion.

辣
牛
湯
河

## Chilli Beef Soup with River Noodles

SERVES 2

225 g (8 oz) rump or sirloin steak, sliced finely across the grain
2 cloves garlic, crushed
pinch of salt
pinch of pepper
pinch of sugar
1 teaspoon sesame oil
1 teaspoon chilli bean paste, or to taste
3 dried Chinese mushrooms, soaked in hot water for 30 minutes
½ tablespoon vegetable oil
40 g (1½ oz) mangetout
½ small red pepper, cored, seeded and finely sliced lengthways
½ small green pepper, cored, seeded and finely sliced lengthways
40 g (1½ oz) Spanish onion, finely sliced
25 g (1 oz) carrots, finely sliced
25 g sliced bamboo shoots
25 g sliced water chestnts
40 g (1½ oz) bean sprouts
400 g (14 oz) fresh river noodles (hofun)
750 ml (1¼ pints) hot beef stock
sesame oil and chopped chillies, to garnish

Place the beef in a shallow dish with the garlic, salt, pepper,
sugar, sesame oil and chilli bean paste. Turn to coat and leave to
marinate overnight in the refrigerator. Drain the mushrooms,
discard the hard stems and slice the caps.

Heat the oil in a wide heavy frying pan. Add the beef slices
and press down with a spatula. Cook until the meat has changed
colour and is slightly browned on both sides, or to taste. Blanch
all the vegetables for a minute. Blanch the noodles for a few
seconds until they separate when shaken with chopsticks, then
drain. Place the noodles in a large bowl and arrange the
vegetables and beef on top. Pour over the stock. Sprinkle with
sesame oil and chillies.

栗
子
煨
豬
肉

## Long-cooked Belly of Pork with Chestnuts

SERVES 4

This dish is very high in saturated fat and should be avoided if you worry about putting on weight. Nevertheless it remains our favourite dish and the one that most evokes our father's home cooking. There was nothing so warming as to come home hungry on a cold winter's day to a big bowl of rice and long-cooked belly of pork. People either love or hate it. In the Teahouse we often get the dish returned by those who have us singled out as a health-food restaurant and are horrified by the fatty meat, but others come back time and again for more. Even health-conscious acupuncturist colleagues will scrape the dish clean. In ancient China fatty meat was a sign of wealth, as it indicated that the household had enough money to feed the livestock well. For those of us who tend toward indulgence the fat of this belly of pork, unlike the equivalent English dishes, becomes steeped in the meat juices and the sweet and savoury flavour of chestnut and soy, producing a succulence that is hard to equal.

20 dried chestnuts, soaked overnight, or canned, added towards the end of cooking
500 g (1 lb) belly of pork, sliced into 2.5cm (1 inch) wide strips
1 litre (1¾ pints) water
1 tablespoon of dark soy sauce
1 tablespoon whole five-spice
750 ml (1¼ pints) stock (see page 18)
½ tablespoon sugar
1 tablespoon Shaoxing wine

Drain the chestnuts, then boil in fresh water for 20 minutes.

Fry the pork gently in a casserole in its own fat until it browns a little on each side. Add the water, bring to the boil and simmer for 20 minutes. Drain off the water then add all the other ingredients and bring back to the boil. Preheat the oven to 160°C, 325°F, Gas 3.

Place the casserole in the oven and stew gently for 1½ –2

hours or more. Check from time to time and add a little water if the liquid seems to have reduced too much. If the dish is too liquid at the end, reduce quickly over a high heat – not for too long or the meat will disintegrate. The meat should be so tender that it melts in your mouth while the chestnuts, in contrast, should be soft but still firm.

## Hair Vegetable and Triple-cooked Pork

髮
菜
煨
豬
肉

SERVES 4

One more of our New Year dishes involves a delicious way to cook belly of pork. It combines a crispy skin with a rich, dark flavour. The purpose of pre-boiling and deep-frying is to remove much of the fat, while making the skin crisp.

8 dried Chinese mushrooms, soaked in hot water for 30 minutes
500 g (1 lb) lean belly of pork, cut into 10 x 5 cm (4 x 2 inch) chunks
1 litre (1¾ pints) water
2 slices root ginger, finely chopped
1 clove garlic, crushed and finely chopped
2 teaspoons whole five-spice
1 teaspoon Sichuan peppercorns
4 heads of star anise
4 tablespoons mushroom soy sauce
2 tablespoons hoisin sauce
2 tablespoons Shaoxing wine
vegetable oil, for deep-frying
2 tablespoons oyster sauce
1 teaspoon light soy sauce
2 teaspoons sesame oil
½ teaspoon salt
1 teaspoon sugar
25 g (1 oz) hair vegetable, washed and drained

Drain the mushrooms, discard the hard stems and cut the caps into 3 pieces. Place the meat in a pan with the water. Add the ginger, garlic, whole five-spice, Sichuan peppercorns, star anise, 2 tablespoons of the mushroom soy, the hoisin sauce and 1 tablespoon of wine. Bring to the boil and cook for 40 minutes, reducing the liquid. Drain the meat and leave to cool, reserving the liquid.

Heat the oil in a wok. Deep-fry the meat over a low temperature for 5 minutes. Be careful not to let it burn. Remove the meat with a slotted spoon and leave on kitchen paper to drain and cool. Cut the meat into thick slices. Heat a tablespoon of the oil in a casserole and stir-fry the mushrooms for 30 seconds. Add the oyster sauce, remaining mushroom soy and the light soy sauce, the remaining wine, the sesame oil, salt and sugar. Add the reserved liquid and bring to the boil. Turn down the heat and simmer for 10 minutes. Then add the hair vegetable and continue to simmer for 5 minutes, stirring gently.

豆
豉
海
鮮
拉
麵

## Black Bean Seafood

SERVES 2

This is the dish that our father's dreams were made of. After Singapore noodles, it must be the most popular dish in the Teahouse, favoured by our more discerning customers. The juxtaposition of the fresh-tasting seafood, the strong savouriness of the black bean and the substantial egg noodles gives a taste and texture full of vibrant contrast. Black beans come tinned or in packets. The packets are preferable as they do not have any additional ingredients. Before use they should be soaked in hot water for 10 minutes. Drain and discard the water.

1 squid
vegetable oil, for deep-frying
8 tiger prawns, shelled and deveined
3 cloves garlic, crushed
a little fresh chilli
3–4 tablespoons black beans, soaked and drained
125 g (4 oz) Spanish onion, finely sliced
½ red pepper, cored, seeded and finely sliced
½ green pepper, cored, seeded and finely sliced
15 small cooked mussels
½ tablespoon dark soy sauce
2 tablespoons oyster sauce
1 teaspoon sugar
500 g (1 lb) oil noodles
2 tablespoons Shaoxing wine or dry sherry
2 teaspoons sesame oil

Cut the squid in half and score diagonally on the inside to make a diamond pattern. Then cut into small pieces about 2.5 cm (1 inch) square.

Heat the oil in a wok until almost smoking. Stir-fry the prawns and squid together for 30 seconds. Remove the seafood with a slotted spoon and pour off the oil, leaving 1 tablespoon. Add the garlic, chilli and the black beans and turn together for 30 seconds. Add the onion, peppers and mussels, soy sauce, oyster sauce, sugar and noodles. Return the seafood to the pan. Mix thoroughly and stir-fry for 3 minutes. Add the wine and sesame oil and turn together for another 30 seconds. Serve immediately.

叉
燒
蜜
肉

## Honey Roast Pork

One of the cheapest dishes at the Teahouse is the fresh noodle soup garnished with spinach or bak choy and cha shao. Cha shao is an old favourite much favoured in Chinese restaurants in England. Children also find it very tasty, but most westerners are unaware how versatile it is. It can be served on its own, stir-fried with noodles or vegetables topped with nuts, or even cold in a mixed platter for starters. This recipe will not produce pork as red as that served in most restaurants as we do not use chemical colourants.

500 g (1 lb) pork fillet, cut into 2 pieces about 18 x 6 cm (7 x 2½ inch)

MARINADE
2 cloves garlic, crushed and finely chopped
1 cm (½ inch) piece of root ginger, finely chopped
1 tablespoon dark soy sauce
1 tablespoon yellow bean paste
2 tablespoons hoisin sauce
1 tablespoon sugar
1½ tablespoons vegetable oil
1 teaspoon red bean cheese
2 tablespoons clear honey
1 teaspoon five-spice powder

PER PORTION OF NOODLE SOUP
400 ml (14 fl oz) vegetable stock (see page 19)
small handful of spinach or bak choy
125 g (4 oz) fresh egg noodles
5 slices cha shao pork
chopped spring onions, to garnish

Place the pork in a shallow dish. Mix all the ingredients for the marinade in a bowl and then rub on to the meat. Leave to marinate for at least 2 hours and preferably overnight.

Preheat the oven to 220°C, 425°F, Gas 7. Place the pork on a wire rack over a roasting tin filled with 2.5 cm (1 inch) of water to catch the drips, and roast for 15 minutes. Turn the meat over, reduce the heat to 180°C, 350°F, Gas 4 and roast for another 30 minutes. Remove the pork and cut across the grain into thin slices. The meat should be framed in dark brown which contrasts appealingly with the lightly roasted colour of the inside.

To make the soup, heat the stock and blanch the spinach. Boil the egg noodles for 30 seconds, drain and place in a large soup bowl. Pour on the hot stock. Arrange the spinach and pork on the top of the soup. Garnish with chopped spring onions.

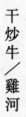

## Beef or Chicken River Noodles

SERVES 2

River noodles or hofun are the noodles that you will see the staff
of Chinese restaurants eating for their meals. They are rarely
offered to the public on account of their gooey consistency, but
after decades of Chinese food we feel that westerners are now
ready to appreciate their sensuous delights! For those on non-
wheat diets they are a real boon.

300 g (10 oz) lean beef or chicken, thinly sliced and cut into 5 cm
(2 inch) squares
½ teaspoon salt
pinch of pepper
5 tablespoons vegetable oil
500 g (1 lb) fresh river noodles or 225 g (8 oz) dried noodles
½ tablespoon finely chopped root ginger
½ small green pepper, cored, seeded and cut into fine strips
½ small red pepper, cored, seeded and cut into fine strips
½ Spanish onion, finely sliced
1 teaspoon chilli sauce
½ tablespoon dark soy sauce
½ tablespoon light soy sauce
1 tablespoon oyster sauce
1 tablespoon Shaoxing wine
½ tablespoon sesame oil
sesame seeds

Rub the meat with the salt, pepper and ½ teaspoon of oil. If
using dried hofun, parboil them for 7–8 minutes, or according to
the packet instructions. Drain, then soak the noodles in cold
water to prevent sticking. If using fresh you can use them
without pre-cooking, although the stir-frying takes a little
longer. (In the restaurant we put them in the microwave for 2
minutes, then they simply need to be heated and turned in the
wok for a few minutes in the final assembly.)

Heat the remaining oil in a wok over a high heat until it just
begins to smoke. Add the meat and stir-fry for 10 seconds, then

turn down the heat and stir-fry until the meat changes colour. Immediately pour off the oil, leaving 1 tablespoon. Remove the meat and reserve. Add the ginger, all of the vegetables, the chilli sauce, soy sauces, oyster sauce and the fresh or par-cooked noodles to the pan. Turn up the heat as high as possible, turning the mixture together for 1 minute (longer if using fresh noodles which have not been put through the microwave). The noodles will tend to stick together and adhere to the pan. Beat gently with the back of the wok ladle and keep them moving, although not too vigorously as the noodles may break. If the mixture is too dry and keeps sticking add a little more oil. Return the meat to the pan, add the wine and sesame oil and stir for another minute. Turn out on to a dish and sprinkle with sesame seeds.

# Singapore-style Dishes

In Singapore, roadside cafés and small and elegant restaurants alike give you three choices when ordering noodles – wet, dry or soup. Wet means that the noodles will arrive with the meat or vegetables of your choice, covered in a sauce or gravy. Dry means precisely that, that they are stir-fried without a wet sauce. Soup noodles are soup noodles, but as you will see, they are very distinctive! Unlike Chinese dishes, where the flavours tend to be mixed on the spot, the Singapore flavours are prepared in advance by boiling the spices in oil to create a paste. The paste should last two weeks if kept in a jar in the refrigerator. It is a very convenient way of serving up fantastic meals in seconds.

新
加
坡
鮮
辣
湯

## Laksa

SERVES 2

This dish is normally known as 'Singapore Laksa', one of the soup noodles. Tim and Jenny have created a lighter distinctive version, but as it is not entirely authentic we dare not call ours 'Singapore'. The curry powder has to be the golden Malaysian variety: nothing else will do.

LAKSA PASTE

(makes enough for 10 soups. Store in the refrigerator in an airtight container. It will keep for up to 2 weeks)
8 cm (3½ inch) piece of root ginger, finely chopped
3 stalks fresh lemon grass, finely chopped
3 red chillies, finely chopped
2 tablespoons plain flour
1 tablespoon Malaysian curry powder
3 tablespoons ground coriander
1 tablespoon turmeric
1 tablespoon paprika
1 teaspoon chilli powder
175 ml (6 fl oz) vegetable oil
1 small Spanish onion,chopped
3 cloves garlic, crushed and finely chopped
2 tablespoons dried shrimps, ground with a pestle and mortar
2 tablespoons balachan (shrimp paste), finely chopped

Place the ginger, lemon grass and chillies in a food processor and process until pulped. Mix together the flour, curry powder, coriander, turmeric, paprika and chilli powder.

Heat the oil gently in a wok, add the onion, garlic and the pulped ginger mixture and stir-fry over the lowest possible heat. Add the dried shrimps and balachan and stir-fry for about 20 minutes, stirring continuously. If the mixture begins to burn the heat is too high. Finally add the powdered spices mixture and stir thoroughly into the oil.

Pour the mixture into a container and leave to cool. Store in the refrigerator in an airtight container (it will keep for up to 2 weeks).

## Laksa

SERVES 2

1 squid, cleaned and halved
300 g (10 oz) rice stick noodles
2.5 cm (1 inch) cube of deep-fried bean curd (see page 261),
halved diagonally
3–4 tablespoons Laksa paste (see previous page)
600 ml (1 pint) chicken or vegetable stock (see page 18)
¼ teaspoon salt
½ teaspoon sugar
3 tablespoons coconut milk
½ teaspoon fish sauce
8 tiger prawns, shelled and deveined
15 small cooked mussels
handful of bean sprouts
sprig of Thai mint or coriander

Open out the squid and score with diagonal lines on the inside
to make a diamond pattern. Then cut into small pieces about 2.5
cm (1 inch) square. Soak the rice stick noodles in hot water for
about 10 minutes until just soft. Drain and place in 2 large soup
bowls. Divide the bean curd into half along the diagonal.

Heat the Laksa paste gently in a wok and then add the stock,
salt, sugar and coconut milk immediately. Stir and mix well.
Bring to the boil. Add the fish sauce, prawns and mussels and
bring back to the boil. Simmer for 1 minute. At the last minute
add the bean sprouts. Pour into the soup bowls. Arrange the
seafood and bean curd on the top and garnish with a sprig of
Thai mint.

## Singapore Noodles

新
加
坡
炒
粉

SERVES 2

This is the dish that we fell out over. Vivienne felt it was full of
all the leftovers, and that Orientals should leave curry to the
Indians, but she is slowly being converted. It is certainly the
most popular dish in the Teahouse. So many of our customers
cannot be wrong!

400 g (14 oz) rice stick noodles
2 tablespoons vegetable oil
1 egg, beaten
125 g (4 oz) cooked chicken or cha shao pork (see page 256), cut
into fine strips
1 spring onion, sliced
50 g (2 oz) Spanish onion, sliced
50 g (2 oz) red pepper, cored, seeded and sliced
50 g (2 oz) green pepper, cored, seeded and sliced
handful of bean sprouts
125 g (4 oz) cooked shrimps
1 tablespoon curry paste (see below)
salt
sugar

CURRY PASTE (ENOUGH FOR ABOUT 10 PORTIONS)
1 clove garlic, roughly chopped
4 slices root ginger, roughly chopped
2 stalks lemon grass, roughly chopped
10 tablespoons vegetable oil
½ onion, finely chopped
½ tablespoon paprika
1 tablespoon tumeric
4 tablespoons Malaysian curry powder

First make the curry paste. Process the garlic, ginger and lemon
grass in a food processor. Heat the oil in a wok and fry the onion
over a low heat for 10–15 minutes. Carefully strain the oil and
reserve. Discard the onion. Warm the oil again and add the

processed ingredients. Cook gently for 5 minutes before adding
the spices. Continue to cook for 1 more minute.

Soak the rice noodles in hot water for 10 minutes or until al
dente. Drain and set aside. Heat the oil in a wok, swirling it
around until it just begins to smoke. Pour in the egg. It will rise
up the pan. Stir to scramble it. Add all the other ingredients and
stir-fry, mixing the paste thoroughly with the noodles. Serve
immediately.

# The Essential Larder

*Japanese names are given in square brackets.*

### Agar agar   瓊脂 洋菜 [寒天]

Agar agar is a translucent seaweed used for setting jellies, junkets and desserts. It is available in bars, often referred to as kanten bars, in flakes or in powder. It can be a little difficult to use, especially in the raw form, but is a good vegetarian substitute for gelatine. Agar agar needs to be boiled, stirring continuously until it melts, and then strained before mixing with other ingredients.

### Balachan   [马拉虾膏]

This is an evil-smelling fermented shrimp paste, responsible for the strong seafood flavour in Malaysian and South Sea spice pastes and dips. It is essential to South-east Asian cuisine. A liquid version is very popular in the Philippines, Vietnam and Thailand.

### Bamboo shoots   竹笋

Bamboo shoots are available in cans, ready sliced, and make a good addition to the texture of stir-fried dishes. They will last for weeks if kept covered with fresh, regularly changed, water in the refrigerator.

## Beans

### Aduki beans   紅豆 赤小豆

Small red beans which are often used in sweet soups. They are best known sweetened and pureed when they are used as a sweet filler for cakes and desserts.

### Black beans   黑豆

These tiny, potent little beans have become very familiar with the spread of Chinese restaurants. They are best bought in bags or packets. In this form they are soft, but must still be soaked for 10 minutes. The bean is preserved with salt and should be used sparingly, especially when soy sauce is also added. Salted black beans will balance the clean taste of fresh seafood.

Black beans also come in some proprietary stir-fry sauces where they are mixed with sugar, soy sauce and other ingredients.

## Bean curd (tofu) 豆腐

Bean curd is a soybean powder product that comes in many shapes and forms. It is a versatile and invaluable form of protein, so it is especially important for vegetarians to master a working knowledge of the different bean curd products and the different methods of cooking. Japanese bean curd is softer and tastier marinated and eaten raw than the more solid Chinese counterpart. It is also suitable for clear soups. Being soft it is not suitable in stir-fry dishes as it tends to disintegrate. One of the beauties of bean curd is that it will adopt the flavour of the sauce in which it is cooked. The secret is to keep it intact long enough! One of the most common ways of ensuring this is to cut it into 3 cm (1½ inch) squares and then deep-fry it until golden brown. It becomes slightly crunchy and maintains its shape while still absorbing some of the taste of the food in which it is cooked. Deep-fried bean curd can be bought ready prepared.

### Dried bean curd (sticks and skins) 腐竹 〔腐竹或腐皮〕
For long-cooking or prolonged braising it is good to keep dried bean curd in your larder. Bean curd sticks and skins are made from dried soybean milk, hardened into a glossy tan-coloured material that can be used in stir-frying. They must be soaked in plenty of hot water, changing the water when it becomes cloudy – do not use boiling water, as this will damage the bean curd. They are ready to use when they become soft and white. In a hurry, this can be done in about half an hour, but they can also be left to soak overnight.

### Fermented bean curd (red or white bean curd cheese) 紅腐乳
This suspicious-looking product comes in jars or cans full of a slimy substance – cubes of bean curd fermented in rice wine and salt. My father, who was never known to reprimand, let alone smack us, as children, would delight in surreptitiously giving us teaspoons of this disgusting substance as his kind of revenge. It is available in both red and white in different grades. The red is extremely strong, and apart from being used to torment children, a teaspoonful added to a stir-fry gives a tremendous depth of flavour.

### Red bean cheese 紅腐乳
*see* Fermented bean curd.

### Silky bean curd  嫩豆腐
This is a softer variety of bean curd which can be eaten raw or added to a clear soup stock. It is difficult to stir-fry without it falling apart. The Japanese variety is widely available in the West. The Chinese version is made with peanuts.

### Sweet red bean paste  紅豆沙
*see* Beans: Aduki beans

### Yellow bean (paste)  黃豆醬
Yellow beans can be bought in cans or jars as the cooked bean itself, or in sauce form. It has a strong full flavour which is often used as an addition to more complex sauces, or simply in long-cooked dishes.

### Black fungus  黑木耳
*see* Wood ear

### Bonito flakes  [鰹節]
These are dried tuna flakes which are used to make dashi, the basic Japanese broth, or scattered as a seasoning over bean curd and vegetables.

### Chestnuts (dried)  干栗子
Most good Chinese supermarkets stock packets of them. They are quite hard and need to be placed in boiling water and soaked for an hour and then simmered for another hour before use. Added to long-cooked meats they impart a natural sweet, dry taste.

### Chilli paste  辣醬
Chilli paste is a fiery sauce made with crushed fresh chilli peppers and salt. It is most often used as a dip for crisp foods and cold vegetables and meats.

### Chinese chives  韭菜
Chinese chives are a long green, thin vegetable with an aromatic, pungent flavour for which there is no substitute. Chopped finely and added to stuffings for dumplings or stir-fried with other vegetables they are unforgettable. However, they are only available seasonally. A mixture of chives and coriander makes a good substitute.

### Chinese dried mushrooms  香菇  冬菇
Chinese dried mushrooms must be the most substantial and

meaty of all vegetables! You can do anything to these large, black, thick-capped fungi and they won't fall apart. When braised or long-cooked they adopt that kind of slithery texture that the Chinese love, and they have just enough musty, earthy flavour to add a unique dimension, but not too much to be prohibitive to those with a less adventurous palate. Shiitake mushrooms are available both fresh and dried.

**Chinese white radish**　白蘿蔔　大根
Chinese white radish looks like a massive white carrot and is commonly used in vegetable stocks. It is not quite so sharp as the small red radish, but has the same crisp watery taste.

**Daikon**　白蘿蔔　大根
*see* Chinese white radish

**Dang gui**　當歸
Dang gui is the root of Chinese angelica, one of the most commonly prescribed Chinese herbs, thought to act on the kidneys and the blood. The 'head' and the 'tail' of the root are differentiated; the tail is thought to have a stronger action in moving the blood. It is especially good for gynaecological problems, especially after childbirth, and is also reported to be good for male impotence. In food dang gui is often combined in braised dishes or stews with lamb or chicken.

**Dashi**　[出し]
The basic Japanese broth, made from kelp and dried tuna flakes.

**Dried shrimps**　乾蝦米　乾蝦仁
Dried shrimps are widely used to flavour vegetables, savoury dishes and soup stocks. These bright pink shrimps have been salted and dried and come in different sizes. Soak in warm water for at least 30 minutes before stir-frying or simmering with the other ingredients.

**Fish sauce**　魚露
Our first chef in the Teahouse was influenced by Japanese cooking styles, and very fond of adding fish sauce to his dishes and stocks. It is a thin, translucent brown liquid that gives a light, fragrant saltiness to food. Its use in Thai, Vietnamese and Phillipine cuisine might be compared to the use of soy sauce in China.

**Five-spice powder**   五香粉
Five-spice is sold both whole and powdered. It is a dynamite
combination of five strong-tasting ingredients: star anise, fennel
seeds, cloves, cinnamon and Sichuan peppercorns, dominated by
the star anise. It is particularly good added to long-cooked
dishes, or a marinade for spare ribs, but use it sparingly.

**Ginko nuts**   白果   [銀杏]
These small white nuts of the maidenhair tree can be bought
shelled, unshelled, or even canned. Unshelled nuts are time-
consuming to prepare. The shell must first be cracked and then
the nut boiled for a few minutes. This loosens the inner skin
which then can be rubbed clear. Ginko nuts can be added to
soups and stews and have a flavour that is simultaneously bland
and bitter.

**Hair vegetable**   髮菜
Hair vegetable, or facai, gets its name from its long, fine, black
strands. It is quite expensive and attributed with life-enhancing
qualities. Facai can also mean 'make a fortune', so this vegetable
is often served at festivals and celebrations for good luck.

**Haw flakes**   山楂片
Haw fruits, flakes and jellies are an integral part of traditional
life in Beijing. As a stewed fruit condiment, stuffing for griddle
cakes, or glazed with caramel and speared with sticks on the
street stalls, they are a part of everyone's childhood. Sadly, in the
West we can only enjoy them in dried flakes sold as children's
sweets.

**Hoisin sauce (also known as barbecue sauce)**   海鮮醬
Hoisin is a thick soy-based product combined with flour, garlic,
chilli, sugar and other ingredients. It is commonly used in
barbecue marinades for its sweet and savoury flavour and
glowing colour, but it can also be added to other stir-fry recipes.
Mixed with peanut butter and sesame oil it makes a good dip.
Once opened, store the sauce in the refrigerator.

**Hot bean sauce**   豆瓣辣醬
A delicious combination of yellow and black beans with garlic,
sesame and lots of chilli. If you like your food hot and spicy this
is a must for stir-fries.

**Huang qi**   黃耆
Huang qi, or radix astragali, is a root commonly used in chicken

soup to tone Qi (see page 164) and to strengthen the body's defences against infection. It is also one of the dishes given to women after childbirth.

**Jiu cai** 韭菜
*see* Chinese chives

**Kombu** [昆布]
A large-leaved seaweed in the kelp family which is often used in Japanese cuisine, especially in soups and stews. It must be wiped with a damp cloth before use.

**Lemon grass** [香茅]
Lemon grass is a tall thick grass-like plant that has a strong flavour of citron. The lower white juicy base is used to make South-east Asian spice pastes, soups and stews.

**Mirin** [味醂]
Sweet cooking sake, used in Japanese cooking.

**Miso** [味噌]
Fermented soya bean paste, used in Japanese coooking. There are several grades of miso, the strongest being red miso which is very dark. *See also* Shiro miso.

**Mouli**
Similar to Chinese white radish.

**Mung beans (Green beans)**
These are the smallest of the beans and are used for a multitude of purposes. They can be sprouted for bean sprouts, or bought as fen si, the silken noodles. In their plain form they may be made into sweet-flavoured stews that are specially good to cool the summer heat.

**Naruto** [鳴門]
Literally means spiral. These Japanese fishcakes have a pink spiral in the centre made from food colouring.

## Noodles

**Egg noodles** 雞蛋麵
Egg noodles are made from wheat flour and eggs and can be bought in numerous thicknesses and shapes. They are sold fresh as oil noodles in Chinese supermarkets and as ramen in Japanese. The oil noodles can be stir-fried without boiling or other

preparation. The ramen must be boiled first. The dried variety are most commonly used in Chinese restaurants in Britain. To make the well-known Cantonese 'two sides brown' deep-fried noodles (see page 124) you have to use the very fine round version.

**Fen si noodles (Green bean silk noodles)**　粉絲　粉條
Although these noodles are made from the green bean, they are translucent. Soak them for 5 minutes in boiling water until al dente, then rinse under cold running water. These make a wonderful summer noodle. Alternatively, add them to a soup at the last minute.

**Oil noodles**　油麵
*see* egg noodles.

**Ramen**　[ラーメン]
Japanese-style egg noodles available dried, fresh and frozen. Ramen are typically added to soup stocks and garnished with seafood, meats and vegetables.

**Rice stick noodles**　米粉
British people all seem to know rice stick noodles from the popular dish of Singapore noodles, a stir-fried assembly of leftovers in a curry sauce. The rice sticks must be soaked in hot water until they are soft but still al dente.

**River noodles (dried and fresh hofun)**　河粉
Hofun are flat rice noodles which are, as yet, not very well known in the West. When well cooked they are one of the tastiest noodles available, and are often what the staff cook for themselves in the Chinese kitchen. Fresh hofun are by far the most superior. They need to be blanched for a couple of seconds until they can be shaken apart with chopsticks. Take great care not to overcook them, or they will fall apart when you come to stir-fry them. Dried hofun have to be cooked longer, following the instructions on the packet. These are even more likely to fall apart if overcooked.

**Soba**　[蕎麦]
Japanese brown buckwheat noodles. Some varieties are flavoured with tea. Cook in boiling water for 7 minutes, then drain and rinse.

**Somen**　[素麺]
Japanese white wheat noodles, available in different thicknesses.

### Udon  [饂飩]
Japanese thick white noodles made from wheatflour. These are served in the winter in Japan.

### Wun tun noodles  餛吞麵條
Wun tun noodles are fresh egg noodles used for wun tun soup. They are strongly flavoured yellowy wheat-flour noodles that only need to be boiled for a minute or so before adding to the stock.

### White noodles  上海面
These are often sold as Shanghai noodles but also come under various other brand names. They are fresh noodles that have to be blanched briefly before serving.

### Nori  [海苔]
A crisp seaweed used in Japanese cooking to garnish soups and wrap sushi.

## Oils

### Red chilli oil  紅辣油
A few drops of this hot oil made from the red chilli are often added to stir-fries to liven up the sauce. The oil is made by frying small red chillis in oil very slowly, and it is very hot. It is similar in flavour to tabasco and is widely used in Sichuan cooking.

### Sesame oil  芝麻油  香油
Sesame is one of the most immediately recognizable flavours in Chinese cooking. Just a few drops at the end adds a nutty, aromatic flavour to the final dish. It is rarely used for stir-frying as it has a low burning point.

### Oyster sauce  蠔油
A thick brown Cantonese sauce made from soy sauce and oysters and widely used in southern cooking. A tablespoon added to any savoury sauce will give the sauce an added, almost meaty depth. Some brands do not add MSG. There is also a vegetarian version produced by Amoy.

### Pickled cabbage  冬菜
Also known as winter pickle, this is brownish-green in colour, savoury and mildly salty. It is sold in jars.

**Red dates**　紅棗
A dried date that is used in sweet soups. Red dates are thought
to enrich the blood and calm the heart and the spirit.

## Rice

**Glutinous Rice**　糯米　江米
A round-grained rice used for stuffings and puddings such as
eight-treasure rice or pearl dumplings.

**Thai fragrant rice**　泰國香米
Thai fragrant rice is arguably the tastiest rice available. It comes
in large fluffy grains that have a light and heady aroma. For 2–3
people use 300 g (10 oz) to 400 ml (14 fl oz) water. Wash the rice
thoroughly. Add the water and cover. Bring to the boil, turn
down the heat and simmer for 10 minutes. Do not remove the
lid. Leave to stand for 5 minutes before serving.

**Rice noodles**　米粉
*see* noodles

**Rice vinegar**　米醋
Rice vinegar is the delicate vinegar often added to give a hint of a
sour flavour to a sauce.

**Rock sugar**　冰糖
This is a pure crystal sugar which has to be ground in a pestle
and mortar before using. It has a light, almost barley sugar taste,
and should be used in long and red cooking as it thickens and
glazes the sauce.

**Sake**　[酒]
This is the Japanese rice wine which is served along with the
main meal in a pot warmed in a bowl of water. In cooking it
counteracts strong odours.

**Sesame oil**
*see* Oils

**Sesame paste**　芝麻醬
Sesame paste is commonly used as a dressing for cold food. It
comes packed into a jar and covered with oil and has to be mixed
with hot oil or water before using. Tahini or sesame oil mixed
with peanut butter can be substituted.

**Sesame seeds (black or white)**　芝麻　〔黑芝麻或白芝麻〕
White sesame seeds are toasted or eaten raw scattered over griddle cakes, stir-fries, salads or desserts. Black sesame is often ground and cooked as a soup. It is thought to nourish the liver and kidneys.

**Shaoxing wine**　紹興酒
Shaoxing or Chinese rice wine is very commonly used in stir-frying. A tablespoon will be thrown in at the last minute and swirled around the pan before serving. You can substitute cooking sherry.

**Shiro miso**　[白味噌]
Shiro miso is the lightest coloured of all the grades of miso available and has a deliciously mild flavour. It turns white when water is added. *See also* Miso.

**Shiitake Mushrooms**　[椎茸]
*see* Chinese Mushrooms

**Sichuan peppercorns**　花椒
These reddish-brown peppercorns are native to Sichuan. They are much stronger and more fragrant than ordinary peppercorns and are essential for anyone who wants to understand regional variations in Chinese cooking. The peppercorns should be dry-toasted in a wok until the aroma is released and the peppercorn turns a little brown. Then grind them in a mortar and pestle.

**Sichuan pickle (Zhacai)**　榨菜
Sichuan pickle are the preserved knobs that grow on the stems of mustard greens. Preserved in salt and chilli powder it combines peppery hot and salty flavours. Finely chopped it can be used to spice up a bland stew or flavour a clear stock.

**Snow pickle**　雪菜　雪里紅
These are salted mustard greens, and have a salty, mildly sour flavour.

**Soy sauce**　醬油
These days it is probably unnecessary to introduce this staple of the Chinese kitchen. It is made from fermented soya beans, wheat, yeast, salt and sugar, and is one of the basics of Chinese seasoning. Light soy tends to have less additives and a more delicate flavour. A good brand has a clear brown colour and is best used in soups or when the food itself has a flavour that it is

important not to conceal. Dark soy is richer in colour and stronger and sweeter in taste. Use it with meat and especially when long-cooking or braising.

**Star anise** 八角 大料
This is a dried eight-pointed star-shaped spice with a shiny brown seed in every point. Its strong aniseed odour makes it one of the stronger flavours of the five spices in five-spice. Star anise is at its best in long-cooked dishes such as long-cooked belly of pork (see page 250).

**Straw mushrooms** 草菇
We are not great fans of these canned slimy-textured mushrooms, despite continuous pressure from our chefs to use them. Along with soggy beansprouts they best represent the taste and texture of takeaway food.

**Tamari** [溜まり]
Dark, sweetened soy sauce without the wheat.

**Teriyaki** [照り焼きのたれ]
A Japanese marinade for lean meats made from soy sauce, sake, mirin and sugar.

**Tangerine peel (dried)** 陳皮
Dried tangerine peel gives a strong orangey flavour to meats and stews. Soak for 30 minutes in warm water before use. Once the flavour has been extracted discard the peel as it is not particularly tasty itself. It is easy to make your own.

**Tiger lily buds** 黄花
Also known as golden needles. These add a musky flavour to stir-fried noodles or soups. They must be soaked for 30 minutes in hot water. Remove the knobbly bits before using.

**Vegetarian oyster sauce**
*see* oyster sauce

**Wakame** [若布]
A silky seaweed often used in Japanese soups.

**Wasabi** [山葵]
Wasabi is a green horseradish paste that is not related to the western horseradish. It is usually sold in powder form and has to be mixed with water before being eaten as a condiment to Japanese sushi.

**Water chestnuts**  馬蹄 荸薺
Water chestnuts are available in cans, ready peeled. They are used more for their special crunchy texture which they retain through cooking, rather than for their taste which is bland and sweetish.

**White fungus**  白木耳 銀耳
White fungus looks like black fungus or wood ear and is used as a food to nourish the lungs. It can be used as a substitute for the prized snow fungus, which is the gland of the northern snow fungus.

**Wood ear**  木耳
One of the grey-black curly things that you've never been able to identify in your soup or chopped up in the spring rolls is probably wood ear. Wood ear is almost flavourless but has the virtue of sustaining its crunchiness through cooking. Texture of course is almost as important as taste in good Chinese food. It is said to be good for the digestion. Also known as Black fungus.

**Wun tun skins**  餛吞皮
Wun tun skins are made from flour and eggs, and can be bought fresh or frozen from Chinese supermarkets. They are thin, pastry-like wrappings which are stuffed and then fried, steamed or cooked in soups.

**Zhacai**  榨菜
*see* Sichuan Pickle

**Zhenjiang vinegar**  鎮江香醋
This is considered a high quality vinegar, although it tastes much like malt vinegar. It is made from glutinous rice and has a much stronger, fuller flavour than the rice vinegars that are normally used in Chinese cooking. You can use red wine vinegar instead.

# Useful Addresses

## Chinese & Japanese Supermarkets

Cheong-Leen Supermarket, (Mail Order)
Tower House, 4–10 Tower Street , London WC2
0171–836–5378

Dragon and Phoenix Co.
15–18 White Lion St,  London N1
0171–837–0146

East West Herbs
Neals's Yard, London WC2
0171–378–1312

Hong Kong Supermarket
31 Wardour Street, London W1
0171–437–6313

Japan Foods
67A Camden High Street, London NW1

JA Centre Supermarket
348–56 Regents Park Road, London N3

Loon Fung Chinese Emporium
39 Gerrard Street, London W1
0171–437–1922

Ninjin
244 Great Portland Street, London NW1

The Peking Supermarket
59 Westbourne Grove, London W2
0171–243–2994

See Woo Hong
19 Lisle Street, London WC2
0171–439–8325

Wing Yip
96–98 Coventry Street, Birmingham
0121–327 3838

Wing Yip
550 Purley Way, Croydon CRO 4RF
0181–688–4880

Wing Yip
295 Edgware Road, London NW2
0181–450–0422

Wing Yip
45 Faulkner Street, Manchester
0161–832 3215

Yaohan Plaza
399 Edgware Road, Colindale, London

## Chinese Herbal Medicine

To purchase individual herbs or have the teas made up it would be advisable to photocopy the appropriate recipe and either take or fax it to a supplier. If you contact a wholesaler you will have to buy ten or more bags of tea.

The Chrysanthemum Clinic
3 Station Parade, Burlington Lane, Chiswick, London W4 3HD
0181–995–1355

Mayway UK Ltd
Chinese Herbal Wholesaler
Tel: 0181–893–6873
Fax: 0181–893–6874

The Register of Chinese Herbal Medicine
9 Lawns Court, The Avenue, Wembley Park, Middlesex HA9 9PN
0181–908–1697

# Further Reading

Beinfield, Harriet and Korngold, Efrem, *Between Heaven and Earth – A Guide to Chinese Medicine* (New York: Ballantine Books, 1991)

Flaws, Bob and Wolfe, Honora: *Prince Wen Hui's Cook: Chinese Dietary Therapy* (Brookline, MA: Paradigm Publishing, 1983)

Goodwin, Jason, *The Gunpowder Gardens – Travels through India and China in search of Tea* (London: Vintage, 1990)

Graham, A., *Disputers of the Tao Open Court* (La Salle, Illinois: Open Court, 1989)

Harper, D., *Early Chinese Medical Literature – The Mawangdui Medical Manuscripts* (London: Kegan Paul International, 1997)

Lai, T. C., *Chinese Food for Thought* (Hong Kong: Hong Kong Book Centre, 1978)

Lao She, *Teahouse*, trans. John Howard Gibbon (Beijing: Foreign Language Press, 1980)

Legget, D., *Helping Ourselves* (Totnes: Meridian Press, 1995)

Lu, Henry C., *Chinese System of Food Cures: Prevention and Remedies* (New York: Sterling Publishing, 1986)

Pitchford, Paul, *Healing with Whole Foods* (Berkeley, CA: North Atlantic Books, 1993)

Sivin, Nathan, *Traditional Medicine in Contemporary China* (Ann Arbor: Center for Chinese Studies, University of Michigan, 1987)

wagamama, *way of the noodle* (London: Boxtree, 1994)

Unschuld, P., *Medicine in China: A History of Ideas* (Berkeley, CA: University of California Press, 1985)

Xu Guang, *Chinese Herbal Medicine* (London: Vermilion, 1996)

# US Conversion Tables

## Liquid Measurements

| | | |
|---|---|---|
| 50 ml | 2 fl oz | ¼ cup |
| 75 ml | 3 fl oz | ⅓ cup |
| 125 ml | 4 fl oz | ½ cup |
| 150 ml | ¼ pint | ⅔ cup |
| 175 ml | 6 fl oz | ¾ cup |
| 250 ml | 8 fl oz | 1 cup |
| 300 ml | ½ pint | 1¼ cups |
| 350 ml | 12 fl oz | 1½ cups |
| 500 ml | 16 fl oz | 2 cups |
| 600 ml | 1 pint | 2½ cups |
| 750 ml | 1¼ pints | 3 cups |
| 900 ml | 1½ pints | 3½ cups |

## Dry Weights

**FLOUR**

| | | |
|---|---|---|
| 60 g | 2 oz | ½ cup |
| 125 g | 4 oz | 1 cup |
| 175 g | 6 oz | 1½ cups |
| 500 g | 1 lb | 4 cups |

**SUGAR**

| | | |
|---|---|---|
| 30 g | 1 oz | 2 tbsp |
| 125 g | 4 oz | ½ cup |
| 250 g | 8 oz | 1 cup |

**RICE**

| | | |
|---|---|---|
| 25 g | 1 oz | 2 tbsp |
| 125 g | 4 oz | ½ cup |
| 225 g | 8 oz | 1 cup |

# Appendix
## An Introduction to Chinese Medical Terminology

### Yin, Yang and Qi

The art of oriental dietary therapy or medicine lies in interpreting the signs of the body, so that the underlying condition of an individual can be assessed in relation to an appropriate diet or medical intervention. Unlike western medical traditions, either mainstream or alternative, it frequently avoids universal recommendations, but tailors the recipe to the context – the symptoms and constitution of the patient. Exactly how the signs are interpreted may change from one period or one place to another, but there are fundamental ideas that are always shared. Yin, Yang and Qi are the basic terms of Chinese medicine.

In Chapter 4 we have already described how Qi is related to the changing moods of the season. Qi in the body is both the term that describes the sensation of being alive and is the stuff considered most critical to health and well being. In early Chinese medical thought it was understood to enter the body on the breath, bringing vitality and passing along the various anatomical planes to enter the internal organs – the channels of acupuncture. Where Qi stagnates, death and illness ensue; and where it lubricates, there will be life and health:

> Now flowing water does not stagnate, when the door pivots there will be no woodworm because of movement. When there is movement then it fills the four limbs and empties the five viscera, when the five viscera are empty then the jade body will be benefited.
> (*Symptoms of Death on the Yin and Yang Channels*, 200 BC)

Illness can be described as a deficiency of Qi, as blockages of the flow of Qi, or as imbalances of Yin or Yang Qi. Likewise, foods are often described as supplementing, calming or moving Qi.

The polarities associated with Yin and Yang reveal a binary way of thinking that divides all phenomena into two, starting with the dark and sunny sides of a hill – simply two aspects of the same object. Yin and Yang represent simultaneously complementary and opposing aspects of time–space that are in an eternal state of flux, just as sunshine becomes shade and shade, sunshine, or as day and night revolve around. Yang represents activity, light, heat and movement, whereas Yin represents stillness, dark and cold. When an extreme state of Yang is reached then it begins to transform into its opposite.

Fig.1: Some Correlations with Yin and Yang (c.250 BC)

| Yang | Yin |
|---|---|
| Heaven | Earth |
| Summer | Winter |
| Day | Night |
| Action | Inaction |
| Stretching | Contracting |
| Ruler | Minister |
| Above | Below |
| Man | Woman |
| Father | Child |
| Older | Younger |
| Noble | Base |
| Getting on in the world | Stuck where one is |
| Giving | Receiving |

Everybody, every symptom and every foodstuff can be described in terms of its Qi or its action. The terms Yin and Yang themselves are rarely used to describe food directly but, as we shall see below, equivalent polarities such as heat or cold or flavours associated with the movements of Yang and Yin are commonly attributions.

## Body types
People are classified into body types by analysing their superficial physical signs, their personalities and preferences. Closely analogous to the description of phenomena as relatively Yin or Yang is whether they are classified as hot, warm, cool or cold. Signs of heat in the body might be actual physical heat, redness of tongue or body, dislike of a hot environment, a thirst for cold drinks, underweight, dryness of skin and body, dark urine and a tendency to constipation. Emotionally, the over-heated type may be prone to irritability and have an agitated, impatient disposition. At the opposite end of the scale the cold, lethargic person who craves warmth in the environment and in food and drinks, tends to be overweight and have excess water in the body, suffers with loose stools and copious pale urine and has a pallid complexion and tongue, may well be classified as a cold type.

Excess or deficient heat is a polarity which, broadly speaking, is expressed in terms of Yang and Yin. There are a number of simple indicators of the balance of Yin and Yang in the body. Physical resources are an important consideration. Qi can be substituted here for the concept of physical resources. A deficiency in Qi will inhibit our flexibility – our stamina and resilience to illness and emotional stress. Hyperactivity may point to an excess of Yang Qi, perhaps in combination with a deficiency of Yin, while lethargy may relate to the opposite conditions. Sexual vitality can be interpreted in the same way. An experienced practitioner will be able to interpret all these signs and symptoms as revealing the underlying dynamic between the Yin and Yang aspects of the body.

## Damp

Another common description of the body will relate to the quality of fluid retained in the body. People are often described as damp or dry. A damp condition arises when the transformation of moisture in the body is impeded by a number of different factors. A poor diet full of cold food, sweet food and saturated fat, is thought to be a primary cause of this condition. Damp, as well as cold, heat and wind, is also thought to create blockages in the channels of Qi. A person suffering from damp may be prone to water retention; dampness sinks and tends to accumulate around the belly and knees. Common complaints may be a swollen belly or swollen knee joints, tiredness, poor memory and an overall feeling of dragging the body around. In general an avoidance of cold, sweet and fat and a concentration of gently warming and drying foods will begin to resolve a damp condition. Conversely, a dry condition will also be reflected in the quality of the skin and flesh. There may be a lack of oiliness or lustre as well as a lean and wiry body, a dryness in movement and mood accompanied by symptoms of heat. Savoury, cooling foods will tend to moisten a dry condition.

Few people neatly fit these criteria, but it is usually possible to identify tendencies toward one extreme or other. Most people will readily identify their type themselves. If there is a mixture of mild hot and cold, damp and dry or energetic and tired symptoms, it probably indicates reasonable health. Sometimes it is important to distinguish between an acute and a constitutional condition. In fever, extreme signs of heat may coexist with a fundamentally cold body type. A person may also change their body type. A woman who has been a cold type all her life might suddenly become hot for a protracted period during menopause. But these are more extreme problems that belong to the domain of the clinician.

## Classification of Foods

By consulting Table 1 the reader will find that foodstuffs are described in such terms as tonifying Yin, moving Qi or clearing damp, some of the conditions described above. To design a nourishing way of eating it is necessary to match the individual body type to their food. Foods are also classified according to their thermostatic qualities (hot, warm, neutral, cool and cold), by flavour (pungent, sweet, salt, sour and bitter), the direction in which they induce movement within the body, the organ system that they support as well as simply the symptom that they can influence. After ascertaining what body/personality type you are then find a food to match. If you are internally cold, then find food that generates heat. If you are hot, eat cooling foods and drinks; if damp, choose drying foods; if dry, choose moistening foods.

## Thermostatic qualities

Food that generates heat or cold is not necessarily the same thing as hot or cold food. It will rather generate sensations and symptoms of heat or cold in the body. Lamb, for example, is considered warming regardless of whether it is served hot or cold. Hot mint tea is the most cooling of drinks to serve in summer. An excess of ice-cold cola can create inner heat. In general, a meal should be well-balanced and comfortable to eat. Very hot foods should be accompanied by cooling foods, very spicy with bland. The way the food is cooked is also significant. Raw or lightly cooked foods are cooling, whereas long-cooked or seared foods will tend to heat.

## Five Phase Associations

The term 'Five Elements' is the most commonly used translation for the Wuxing (Wood, Fire, Earth, Metal and Water) which we here translate as Five Phases. It is unfortunate that the word 'elements' tends to suggest a static and simple material or constituent, whereas the Wuxing represent the dynamic of movement. Fire, for example, heats and rises, water sinks and finds the lowest level. And, as we shall see in a moment, it is these qualities of movement that influence the sets of associations that are most important to dietary therapy.

Summer, the season associated with fire, is hot and full of flourishing and rising movement. In winter, as with water, everything in nature sinks and contracts. Every phase has an associated flavour, internal organ and physiological function associated with the organ. Sour is associated with wood and the liver, bitter with fire and the heart – and it is this spectrum of associations that forms a large part of the essential background knowledge in Chinese medical thought and dietary therapy. It is not a system to be slavishly followed, but one of many which provide primary reference points to guide the judgement.

Fig. 2: Correlations of the Five Phases

| ELEMENT | **Wood** | **Fire** | **Earth** | **Metal** | **Water** |
|---|---|---|---|---|---|
| SEASON | Spring | Summer | | Autumn | Winter |
| DIRECTION | East | South | (Centre) | West | North |
| COLOUR | Green | Red | Yellow | White | Black |
| VISCERA | Liver | Heart | Spleen | Lungs | Kidneys |
| NORMS | Benevolence | Ceremony | Trustworth-iness | Right | Wisdom |

White Tiger Discussions (first century AD)

## The Direction of Movement

The ability of a food to promote movement within the body is a significant element in designing a diet. Food can be emphasized for being able to move Qi in the channels, to move the blood, or calm the spirit. Its action can also be described as promoting upward, downward, inward or outward movement. The outward movement of pungent foods will induce sweating, the inward movement of salt will moisten the body, of bitter will dry and drain excess moisture and swelling, upward movement will counteract prolapse or diarrhoea and downward will settle vomiting, asthma or hiccup. In less acute circumstances you may be guided by your body type. If you have a swollen belly and waterlogged flesh, then you should choose foods which move upward, as well as those that dry dampness.

## Organ Systems

The organs of Chinese medical thought are not at all identical to the organ as described in western medicine. They are rather a range of functions understood to be associated with the path of the acupuncture channel and the organ itself. The lung, for example, relates to the lung organ and can also be influenced from the anatomical plane that travels from the lateral aspect of the thumb to the chest. It is naturally associated with breathing, but it is as much associated with the quality of the skin, one medium through which Qi is inhaled, as it is with the lungs. Breathing through the skin is a familiar concept with cosmetic salespeople, but in the tradition of self-cultivation it also suggests ingesting vitality through the skin with practices such as Qigong, meditation and Tai Jiquan.

There are altogether five solid organs which relate to organs that we are familiar with – the lungs, kidneys, liver, heart and spleen. There are also five hollow organs: the large intestine, bladder, gall bladder, small intestine and stomach. The functions associated with these viscera in Chinese medical thought are much too complicated to go into detail here, although the spleen probably deserves special mention for being a mis-translation of the pancreas. This is the organ most implicated in the traditional physiology of digestion and the extraction and transportation of nourishment in the body. To learn more about the organ systems see the bibliography (page 274).

## Flavour

Of all the associations with the Five Phases, flavour must be most important to the concerns of a dietary regime. In this context flavour is no longer simply the judicious combination of tastes. The flavours assigned to foods are linked to their therapeutic effect. They tend to reflect their taste, but quite often the food itself has very little taste of its own. In such cases a flavour is probably attributed according to an observed physical response, or the constellation of its other attributes. With five basic flavours acknowledged each one is linked with the sets of associations with the Phases and therefore also with organs and their functions.

Pungent is the most Yang of flavours and is expansive, upward and outward in its movement. It stimulates Qi and blood and enters the lungs and large intestine, drying fluids and clearing mucus. In this book the pungent flavour will be found in ginger and garlic, onions, chives, leeks and hot pepper. Pungent is generally thought of as heating, but there are those pungents that, when moderated by other qualities, have been classified as neutral and cooling.

Sweet is slightly Yang in nature and promotes an upward and outward movement. It enters the stomach and spleen. Mildly sweet foods, such as grains, nuts, fruits and many vegetables, form the main bulk of any diet. Stronger sweet flavours have a very warming and nourishing effect, but should be avoided by people with signs of damp. Those who crave sweet food would be well advised to choose from the list of mildly sweet foods.

Sour and salty are slightly Yin in flavour, and are therefore cooling. They promote a downward movement in the body. Salt will moisten the body while sour gathers and contracts, cleansing the body and moving the blood. Salt enters the kidneys and sour the liver.

Bitter is the most Yin of flavours. It causes contraction and makes Qi descend and move inward, reducing fever and calming agitation. It is also drying and is good for dampness. Bitter enters the heart and clears heat, calming the spirit.

In truth, each food may have several flavours and qualities which tend to moderate its action. Very few are pungent, hot and move upward, or bitter, cold and move downward. Those that are, like chilli and ginger, or lettuce, we will instinctively be aware of. Other, less extreme, foods will tend toward one end or other of this scale, but equally may be used for their action on specific symptoms or a particular channel.

It is hoped that the reader will be sufficiently interested by the ideas in Chapter 4 and in this Appendix to try some of the recipes and read more about the subject. Regardless of whether we accept all the theories and recommendations, an appreciation of how the oriental approach to diet caters for the individual will leave us with a richer and more satisfying relationship with the food that we eat.

## Table 1: The Classification of Foods

No western-language directory of the oriental classification of foods systematically includes historical sources. These lists are therefore a summary of contemporary books listed in the Further Reading section of this book, substantiated by information from Li Shizhen's *Bencao Gangmu* and the advice

| FOOD | FLAVOUR | CHANNEL ENTERED |
| --- | --- | --- |
| **Beans and Vegetables** | | |
| Aduki bean | Sweet and sour | Small intestine and heart |
| Asparagus | Bitter | Kidney and liver |
| Aubergine | Sweet | Lungs, stomach and spleen |
| Bamboo shoot | Sweet | Liver, lungs and stomach |
| Bean curd | Sweet | Large intestine, spleen and stomach |
| Beetroot | Sweet | Heart and liver |
| Black bean | Sweet | Kidneys |
| Black fungus | | Large intestine |
| Black sesame seeds | Sweet | Liver and kidneys |
| Broad bean | Sweet | Spleen and stomach |
| Broccoli | Bitter, pungent | |
| Cabbage | Sweet | Stomach and spleen |
| Carrot | Sweet | Tonifies liver and spleen |
| Celery | Sweet and bitter | Liver and stomach |
| Chinese cabbage | Sweet | Large intestine and stomach |
| Chinese mushroom | Sweet | Stomach |
| Chinese white radish | Pungent and sweet | |
| Chive | Pungent | Liver, kidneys and stomach |
| Coriander | Slightly pungent | Lungs, stomach and spleen |
| Cucumber | Sweet | Stomach and kidneys |
| Fennel | Pungent | Bladder, kidneys and stomach |
| Garlic | Pungent | Large intestine, lungs, spleen and stomach |
| Ginger (fresh) | Pungent | Stomach, spleen, lungs |
| Ginseng | Sweet, bitter | Lungs and spleen |
| Kelp | Salty | Bladder, kidneys, liver and stomach |
| Leek | Pungent | Lungs and liver |
| Lettuce | Sweet and bitter | Stomach and large intestine |
| Mung beans | Sweet | Heart and stomach |
| Potato | Sweet and sour | Liver and stomach |
| Pepper (red/green) | Pungent | Spleen and heart |
| Pumpkin | Sweet and pungent | Liver and spleen |

of our friend and colleague Dr Xu Guang. The table is presented as background to the text and recipes and not as the only classification system. It is hoped that it will encourage further reading and a richer understanding and love of food.

| MOVEMENT | NATURE | CLINICAL USE |
| --- | --- | --- |
| Neutral | Neutral | |
| Upwards | Slightly warm | |
| Neutral | Warm | |
| Downwards | Cold | |
| Downwards | Cool | Tonifies Yin and Qi |
| Upwards | Neutral | |
| | Warm | Tonifies Yin and blood |
| Upwards | Neutral | |
| Upwards | Neutral | |
| Upwards and inwards | Neutral | |
| | Cool | |
| Upwards | Neutral | Stomach and duodenal ulcer. Poor appetite |
| Upward | Neutral | Indigestion, dry eyes, blurred vision |
| Downwards | Neutral, clears heat and damp | Irregular periods, heavy bleeding, headaches caused by liver Yang rising |
| | Neutral | Clears damp and heat and drains water |
| Upwards | Neutral | Tonifies Qi |
| | Cool | Clears damp |
| Outwards | Warm | |
| Outwards | Warm | Moves stomach Qi downwards, indigestion |
| Neutral | Cool | Clears heat poison and damp heat. Oedema and cold sores |
| Outward | Warm | |
| Outward | Warm | Prevents flu and colds. Diarrhoea and coughs caused by TB |
| Outward | Warms stomach | Feverish colds. Vomiting from shellfish/fish poisoning |
| Upward | Warm | |
| Downwards | Cool | Strengthens Yin and blood |
| Outward | Warm | Counteracts cold and improves blood circulation |
| Downward | Cool | Counteracts damp and heat and drains water |
| Neutral | Cool and sweet | Cools heat and drains water |
| Upwards | Slightly cool | Nourishes Yin. Clears heat in stomach. Improves appetite. Gum bleeding |
| Outward | Hot | |
| Neutral | | Clears damp |

| FOOD | FLAVOUR | CHANNEL ENTERED |
| --- | --- | --- |
| Spinach | Sweet | Large intestine and stomach |
| Spring onion | Pungent | (white root) Lungs and stomach |
| | | |
| Sweet potato | Sweet | Kidney and spleen |
| Tomato | Sweet and sour | Liver and stomach |
| White fungus | Sweet | Lungs |

**Fruit, Nuts and Grain**

| FOOD | FLAVOUR | CHANNEL ENTERED |
| --- | --- | --- |
| Almond | Bitter | Lungs and large intestine |
| Apple | Sweet and sour | Large intestine, spleen |
| Banana | Sweet | Spleen and stomach |
| Black sesame | Sweet | Kidneys and liver |
| Chestnut | Sweet | Kidneys and spleen |
| Coconut | Sweet | |
| Dates (red) | Sweet | Spleen and stomach |
| Hawthorn Berry | Sweet and sour | Spleen, stomach and liver |
| Lychee | Sweet and sour | Liver, spleen and kidneys |
| Peanut | Slightly sweet | Spleen and lungs |
| Pear | Sweet and sour | Lungs and stomach |
| Pine nuts | Sweet | Lungs and large intestine |
| Rice | Sweet | Spleen and stomach |
| Sesame oil | Sweet | Large intestine |
| Walnut | Sweet | Kidneys, large intestine |
| Water chestnut | Sweet | Lungs and stomach |
| Water melon | Sweet | Heart, stomach, bladder |

**Fish and Meat**

| FOOD | FLAVOUR | CHANNEL ENTERED |
| --- | --- | --- |
| Beef | Sweet | Large intestine, spleen and stomach |
| Carp | Sweet | Spleen, stomach and small intestine |
| Duck | Sweet and salty | Kidney and lungs |
| Egg (chicken) | Sweet | Heart, kidneys, liver and stomach |
| Chicken | Sweet | Spleen and stomach |
| Lamb | Sweet | Kidneys and lungs |
| Liver (pork) | Bitter and sweet | Liver |
| Liver (lamb) | Bitter and sweet | Liver |
| Mussel | Salty | Liver and kidney |
| Pork | Sweet and salty | Spleen, stomach and kidneys |

| MOVEMENT | NATURE | CLINICAL USE |
| --- | --- | --- |
| Neutral | Cool | Nourishes blood |
| Outward | Warms Yang Qi | Feverish colds. Painful diarrhoea. Scanty urine from Yang deficiency |
| Downwards | Warm | Nourishes Yin and Qi |
| | Cold | Nourishes Yin |
| | Neutral | Clears damp |
| | Cool | Clears phlegm. Coughing and constipation |
| Downwards | Cool | Tonifies spleen. Thirst, diarrhoca |
| Downwards | Cold | Constipation, dry cough |
| | Neutral | Tonifies Yin and blood |
| Upwards | Warm | Back pain. Diarrhoea |
| | Warm | Tonifies Yin |
| Upwards | Warm | Nourishes blood and Qi and calms the spirit. Fatigue |
| Upward | Slightly warm | Aids digestion. Period pain. High cholesterol and blood pressure |
| Upwards | Warm | Coughs with Qi deficiency. Shortage of breath. Chronic diarrhoea |
| | Neutral | Oedema. Increases milk after childbirth |
| Downwards | Cool | |
| | Cool | Coughs and constipation |
| | Neutral | Diarrhoea. Poor appetite. Tonifies blood and Qi |
| Neutral | Cool | Constipation |
| | Hot | Constipation. Lower back ache and impotence. Tonifies kidney and Yang |
| Downwards | Cold | |
| Downwards | Cold | Irritability and oedema |
| Upwards | Warm | Tonifies blood. Anaemia |
| Upwards | Neutral | Oedema. Shortage of milk after childbirth. Drains water |
| Downwards | Neutral | Tonifies Yin |
| | Neutral | Tonifies Yin and blood |
| Upwards | Warm | Tonifies Qi and blood |
| Upwards | Warm | Tonifies Yang of kidneys |
| Upwards | Warm | Tonifies blood |
| Downwards | Cool | Tonifies blood |
| Downwards | Warm | Weakness from chronic illness. Impotence. Tonifies blood |
| Upwards | Neutral | Tonifies Qi and Yin, especially after childbirth |

*Appendix*

| FOOD | FLAVOUR | CHANNEL ENTERED |
| --- | --- | --- |
| Prawn | Sweet | Kidneys and liver |

**Other**

| | | |
| --- | --- | --- |
| Honey | Sweet | Spleen, large intestine and lungs |
| Salt | Salty | Kidney, large and small intestine, stomach |
| Soy sauce | Salty | |
| Star anise | Pungent and sweet | |
| Sugar | Sweet | Spleen |
| Tangerine peel | Pungent and bitter | Lungs and spleen |
| Vinegar | Sour and bitter | Liver and stomach |

| MOVEMENT | NATURE | CLINICAL USE |
|---|---|---|
| Upwards | Neutral/warm | Tonifies kidney and Yang. Shortage of milk after childbirth. Impotence |
| Upwards | Neutral | Tonifies Qi. Increases appetite. Insomnia |
| Inward | Cold | |
| | Cool | Clears damp and promotes Qi circulation |
| Outward | Warm | |
| Upwards | Neutral | |
| Upwards | Warm | |
| | Warm | Improves blood circulation |

# Index

# Index

## Index

Noodles 205
miso paste 265
 Butajiru Pork and Vegetable Stew 207
 Masu no miso-ni: Miso Braised
  Aubergine 202
 Sake no Dengaku: Miso Glazed
  Salmon 209
Mongolian Hotpot 25, 60, 68
mooli 265
 see also Chinese white radish
mountain spring water 193
Moyashi no Gomazu-ae: Bean Sprout
 Salad 216
MSG (monosodium glutamate) 9, 18,
 106, 193, 226, 227
Mugicha tea 192
mung beans 148, 265
 Mung Bean Dessert 159
 see also green beans
mushrooms see button mushrooms;
 Chinese mushrooms; Shiitake
 mushrooms; straw mushrooms;
 wood ear
Mushu Rou Yellow Cassia Roll 47
mussels
 Laksa 257
 Slow-braised Seafood Noodle 123
mustard greens 66

naruto fish cake 265
 Cha Su Ramen: Roast Pork Ramen
  200
No 1 Banana Pancake 173
noodle bars 192–3
noodles 203
 buying 13–14
 Cantonese 105, 106
 Chicken Soup Noodles 240
 dried 12, 13, 265
 Drum Mountain Vegetable Noodles
  238
 dry 255
 Duck Soup 243
 egg 265
 fresh 12–13, 227
 Nun's Vegetable Soup 236
 Shallow-fried Noodles or Two Sides
  Brown 124, 265
 Shanghai see white noodles
 Singapore 13, 227, 228, 255, 266
 Singapore Noodles 258
 Slow-braised Seafood Noodle 123
 soup 255
 Torinamban Udon (Soba): Chicken
  and Shiitake Mushroom on White
  Wheatflour or Buckwheat Noodles
  199
 Tsukimi Soba: Moon Viewing in
  Buckwheat Noodles 197
 wet 244

Zaru Soba: Sieved Buckwheat
 Noodles 205
 see also dan dan noodles; fen si
  noodles (green bean silk noodles);
  oil noodles; ramen; rice stick
  noodles; river noodles (hofun);
  soba; somen; udon; white noodles;
  wun tun noodles
nori 267
 Tusukimi Soba: Moon Viewing in
  Buckwheat Noodles 197
Nun's Vegetable Soup 227, 236

oil noodles 12, 13–14, 200, 265
 Drum Mountain Vegetable Noodles
  238
 Hot-tossed Noodles 86
 Lamb and Leek Manchurian Pot-
  cooked Noodles 49
 Paifang Noodles 84
oil sticks (Soya Milk and Oil Sticks) 29
oils 9, 15, 16–17, 267
okra (Okura Sarada Simple Okra Salad)
 218
Old Pockmarked Mrs Chen's Bean
 Curd 91
one-dish noodle meals
 Ants Climbing the Trees 83
 Cantonese River Noodles with Beef
  in Black Bean Sauce 126
 Dan Dan Noodles 85
 Eastern River Salt-baked Chicken
  128
 Hot-tossed Noodles 86
 Paifang Noodles 84
 Shallow-fried Noodles or Two Sides
  Brown 124
 Slow-braised Seafood Noodle 123
onions
 Beijing Zhajiang Noodles 45
 Butajiru Pork and Vegetable Stew
  207
 Cold-tossed Chinese Chives and
  Bean Curd 154
 Congee with Three Mushrooms 170
 Curry Paste 247
 Nun's Vegetable Soup 236
 Pepper and Sesame Whitebait 95
 see also Spanish onions
oranges
 Peace and Comfort for Old and
  Young 119
 Tangerine Duck 51
oriental dietary therapy 9, 131–6
oriental supermarkets 11
oyster sauce 11, 267

Paifang Noodles 84
pancakes 105
 Dorayaki: Red Bean Pancakes 221

298

# Index

# Index

# Index